The POWER
of PICTURE BOOKS in
Teaching Math, Science, and Social Studies

GRADES PreK–8

SECOND EDITION

Lynn Columba
LEHIGH UNIVERSITY

Cathy Y. Kim
MUHLENBERG COLLEGE

Alden J. Moe
ROLLINS COLLEGE

Holcomb Hathaway, Publishers
Scottsdale, Arizona

Library of Congress Cataloging-in-Publication Data

Columba, Lynn.
    The power of picture books in teaching math, science, and social studies :
grades prek–8 / Lynn Columba, Cathy Y. Kim, Alden J. Moe. — 2nd ed.
        p.   cm.
    Includes bibliographical references.
    ISBN 978-1-890871-92-5
1. Mathematics–Study and teaching (Elementary)—Audio-visual aids.   2.
Science—Study and teaching (Elementary)—Audio-visual aids.   3. Picture
books for children—Educational aspects.   I. Kim, Cathy Y.   II. Moe, Alden J.
III. Title.
    QA19.P53C65 2009
    372.35'044—dc22

                                                                2009021777

Holcomb Hathaway, Publishers, Inc.
6207 North Cattletrack Road
Scottsdale, Arizona 85250
480-991-7881
www.hh-pub.com

10 9 8 7 6 5 4 3 2 1

ISBN 978-1-890871-92-5

Contents

Discovering Mathematics, Science, and Social Studies   101

Grades 2-3

Experiencing Mathematics, Science, and Social Studies   133

Grades 4-5

Investigating Mathematics, Science, and Social Studies   179

Grades 6-8

Appendix   223

Preface

This book was inspired by the many great books sitting on our bookshelves and bedside tables, by the books we have read at local bookstores, and by the books we have brought to share with one another on Monday mornings. We three authors share one passion—the passion for books written for children, particularly picture books. Our genuine and sincere responses to literature and the spirit of full collaboration gave birth to this book.

The children's books in this text were selected because they are written and illustrated beautifully and because they possess the potential to teach some essential concepts of mathematics, science, and/or social studies. Patricia Polacco's *The Keeping Quilt* (1988, 1998) we have used for years because of the poignancy of the faith and love shown by members of the immigrant family in the book—it is an excellent story. It also provides the basis for a wonderful lesson on geometric shapes and other fundamental aspects of geometry. Others, such as *Prince William* (Rand, 1992) or *The Water Hole* (Base, 2001), deal with environmental issues and the conservation of our natural resources, all in the process of telling a good story. *Flight: the Journey of Charles Lindbergh* (Burleigh, 1997) provides the teacher with the opportunity to introduce difficult scientific concepts such as Bernoulli's principle, a challenging concept even for adults.

Many of the books we have selected here are award winners, while others, like *Growing Vegetable Soup* (Ehlert, 1987), have stood the test of time and are still widely available in libraries. Some of our books provide explicit content in mathematics, such as *Spaghetti and Meatballs for All* (Burns, 1997), or science, such as *Sun Up, Sun Down* (Gibbons, 1983). Many of the books selected were not written specifically to teach mathematics or science or social studies; we have included them because they tell a good story and because they may inspire further learning on the part of the students. Many other books could have been included, and creative teachers will use them in lessons much the same way we have used the books selected here.

In this second edition, we have added newly published and/or newly discovered books, some with wonderful social studies concepts, at the suggestion of readers who requested connections to content area subjects beyond mathematics and science. Sophisticated and complex social studies concepts—such as staple food crops through *Weslandia* (Fleischman, 1999), the underground railroad through *Henry's Freedom Box* (Levine, 2007), and the Harlem Renaissance through *Sweet Music in Harlem* (Taylor, 2004)—are presented. When possible, these social studies concepts are also integrated with mathematics or science concepts appropriate to the grade level. Look for new and exciting teaching ideas and learning opportunities in the new lessons.

Chapters 1 through 5 of this book set the stage for using picture books in teaching math, science, and social studies. In these chapters, we discuss the effective, imaginative integration of literature into the classroom. We help teachers create an environment to ensure that when children and books come together, the experience is enjoyable and thought-provoking. We discuss selection criteria, including distinguishing by purpose, by audience, by structure, and by content. In addition, we show how using children's literature can help teachers meet national standards for math, science, social studies, and language arts.

In Chapters 6 through 9 we provide individual "lessons" for using quality books to extend mathematical, science, and social studies concepts. These chapters cover, respectively, pre-kindergarten through grade 1, grades 2–3, grades 4–5, and grades 6–8. Each lesson includes the following:

- brief summary of the book
- mathematics, science, and/or social studies standards addressed
- objective of the lesson
- applicable language arts experience
- literacy and arts connections
- key concepts
- materials needed to teach the lesson
- procedures for teaching
- possible assessment activities

In the new edition, look for extended assessment plans for selected lessons that exemplify a range of authentic and effective ways to measure student learning. Expanded examples of these assessment tools are presented in the following lessons:

- Questioning and learning log example in *Henry's Freedom Box* in Chapter 8, Lesson 8.14 (grades 4–5)
- Observation example in *Jump, Frog, Jump* in Chapter 6, Lesson 6.7 (grades preK–1)
- Performance example in *The Keeping Quilt* in Chapter 7, Lesson 7.6 (grades 2–3)
- Rubrics example in *Spaghetti and Meatballs for All!* in Chapter 8, Lesson 8.3 (grades 4–5)

Following each lesson, we offer information for "making connections" to other concepts and/or to other books, the titles of which we have included. Finally, we suggest websites related to the lesson concepts for supplementary information.

As educators of teachers, we share our perspectives about the science of teaching and learning in this book. In the lessons we have compiled here, we emphasize the constructivist approach, which places the learner at the heart of the learning experience. Learners are encouraged to make connections to their prior knowledge, to speculate and problem solve, to formulate hypotheses and collect data to confirm them. We use books to help relate human experiences to math, science, and social studies concepts, and we believe this integration will help to motivate all learners.

When we examine the literature on the science of teaching, we are influenced by such experts in the field as Jean Piaget, Lev Vygotsky, Jerome Bruner, and others who have described how children learn, the nature of their developmental stages of learning, and the best means to facilitate their learning at the various stages of development. Additionally, we are influenced by the more recent work of scholars such as Richard C. Anderson and David Pearson, who vividly describe how students comprehend text and who substantiate the tremendous importance of a teacher's influence on the growth of reading. Finally, we are guided by individuals such as Bernice Cullinan, Charlotte Huck, and other children's literature specialists, who help us understand what makes a good book and how to best use them with young readers. In our own teaching, we have come to understand that the methods by which teachers organize for instruction, select and introduce books, and guide students through the learning process are critically important.

We have all observed a master teacher in action. Truly, it is wonderful to see a teacher pose thoughtful questions and help students explore insightful responses, move students in and out of small and large group learning experiences, and both explicitly and subtly facilitate students' understanding of crucial concepts. Often research on instruction fails to capture and describe the art of what we do as teachers. Teaching is sometimes described as a performance, and we hope the collection of beautiful books we discuss here will help to inspire that performance. Some describe teaching as helping students construct meaning, and we hope that our book helps students to make self, text, and world connections that are essential to the comprehension process. Teaching can also be described as the creation of engaging learning opportunities, and we hope that the book experiences in our lessons will motivate students to learn the content area concepts presented. By sharing our book with teachers, we hope we have contributed to the artistry of teaching. Together with those who use this book, we hope to unleash the power of literature!

Acknowledgments

We would like to thank the following reviewers, who read and commented on this or the first edition manuscript while we worked: Danillo Baylen, University of West Georgia; Barbara Chatton, University of Wyoming; Joyce Cockson, Freelance Consultant, Omaha; Frank D'Angelo, Bloomsburg University; Marie DiBiasio, Roger Williams University; Laurie Edmondson, Drury University; Shirley B. Ernst, Eastern Connecticut State University; Marcia Faucher, Roger Williams University; Renee Golanty-Koel, California State University, Sacramento; Judith Hakes, Angelo State University; Laura S. Hayes, Berry College; Leslie Marlow, Berry College; Sonya M. Martin, Drexel University; Mark McJunkin, Arkansas State University; Eula Ewing Monroe, Brigham Young University; Patricia Moyer-Packenham, George Mason University; Frankie Oglesby, Judson College; Connie Parker, Dearborn Public Schools; Jenny A. Piazza, Colorado State University–Pueblo; Debra Price, Sam Houston State University; Joyce Shatzer, Murray State University; Kathy Horak Smith, Tarleton State University; Laura B. Smolkin, University of Virginia; Janice Strop, Cardinal Stritch University; Laurie Swartwout, Cardinal Stritch University; Madge Thombs, Roger Williams University; and Maria Varelas, University of Illinois at Chicago. Their constructive comments helped us to improve the book, and we appreciate their help.

Lynn Columba
Cathy Kim
Alden J. Moe

CHAPTER 1

1

The Magical World
of Picture Books

1

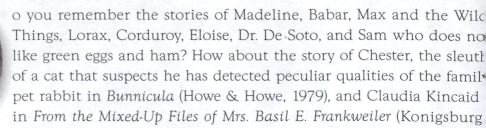

o you remember the stories of Madeline, Babar, Max and the Wild Things, Lorax, Corduroy, Eloise, Dr. De Soto, and Sam who does not like green eggs and ham? How about the story of Chester, the sleuth of a cat that suspects he has detected peculiar qualities of the family pet rabbit in *Bunnicula* (Howe & Howe, 1979), and Claudia Kincaid in *From the Mixed-Up Files of Mrs. Basil E. Frankweiler* (Konigsburg, 1967) who tempts her rich little brother Jamie to accompany her as she runs away from home? More recently, you may have read about the adventures of David in *No, David!* (Shannon, 1998), Mary Alice Dowdel from *A Year Down Yonder* (Peck, 2000), Billie Jo in *Out of the Dust* (Hesse, 1997), and Tree-ear in *A Single Shard* (Park, 2001). All of these stories, for different reasons, touched our hearts; they all have connected with some aspect of our lives.

How do we explain the power these stories seem to hold? Furthermore, how can we use the power of stories to teach content area topics, particularly mathematics, science, and social studies where stories have not been explicitly linked to conceptual learning? In this chapter, we explore some of the reasons why we are attracted to stories, why we ought to use them, and how we as readers respond to stories as we help our students develop into readers, writers, and lifelong learners.

The Power of Stories

ot all readers may be able to articulate what makes a story good. However, we can certainly recognize a good story when it is told. Not all may agree on *exactly* what a good story is, but some characteristics of a good story make the reader want to tell the story to someone else.

We asked our students in children's literature courses the question: "What makes a story a good one?" From their responses, we developed the following description of a good story:

> A good story is creative, suspenseful, imaginative, meaningful, poetic, humorous, adventurous, vivid and colorful, mysterious, engaging, gripping, relaxing, touching, emotional, inspirational, conversational, easy to understand, and beautifully written. A good story also puts the readers inside the story, forces readers to think, encourages them to think about difficult and complex issues, and allows them to recall many good memories of literary experiences.

The power of stories in human life has been documented by many scholars (Bruner, 1986; McEwan & Egan, 1995; Wells, 1986). Wells (1986) writes, "Storying is one of the most fundamental means whereby human beings gain control over the world around them . . . storying is not a conscious and deliberate activity, but the way in which the mind itself works" (p. 197). Narratives mirror life and emotions, our own self presented in familiar *and* peculiar ways. "[S]tories do not simply *contain* knowledge, *they are themselves the knowledge we want students to possess*" (emphasis in original) writes Jackson (1995) to echo that sentiment.

Language of narratives, both oral and written, has a powerful impact on the lives of human beings. Most of us grew up listening to and telling stories from a very young age; the sense of story that we develop is an intimate part of ourselves

Children's responses to narratives are natural, not forced. The power of stories, when combined with children's instinct to make them their own, makes narratives one of the essential ways to teach and to learn. Using this power of stories through books to inspire, motivate, and relate to students as they learn content area topics in mathematics, science, and social studies, then, seems to be not only a natural but also an essential step. Picture books exploring mathematical, science, and social studies concepts are often an unexploited resource and a natural tool for developing mathematical power and scientific ways of thinking, as well as learning about different societies and cultures. As you will see throughout this book, we can effortlessly and effectively use these books to teach difficult and complex concepts to students in grades PreK to 8.

The Power of Picture Books

Picture books are probably the very first form of literature that children encounter as part of their literary experience. Picture books, named for their format rather than content, marry text with illustrations. Many times, a picture book's text and illustrations do not stand alone; rather, each needs the other to complete the story. Surely, you have many picture books that you love and many reasons for loving them. You may love some for the brilliant stories; you may love others for the beautiful language. You may love some for the masterful illustrations; you may love some for the element of surprise or twist at the end of the book. From bright and bold picture books for the very young to highly sophisticated and articulate fiction and nonfiction picture books for older students, picture books satisfy a wide range of readers (even adults).

Picture books eloquently present concepts, both simple and complex, to readers of all levels. It is our intention in this text to highlight these quality books, particularly those that present mathematics, science, and social studies concepts in amazing, beautiful, and brilliant ways. For example, Paul Fleischman's (1999) *Weslandia* is one such book. Wesley, an outcast from his social group, creates a civilization of his very own by planting a staple food crop in his backyard. The strange plant, which Wesley names "Swist," is used to create everything that Wesley needs to maintain the newfound civilization. Games are created with the parts of the plant. Fragrant oil is extracted to sell to children in the neighborhood. From the woody bark, fiber is woven for garments. And of course, fruit from the plant is eaten. Wesley's creativity extends to developing a new number system based on the number eight and a new language based on the 80-letter alphabet. The vivid illustrations are brilliant; they draw the reader into Weslandia. The idea underlying the creation of a new civilization is sophisticated and intelligent.

Reader Response Theory

Readers like different stories and even like the same stories for different reasons. Classic works of literature are banned by some, admired by others; your best friend *really* does not like the very book that changed your life; you cannot imagine why a particular book is chosen by your monthly book club; you disagree with your professor's selections for the modern fiction class; and it baffles you to see a colleague pick a set of books for literature circles when you don't necessarily see the literary merit of those books.

Literary theorists and scholars explain diverse responses to the same text with reader response theory. Essentially, the theory claims that the meaning of a text derives from the dynamic relationship between the reader and the text (Farrell & Squire, 1990; Fish, 1980; Rabinowitz, 1987; Rosenblatt, 1978, 1996). Reader response theory provides a variety of possible ways in which the *reader* contributes to the meaning-making process. This view of reading departs from the traditional definition in which the reader's task is to simply figure out what the author means from the text. In this more traditional view, there is an assumption of authorial power, of *one* meaning that is to be extracted from the reading process. Reader response theory challenges this view to include readers as *they* construct meaning during the reading process.

ROSENBLATT'S TRANSACTIONAL THEORY

Rosenblatt (1978, 1996) was one of the earliest and perhaps most influential proponents of reader response theory. She proposes the idea that reading is "transactional" in nature and argues that the meaning is transacted between the reader and the text in a given context, as shown in Exhibit 1.1. The meaning that *a* reader constructs from reading *a* particular book for *a* given reason varies depending on *who* the reader is, *what* the reader is reading, and *why* or *how* that reading is done.

The reader

Readers vary in innumerable ways. Factors that impact the reader include gender, age, reading ability, ethnicity, religion, interest, attitude, and experiences with literature. Who we are determines our responses to the text as well as the meaning we construct from the text.

Surely, you already have many examples of these reader variations from your own literary experiences. One example that we can share as university and college educators is our students' responses to children's books they read. We often return

---

EXHIBIT 1.1   Meaning is transacted between the reader and the text in a given context.

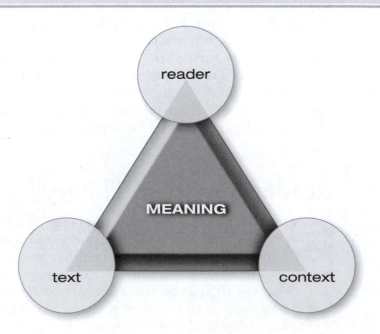

to the books they read as children, and, as you can expect, the responses they generate from these familiar books range greatly. Some books with prior negative or neutral responses turn out to be huge hits; some elicit puzzlement regarding why they were the students' childhood favorites. Some students finally understand the deeper meanings of some books; some find humor in the books for the very first time. Age, undeniably, affects the way we read and how we respond to books.

The text

What we read, too, influences our reader response. In the view of the transactional theory, the text is a counterpart to the reader, necessary in how the literary work comes alive (Karolides, 1997). Contrary to the traditional view of the text as an entity with a determinate meaning inscribed by the author, Rosenblatt (1978) sees the text as dynamic and fluid, requiring the reader to activate the signs. Both play a vital role as necessary ingredients in the process of reading.

A number of factors lead to text variations:

- the content included in the text
- the genre in which the content is presented
- the text structure used in writing
- the easiness or difficulty of the text to comprehend
- the way the author signifies the meaning based on his or her intentions

The text, composed of various particulars, does contribute to a reader's unique meaning-making process.

The context

We define context in just as many ways. Self-selected reading experiences, for example, elicit different responses than assigned readings. Reading for pleasure rather than for information is yet another context variation. A teacher's attitude about reading as well as her enthusiasm for a book or an author may also determine a particular reader response in the students.

Classroom implications of reader, text, and context variation

As discussed earlier, reader response theory informs us that there *are* various meanings readers can construct even as they read the same text. Children arrive at our classrooms as people with different backgrounds, interests, abilities, and levels of motivation. Reading experiences in the schools must allow for these different readers to respond in their unique ways to texts:

- Did they enjoy the story?
- In what ways did they identify with the characters?
- What questions might they have for the characters or the author?
- Did the story remind them of any other personal experiences? Other stories?
- What is the meaning of the story?

These are some of the questions that may help generate unique reader responses during and after reading the text. Students should also learn to acknowledge that there may be many ways to read, understand, and respond to the text and learn to discuss these multiple responses in productive ways with other readers.

In addition to reader variations, classroom teachers should consider the implication of text variations. Literacy experiences in a classroom must include a variety of fiction and nonfiction books in a variety of genres written for a range of readers about topics that interest children. Children who prefer certain types of texts ought to be able to access them in the classroom. As well, they ought to be encouraged to venture into other types of texts. Teachers should model their own engagement with a wide range of texts in their read-alouds, shared readings, and guided readings with their students. Strategies for reading and responding to both fiction and nonfiction should be made explicit in the context of literacy instruction to encourage students to expand what is familiar to them.

TYPES OF RESPONSES: READER STANCES

In addition to articulating the reader, the text, and the context triad (see Exhibit 1.1), Rosenblatt's transactional theory of reader response contributes in another major way to understanding the reading process. Rosenblatt (1978) identifies two extremes in the range of responses to literature that she refers to as stances: *aesthetic* and *efferent*. The two stances do not exist in isolation, but rather as a spectrum of possible responses. As well, a reader in a given reading event can slide from one stance to the other, making the reading process a truly complex one.

Aesthetic stance refers to artistic and personal responses to a text. The experience that takes place *during* reading as the reader interacts with the text is the focus. Quite easily, we can see that reading for pleasure links intimately with the aesthetic stance. First and foremost, we read books, or at least we should, to be entertained. One of the contributions that Rosenblatt makes with the presentation of the aesthetic stance is to foster reading for pleasure in the classroom. Children should read to be entertained and to be engaged, to experience the pleasures that accompany the reading event.

Huck and Kiefer (2003) add that there are other personal values inherent in literature and the reading experience. As mentioned earlier in this chapter, narratives can be a way of thinking. Reading allows us to be imaginative and to have vicarious experiences through the characters we encounter in books. Reading also provides us insight into human behaviors, as well as comprehension of the universality in human experiences.

In contrast to the aesthetic stance, *efferent stance* refers to the informative experiences in reading. Rather than emotional, the responses to a text from an efferent stance are intellectual. If we can describe the aesthetic stance to be a connection to inner life, the efferent stance makes connections to the outside world. This stance has as its focus: (1) the meaning and (2) what we do *after* the reading event. For example, rather than reading simply for pleasure, readers using the efferent stance are asked to complete a book report or to take a quiz after they "uncover" the meaning from the text.

Traditionally, most reading that takes place, especially at the higher grades, emphasizes the efferent stance and responses. However, Rosenblatt argues that an encounter with a text that begins with the efferent stance can transform to the aesthetic stance given appropriate text within a particular context. For example, a student may be assigned to read *The Top of the World: Climbing Mount Everest* by

Steve Jenkins (1999) (see Chapter 9, Lesson 9.11) to learn about the impact of altitude on the human body, and to learn about the history, environment, and geography of other places, but in the process makes deep connections with the climbers and their incredible will to accomplish a goal. You can picture this student sitting in the reading corner, breathing every word of the book until the very last page has been read. Likewise, we can imagine reading from an aesthetic stance turning into an efferent one. A book that a student selects to read for pleasure can be used as an opportunity to learn about the given topic and ultimately can lead to other inquiry processes. For example, while reading aloud Demi's *One Grain of Rice: A Mathematical Folktale* (1997) (see Chapter 9, Lesson 9.2) for pleasure, imagine stimulating students' interest in the mathematical formula to solve Rani's challenge to the greedy raja. What a rewarding moment for the teacher to see students get excited about a topic worth learning!

The selection and inclusion of quality literature in a variety of genres is the key to an effective and motivating learning environment. The picture books presented in this text allow readers not only to transact the meaning of the text, but also to experience both the aesthetic and the efferent stances described by Rosenblatt.

Becoming Learners

The lives of children are filled with play, talk, curiosity, interaction, exploration, and discovery. To the naïve observer, play and the other activities that children engage in appear to be confusing, but to the growing, developing learner this is an essential part of making sense of the world; it *is* learning. In the following sections, we share our perspectives and our philosophy on how children become learners.

THE ACTIVE LIVES OF CHILDREN

As children learn language and the labels used to name things, actions, and people, they become more and more able to discuss their surroundings. The more they learn, the more they talk. The more they learn, the more they explore. The more they learn, the more they want to learn. In most children, the growth of learning and the growth of language go hand in hand (Cox, 2007). And the child's world is filled with more and more activity—physical, linguistic, and intellectual—as the child's world grows from home, to neighborhood, to community, to city, to state, and beyond. We believe that the actions and explorations of children are a normal part of their growth and development.

Suppose a six-year-old boy, Max, watches his father build a deck and learns that a stack of lumber can be used to create a defined outdoor surface where his family can gather and have fun. He learns that lumber can be used to construct something. Max may later create his own "deck" in a sand pile and explain the process to a friend, and so something about the building process has begun to form (or been expanded) in his mind. If he then discovers *Chewy Louie* (Schneider, 2000), the puppy that eats everything, his notion of building is reinforced as he reads about the family that attempts to rebuild the porch that Chewy Louie has chewed up! Another excellent book Max may read in order to expand on the concepts of building and construction is *The Barn Savers* (High, 1999) (see Chapter 8, Lesson 8.4), which deals with one man's interest in the preservation of old barns in Pennsylvania.

Children, like adults, participate in activities, discussions, and experiments that allow them to "make sense of their world." They are constantly trying to figure out the nature of their ever-increasing environments. Good teachers and good books help them to do so.

THE CURIOSITY OF CHILDREN

Children enter school with expectations that they are going to learn to read, to write, to compute, to learn about any number of things. They come to us with an

eagerness and the belief that we, the teachers, know just about everything. By age five or six, they know that there is a great deal more to the world than what they understand. Because they want to know more, they ask insightful questions like "Where does the white go when the snow melts?" and "Why do dandelions become fuzzy fur balls?" and "Why are polar bears left handed?" and "Why do two tulip bulbs that look alike produce different color flowers?" and "How can an ant carry five times its own weight?" and "How were the pyramids built?" We believe that learning begins with such genuine curiosities and wonderments about the world. Good teachers capitalize on the curiosity of their students.

THE CONSTRUCTION OF MEANING

The notion of meaning, what it is, and how it is achieved has been debated and studied since the time of Jean-Jacques Rousseau almost three centuries ago. We feel that the understanding of an event such as a baseball game, or a specific person like a grandfather, or a specific thing like a hurricane, or a concept like love occurs in stages. Think, for example, how a four-year-old, an eight-year-old, and a twelve-year-old might describe his or her meaning for each of these examples. To expand on just one example, the abstract meaning of "love," we can observe the four-year-old tell his mother that he loves her after the parent has shown an act of kindness. By eight, the child knows that "love" means ongoing kindness, concern, and affection displayed in a variety of ways (e.g., hugging, cooking, playing games, making trips to McDonald's). At 12, "love" begins to mean enduring commitment, the special relationship that parents share, and more. In many ways, books like *Love You Forever* (Munsch, 1989), *A Chair for My Mother* (Williams, 1984), *Promises* (Winthrop, 2000), *The Giving Tree* (Silverstein, 1964), *The Memory String* (Bunting, 2000), and others help children understand these words and concepts and help children construct meaning at various stages in their development (Piaget, 1963).

Schema theory and constructivism

Schema theory has much to offer teachers as they strive to understand the cognitive and affective dimensions of teaching and learning. The roots of schema theory can be traced to Piaget (1926) and Bartlett (1932), who introduced the term to psychology (Anderson, 1977, 1994). In Bartlett's studies, he was surprised by the fact that, when adults read stories, there was not a verbatim recall as was believed at that time. Furthermore, he found that the story recall always included information not found in the stories. More recent studies by Anderson (1977), Spiro (1980), and Stein and Trabasso (1981) show that our understanding of narratives is based on our experiences and our understanding of these experiences. Schema theory provides us with an explanation of how we organize and integrate information in our minds. Spiro (1980) refers to this as "the constructive orientation, with its attendant emphasis on the importance of what one already knows in determining what one will come to know." Schema theory and the constructivist approach to learning are interrelated from these perspectives. Ryan and Cooper (2006) view constructivism as "an approach that recognizes this process of constructing meaning [on the part of the learner]."

Based on both schema theory and the constructivist approach to learning, the activation of appropriate prior knowledge is an essential part of meaning construction in the reading process. Fountas and Pinnell (2001) present three types of connections that readers must make as they interact with text: text-to-self, text-to-text, and text-to-world.

Text-to-self. In text-to-self connections, readers make personal connections with the text using life experiences. In *Ira Sleeps Over* (Waber, 2008), Ira worries about his first sleepover at a friend's house without his teddy bear. After much contemplating, Ira bravely ventures into the experience only to realize that his friend Reggie also has a teddy bear that he cannot sleep without. Children can easily relate to the dilemma facing Ira; such connections are an essential way to understand this story. Likewise, many of Kevin Henkes' books (*Chrysanthemum*, 1991; *Wemberly Worried*, 2000; *Julius: The Baby of the World*, 1990) include stories about children dealing with various personal and peer issues. Children's ability to assume the characters' feelings using their own life experiences, again, is critical to understanding these stories.

Text-to-text. In text-to-text connections, readers bring their prior experiences with literature into their encounters with new books. Content connections may be made between books; knowledge connections about genre or text structure may be made. Familiarity with an author's work may also allow readers to read other books by the same author with more ease and fluency. These intertextual connections are a powerful way to read and respond to books (Hartman & Hartman, 1993). Imagine coupling *Out of the Dust* (Hesse, 1997), a historical fiction about Billie Jo's life in Oklahoma during the Dust Bowl, with *Children of the Dust Bowl: The True Story of the School at Weedpatch Camp* (Stanley, 1992), an informational book detailing the experiences of migrants once they arrive in California. These two books complement concepts about the Dust Bowl in remarkable ways, allowing readers to understand experiences of living in the Dust Bowl from different perspectives.

Text-to-world. Text-to-world connections call for students to bring their prior knowledge about the world to their reading. What conceptual understandings do the students need in order to comprehend the story? Do they possess the particular knowledge? If so, how do we *activate* it? If not, how do we *build* it so they can use it during reading? These are some of the questions teachers should ask as they prepare to help students make text-to-world connections. In *The Gardener* (Stewart, 1997), for example, a Depression-era girl must go to the city and live with an uncle due to the difficult financial situation facing the family. In order for students to fully understand why Lydia Grace must leave her family, the historical context of the Depression is an essential one to provide the readers. This seemingly extraordinary story, in fact, is not an exception; many families made difficult sacrifices in order to survive.

These three connections illustrate that reading is both a personal and an intellectual endeavor. In order to help students construct meaning through their reading, teachers must ensure that these connections to self, to text, and to world are made as students encounter and respond to texts.

The Social Aspects of Learning

The early interactions of young children appear chaotic, but before age three they often engage in parallel play (Beaty, 1994) where each child is engaged in practically the same activity but they do so seemingly independently as they play side by side—each may be playing with building blocks or each may be playing with a stuffed animal. Child development specialists, however, tell us that children have an awareness of the other's actions and that this awareness provides some foundation for the cooperative activities in which they later engage. By the age of three or four, children begin to seek ways of playing together through the use of maneuvers that sociologists call *access rituals* (Beaty, 1994; Clay, 1993). These maneuvers involve nonverbal appeals such as gestures and smiles, verbal requests such as "Can I play too?" or maybe even disruptions. By age seven, children are very much socialized to play together.

The social aspects of play—in school and out of school—provide a framework for how children learn together in classrooms. For example, they may observe an activity such as a teacher's demonstration or another child's behavior and attempt to make

sense of the activity. Vygotsky (1978) has much to say regarding the insights these attempts provide us about cognitive and social development. The *zone of proximal development* refers to the difference between a student's current level of knowledge and the potential the student can attain with help from a skillful teacher. *Scaffolding* is a general term for the support provided to link a student's old knowledge to new knowledge (Berk & Winsler, 1995) to help organize information so that it makes sense and can be retained. Both are important theories and practices for teachers as they facilitate students' cognitive learning through social interactions.

The social aspects of learning provide a powerful force upon which teachers build fruitful learning environments. Through cooperative learning activities (Johnson & Johnson, 1986), small and large group activities, teacher-directed discussions, and even reading aloud, teachers can capitalize on this force. Let us examine a few possibilities that involve children's literature and science, mathematics, or social studies lessons.

An example using the force of air within a collaborative experiment may be appropriate here. After a group discussion about the power of and a reaction to books about hurricanes such as *Hurricane* (Wiesner, 1990) (see Chapter 7, Lesson 7.8), students may be led to a further discussion about the destructive power of air. Using several raw potatoes and a straw for every student, the teacher can demonstrate how the force of "packed air" allows the students to drive a straw through a hard potato. All fifth and sixth grade students can have success with such an experiment—they willingly share failed attempts, successes, and observations using the experiment in this interactive activity.

Many students also find the arithmetic of baseball interesting. Baseball provides many opportunities to use numbers. Prior to reading *My Lucky Hat* (O'Malley, 1999), second and third grade students will enjoy a discussion of the reasons why baseball players must be able to count well. After the reading, students can collectively share responses to questions like "How many strikes do you get when you are up to bat?" and "How many players are there on each team?" or even "How many games are there in the World Series?" Some more advanced students may also want to discuss batting averages and how they are computed.

A powerful example of social learning comes from the social studies lesson using *Sweet Music in Harlem* (Taylor, 2004) (see Chapter 9, Lesson 9.13). As students complete an inquiry project on the notable figures of the Harlem Renaissance and understand the historical significance of their work in music and art, they may begin to understand the contributions made by many Americans who come from diverse backgrounds. The lesson, in turn, is designed to affirm the students' own sense of worth and possibilities for contribution using their ethnic and cultural diversities.

Many students may be inspired to read a book solely on the basis of a teacher's brief and creative introduction to the book. For example, a brief discussion of pets and why a crocodile may *not* be an appropriate pet—followed by reading the hilarious account of a girl who takes her pet crocodile on a bus in *Harriet and the Crocodiles* (Waddell, 1982)—should provide delight for most third grade students. Similarly, if the unrealistic but captivating first page of *James and the Giant Peach* (Dahl, 1961) is shared with a fourth or fifth grade class, it will be enough to evoke strong interest from most students. If the teacher then asks, "Who would like to take this book home and read it?" chances are that she will have many takers. Also, if the teacher can engage sixth grade students in a discussion about the tragedy of the Civil War and how it split families, then students will benefit from *Across Five Aprils* (Hunt, 1964). Similarly, if the first, brief chapter of *Holes* (Sachar, 1998) is read aloud to sixth, seventh, or eighth graders, many students will want to read the book. In each case after the book is read, there is an additional invitation to read the same book, but this time by *another* student.

Conclusion

Books have the potential to make personal connections with the reader; they provide genuine opportunities for readers to see themselves in the characters they meet, to elicit unique emotions and responses to the stories, and even to transport themselves to a whole new world. The power that books hold for potential learning is not difficult to imagine, simply because we all have experienced such learning some time in our lives.

We believe that mathematical, scientific, and social studies concepts can be learned through the interaction between what students already know and what they learn by reading and discussing carefully selected books. The development of new knowledge occurs through a construction of meaning that comes about when *the new information is connected to what the learner already knows*. The teacher's role in this process is that of the guider and facilitator who (1) determines which ideas and concepts are appropriate to teach; (2) selects the books and materials necessary to teach the ideas and concepts; (3) determines the procedures necessary—discussions, demonstrations, and activities; and (4) promotes a climate of learning where cooperation and sharing are expected. We hope that this text unlocks that power for learning for the young mathematicians, scientists, social scientists, and readers.

REFERENCES

Anderson, R. C. (1977). *Schema-directed processes in language comprehension* (Tech. Rep. 50). Urbana: Center for the Study of Reading, University of Illinois.

Anderson, R. C. (1994). Role of the reader's schema in comprehension, learning, and memory. In R. B. Ruddell, M. R. Ruddell, & H. Singer (Eds.), *Theoretical models and processes of reading* (4th ed., pp. 469–537). Newark, DE: International Reading Association.

Bartlett, F. C. (1932). *Remembering*. London: Cambridge University Press.

Beaty, J. J. (1994). *Observing development of the young child*. New York: Merrill imprint of Macmillan.

Berk, L. E., & Winsler, A. (1995). *Scaffolding children's learning*. Washington, DC: National Association for the Education of Young Children.

Bruner, J. (1986). *Actual minds: Possible worlds*. Cambridge, MA: Harvard University Press.

Clay, M. M. (1993). *An observation survey of early literacy achievement*. Portsmouth, NH: Heinemann.

Cox, C. (2007). *Teaching language arts: A student- and response-centered classroom* (6th ed.). Boston: Allyn & Bacon.

Farrell, E. J., & Squire, J. R. (Eds.). (1990). *Transactions with literature: A fifty-year perspective*. Urbana, IL: National Council of Teachers of English.

Fish, S. (1980). *Is there a text in this class? The authority of interpretive communities*. Cambridge, MA: Harvard University Press.

Fountas, I. C., & Pinnell, G. S. (2001). *Guiding readers and writers, grades 3-6*. Portsmouth, NH: Heinemann.

Hartman, D. K., & Hartman, J. A. (1993). Reading across texts: Expanding the role of the reader. *The Reading Teacher, 47*(3), 202–211.

Huck, C. S., & Kiefer, B. Z. (Eds.). (2003). *Children's literature in the elementary school* (8th ed.). New York: McGraw-Hill.

Jackson, P. W. (1995). On the place of narrative in teaching. In H. McEwan & K. Egan (Eds.), *Narrative in teaching, learning, and research* (pp. 3–23). New York: Teachers College Press.

Johnson, R., & Johnson, D. (1986). *Cooperation and competition*. New York: Lawrence Erlbaum.

Karolides, N. J. (1997). The reading process: Transactional theory in action. In N. J. Karolides (Ed.), *Reader response in elementary classrooms: Quest and discovery*. Mahwah, NJ: Lawrence Erlbaum.

McEwan, H., & Egan, K. (Eds.). (1995). *Narrative in teaching, learning, and research*. New York: Teachers College Press.

Piaget, J. (1926). *The language and thought of the child*. New York: Harcourt Brace.

Piaget, J. (1963). *The origins of intelligence in children*. New York: Norton.

Rabinowitz, P. (1987). *Before reading: Narrative conventions and the politics of interpretation*. Ithaca, NY: Cornell University Press.

Rosenblatt, L. M. (1978). *The reader, the text, the poem: The transactional theory of the literary work*. Carbondale: Southern Illinois University Press.

Rosenblatt, L. M. (1996). *Literature as exploration* (5th ed.). New York: Modern Language Association.

Ryan, K., & Cooper, J. M. (2006). *Those who can, teach* (11th ed.). Boston: Wadsworth.

Spiro, R. J. (1980). *Schema theory and reading comprehension: New directions* (Tech. Rep. 191). Urbana: Center for the Study of Reading, University of Illinois.

Stein, N. L., & Trabasso, T. (1981). *What's in a story: An approach to comprehension and instruction* (Tech. Rep. 200). Urbana: Center for the Study of Reading, University of Illinois.

Vygotsky, L. S. (1978). *Mind in society*. Cambridge, MA: Harvard University Press.

Wells, G. (1986). *The meaning makers: Children learning language and using language to learn*. Portsmouth, NH: Heinemann.

CHILDREN'S LITERATURE

Bunting, E. (2000). *The memory string* (T. Rand, Illus.). New York: Clarion.

Dahl, R. (1961). *James and the giant peach* (N. E. Ekholm, Illus.). New York: Knopf.

Demi. (1997). *One grain of rice: A mathematical folktale*. New York: Scholastic.

Fleischman, P. (1999). *Weslandia* (K. Hawkes, Illus.). Cambridge, MA: Candlewick Press.

Henkes, K. (1990). *Julius: The baby of the world*. New York: Greenwillow.

Henkes, K. (1991). *Chrysanthemum*. New York: Greenwillow.

Henkes, K. (2000). *Wemberly worried*. New York: HarperCollins.

Hesse, K. (1997). *Out of the dust*. New York: Scholastic.

High, L. O. (1999). *The barn savers* (T. Lewin, Illus.). Honesdale, PA: Boyds Mills Press.

Howe, J., & Howe, D. (1979). *Bunnicula: A rabbit-tale of mystery* (A. Daniel, Illus.). New York: Atheneum.

Hunt, I. (1964). *Across five Aprils*. Chicago: Follett.

Jenkins, S. (1999). *The top of the world: Climbing Mount Everest*. Boston: Houghton Mifflin.

Konigsburg, E. L. (1967). *From the mixed-up files of Mrs. Basil E. Frankweiler*. New York: Atheneum.

Munsch, R. N. (1989). *Love you forever* (S. McGraw, Illus.). Scarborough, Ontario: Firefly Books.

O'Malley, K. (1999). *My lucky hat*. Greenvale, NY: Mondo.

Park, L. S. (2001). *A single shard*. New York: Clarion Books.

Peck, R. (2000). *A year down yonder*. New York: Dial.

Sachar, L. (1998). *Holes*. New York: Farrar, Straus & Giroux.

Schneider, H. (2000). *Chewy Louie*. Flagstaff, AZ: Rising Moon.

Shannon, D. (1998). *No, David!* New York: Scholastic.

Silverstein, S. (1964). *The giving tree*. New York: Harper & Row.

Stanley, J. (1992). *Children of the dust bowl: The true story of the school at Weedpatch Camp*. New York: Crown.

Stewart, S. (1997). *The gardener* (D. Small, Illus.). New York: Farrar, Straus & Giroux.

Taylor, D. A. (2004). *Sweet music in Harlem* (F. Morrison, Illus.). New York: Lee & Low Books.

Waber, B. (2008). *Ira sleeps over*. San Anselmo, CA: Sandpiper.

Waddell, M. (1982). *Harriet and the crocodiles*. New York: Little, Brown.

Wiesner, D. (1990). *Hurricane*. New York: Clarion.

Williams, V. B. (1984). *A chair for my mother*. New York: Greenwillow.

Winthrop, E. (2000). *Promises* (B. Lewin, Illus.). New York: Clarion.

CHAPTER

2

Mathematics, Science, and Social Studies: Learning Through Integration

n the real world outside of school, we do not compartmentalize our thinking as just mathematics, science, or social studies. Topics in life are always multidimensional; topics themselves are naturally connected to each other in more ways than one. Any topic can be and should be examined from multiple perspectives—historical, cultural, sociological, economical, political, technological, anthropological—to *fully* understand its concept, implication, and application. However, the practice in some schools is to teach knowledge and skills in isolation, as separate and distinct subjects without connections within and among ideas and concepts. The lessons in Chapters 6 through 9 allow natural connections to occur as students learn mathematics, science, and social studies concepts using literature.

Why Integrate?

In simplest terms, integration takes place when two or more disciplines are taught together in order to make explicit the multidimensional nature of concepts and to make connections between and among the concepts. In doing so, an integrated curriculum facilitates *conceptual* learning instead of learning facts in isolation and fragmenting content. Such an approach allows students to apply the content, skills, and processes to think about, discuss, and solve real-life problems and situations. Integration is an attempt at making learning meaningful in authentic contexts, to mirror the complexity of the world in students' learning. Learning experiences should enable students to fully understand how they are situated in the world and to apply their understandings in their day-to-day lives.

In addition, there are other important and practical reasons for integration. Hamston and Murdoch (1996) offer the following list as part of their rationale for an integrated curriculum. Integration:

- Loosens the pressure created by rigid timetables and a stop–start curriculum, assisting teachers and students to use and manage their time more productively.

- Assists students and teachers to develop more efficient means of gathering, organizing, and processing the information increasingly available on a global as well as a local level.

- Helps deal with curriculum that is "bulging at the seams" and challenges teachers to develop ways in which students can reorganize and bring the pieces together.

- Helps us focus on the "big ideas" rather than trivializing the content of our programs.

- Makes more sense to the students' (and teacher's) day by providing a flow of learning rather than a stop–start approach.

- Develops a sense of community.

- Caters more successfully to individual differences and the interests and needs of the learner.

- Encourages students to consider how they learn while developing important concepts and understandings.

- Provides genuine and rich contexts for developing a range of skills and understandings.

In practical terms, integration may take place in a single lesson, in a unit comprising a series of lessons over several days or weeks, or even in a yearlong integrated course. Teachers in PreK–8 classrooms accomplish integration by organizing learning experiences around topics of high interest to students, such as the environment and space, allowing connections to occur across curricular areas (Freeman & Person, 1998). Topics may also be generated using state and local standards, matching what is expected to be taught to "big ideas." No matter the particular topic or theme selected, natural and conceptual connections are made among the disciplines and topics. Simply put, learning becomes connecting in an integrated curriculum.

Literature as the Connecting Agent

Children's literature is a vital component in a comprehensive literacy program. Teachers in other disciplines have long advocated the use of literature as a means for teaching. In an integrated curriculum, the use of children's literature helps to develop content area concepts while providing a means for students to realize the variety of situations in which people use mathematics, science, and social studies concepts, for example, for real-life purposes, thus making their learning personal and meaningful. With the wealth of quality children's literature available, it is becoming increasingly easy to develop and enhance content area concepts through stories and poems.

The use of literature to develop content area concepts is encouraged by experts for the following reasons (Lawrence, Hope, Small, & Martin, 1996):

- **Builds on the positive reaction that most children have to hearing and reading both familiar and new stories.** *The Great Kapok Tree: A Tale of the Amazon Rain Forest* (see Chapter 8, Lesson 8.11) by Lynne Cherry (1990) eloquently presents the sheer beauty of the rain forest and the marvelous creatures that inhabit it through both the words and the illustrations. The kapok tree provides habitats for a variety of living organisms.

- **Integrates learning in a variety of curriculum areas.** *The Great Serum Race* (see Chapter 9, Lesson 9.10) by Debbie Miller (2002) tells the story of how brave men and dogs deliver life-saving serum to Nome, Alaska, to prevent the outbreak of diphtheria in 1925. Battling ice, snow, darkness, and severe temperatures, the serum was delivered in five days, saving hundreds of lives. The concepts presented in this story can be linked to science, mathematics, social studies, and health.

- **Humanizes mathematics, science, and social studies in the eyes of children and parents.** *Prince William* (see Chapter 8, Lesson 8.13) by Gloria Rand (1992) and illustrated by Ted Rand is fiction based on the realities of the aftermath of an oil spill. The little girl's love for one baby seal will warm the heart of every child. *Flotsam* (see Chapter 9, Lesson 9.15) by David Wiesner (2006) is a beautiful wordless picture book about a fantastical underwater adventure that can be used to begin talking about what each one of us can do to save the environment.

- **Challenges the stereotype of mathematics as a sterile, noncreative subject that is unrelated to the arts.** *The Quiltmaker's Gift* by Jeff Brumbeau (2000) and illustrated by Gail de Marcken contains 250 different quilt patterns in the King's puzzle poster on the book jacket, which connects mathematics to art.

- **Provides an alternative vehicle for communicating about mathematics, science, and social studies.** *Barn Savers* (see Chapter 8, Lesson 8.4) by Linda Oatman High (1999) and illustrated by Ted Lewin highlights the preservation of old barns. The "Barn Savers"—the father and his son—salvage the pieces of an old barn for recycling and reusing. Triangles, the most rigid and stable polygon, can be observed in the architectural design of a barn. A network of triangles, also known as a geodesic dome, can be connected to the lesson.
- **Stimulates interest, enjoyment, and confidence in children.** In *Officer Buckle and Gloria* (see Chapter 6, Lesson 6.13) by Peggy Rathmann (1995), a humorous story is told about a police officer obsessed with safety rules and

his K-9 partner, Gloria, who helps to amuse the audience while Officer Buckle delivers his safety speeches. Science and social studies lessons related to personal and social perspectives can be presented through the funny story and its comical illustrations.

Perhaps the most powerful reason for using literature to teach mathematics, science, and social studies is that literature speaks to the heart of the child (Spann, 1992). Learning content area concepts becomes personal and meaningful. This type of instruction helps children realize the variety of situations in which people use these concepts for real, authentic purposes.

Stories told in books with social studies concepts are perhaps most inherently relatable. Stories about people—both famous and ordinary—and their experiences—both remarkable and mundane—are sources of deep connection that readers can make. The unforgettable story of Henry, who mails himself in a box in order to gain freedom from slavery in *Henry's Freedom Box* (see Chapter 8, Lesson 8.14), by Ellen Levine (2007), and illustrated by Kadir Nelson, though extraordinary in every possible way, can provide a student the courage to overcome a challenge.

Using Literature to Teach

In this text, all of the lessons provide opportunities for reading, writing, listening, speaking, and viewing through the use of literature. In addition, integration takes place in one of the following ways: (1) integration of literature to mathematics; (2) integration of literature to science; (3) integration of literature to social studies; and (4) integration of literature to some combination of the three, such as literature to math *and* science. Ideally, the development of several of these concepts can evolve using one quality book. As one particular concept is highlighted and linked to children's experiences, there are *appropriate* and *natural* opportunities to teach other concepts. We have made such an integration among mathematics, science, and social studies using literature whenever possible while avoiding superficial and forced connections. In all lesson types, literature is used to inspire and motivate the development of concepts and to make relevant connections to children's lives.

USING LITERATURE TO TEACH MATHEMATICS

When mathematical concepts are taught in isolation, children often have difficulty learning them. They can "learn" an operation but fail to either understand the mathematical concept or recognize a situation where the concept can be applied. Stories, both narrative and expository in structure, provide contexts in which mathematics concepts can be presented together with opportunities to think critically, solve problems, and make connections to students' knowledge about the world.

The National Council of Teachers of Mathematics (NCTM), in its curriculum standards, also endorses integration. The NCTM standards state, "We favor . . . a truly integrated curricular organization in all grades to permit students to develop mathematical power more readily and to allow the necessary flexibility over time to incorporate the content of these standards. Teaching practice should move toward connecting mathematics, its ideas, and its application—away from treating mathematics as a body of isolated concepts and procedures" (NCTM, 1991, p. 3).

Examples of explicit, meaningful, and relevant connections that can be made to mathematics using quality literature are found in many places.

- *Snowflake Bentley* (see Chapter 7, Lesson 7.5) by Jacqueline Briggs Martin (1998) and illustrated by Mary Azarian introduces students to ice crystals as small miracles, and reveals that no two snowflakes are alike and that each one is startlingly beautiful. The formation of ice crystals into snowflakes and the geometry of the six sides (or points) with lines of symmetry invite the students to share in a scientist's vision and perseverance and the wonders of nature. The unit of study can develop around the mystery of the snowflake's universal hexagonal shape and its infinite number of lovely designs.

- *Sea Shapes* by Suse MacDonald (1994) does a delightful job of connecting geometric shapes to marine animals. Geometric shapes are found in real-life examples in exotic sea creatures. Students can collect fascinating facts about their favorite sea creature and find other geometric shapes and patterns in nature.

These are just two of many dynamic and exciting children's books that invite and motivate children to learn mathematics by responding to stories, characters, and their experiences in children's literature.

USING LITERATURE TO TEACH SCIENCE

Science, too, is everywhere, and when we allow children to *experience* science in ways that relate to their own day-to-day lives, meaningful learning takes place. From simple concept books by Gail Gibbons to more elaborate informational books by Seymour Simon, many books present scientific concepts that children see in their own world. Children can build new knowledge or expand their existing understandings; they can refine and reorganize what they already know; and they can make connections among the concepts as they learn more about them.

Picture books can also bring to life distant worlds and concepts that are not part of children's reality. The rain forests and the exotic forms of life that exist within; the human desire to explore the planets, stars, galaxy, and beyond; the life far beneath the surface of great bodies of water; and the technical complexities that hide in modern conveniences are just some of the many "fantasies" that can be made real through literature.

Many of the science lessons that derive from quality books in Chapters 6 through 9 focus on the *process* of doing science. Children participate in genuine inquiries; they experiment and document their observations; they make hypotheses and predictions, and perhaps even generalizations. Through all of these processes, they gain, expand, and refine their scientific concepts and knowledge. Literature provides an invaluable context and springboard for such scientific processes to take place.

Following are two examples of literature that beautifully and meaningfully highlight these concepts:

- *The Hindenburg* by Patrick O'Brien (2000) details the 37 years of the steerable airships until the disaster that ended the era of the majestic dirigibles. At an intermediate level, the airship's design, construction, and aerodynamics can be developed through these illustrations.

- *A Drop of Water: A Book of Science and Wonder* (see Chapter 9, Lesson 9.9), an Orbis Pictus award winner by Walter Wick (1997), presents many properties of water such as surface tension, adhesion, capillary attraction, molecular motion, freezing, evaporation, and condensation. Using Wick's background as a photographer, brilliant photos accompany all of the concepts.

From narratives to expository, from informational books to biographies, many types of children's literature at all levels are available to use when teaching and learning scientific concepts.

USING LITERATURE TO TEACH SOCIAL STUDIES

Social studies is perhaps the content area subject that integrates most naturally with literature. Historical fictions, for example, have inherent connections to history when events and concepts are presented in authentic, accurate, and personally and emotionally relevant ways (Tunnell and Jacobs, 2007). The stories of the protagonists in historical fictions—with their remarkable or subtle encounters with historical figures and events—allow conceptual learning of social studies concepts. For example, *Sweet Music in Harlem* (see Chapter 9, Lesson 9.13) by Debbie A. Taylor (2004) and illustrated by Frank Morrison uses a legendary photograph of 57 famous jazz musicians standing on the steps of a brownstone in Harlem, taken by a young photographer named Art Kane in 1958. The life of bustling, colorful, and rhythmic Harlem surrounding these musicians is artfully and authentically presented from the perspective of a young boy who lives in the neighborhood. As Tunnell and Jacobs (2007) state so eloquently, "[H]istorical fiction can quicken dry historical facts and breathe life into the people and events of the past." Historical events from both recent and ancient past, lives of famous figures, and sociological patterns from generation to generation are already told in story form. Literature written for children serves as a natural vessel for capturing these stories.

USING LITERATURE TO TEACH MATHEMATICS, SCIENCE, *AND* SOCIAL STUDIES

During most of history, the practices of mathematics and science were indistinguishable. One reason for the integration of mathematics and science is that "the very backbone of much of theoretical science evolved, in a sense, as a branch of applied mathematics and would not exist without it today" (Adams, 1970). Others claim that "integration infuses mathematical methods in science and scientific methods into mathematics such that it becomes indistinguishable as to whether it is mathematics or science" (Berlin & White, 1992, p. 341).

Likewise, social studies and literature share natural affinities, making them ideal for meaningful integration: Events in the past are told in stories; we learn about others in remote places through stories; and myths and legends from ancient civilizations are passed down as stories. Furthermore, having a conceptual understanding of people's impact on the environment allows opportunities for social studies to naturally integrate with science. Neither exists without the other, and the symbiotic relationship between people and their environment, both social and natural, is easy to recognize.

Consider the following ways in which content area concepts in the classroom overlap (Pang & Good, 2000):

- **Discovering patterns and relationships.** Students can compare patterns in human-made objects with patterns in natural objects. The patterns can be represented with manipulatives such as tiles, buttons, beads, and counters. *Dots, Spots, Speckles, and Stripes* by Tana Hoban (1987) vividly illustrates patterns in feathers, flowers, people, and animals. Students can also find relationships between historical events. For example, the timeline of the Harlem Renaissance can be understood in the context of our nation's history in *Sweet Music in Harlem* (see Chapter 9, Lesson 9.13) by Debbie A. Taylor (2004).

- **Solving problems, the inquiry approach.** Students learn to partition equal quantities among different numbers, which is the concept of division. In *The Doorbell Rang* by Pat Hutchins (1986), the story does not initially tell us how many cookies there are, but it does tell us how many there are for each child. As more and more children arrive, they share equally, learning the concept of division.

- **Connecting to real-life situations, authentic problems.** Students might research historic barns and their architecture in their community or state. Then, they construct barns with "junk" or recycled materials as they explore conservation and restoration, using the *Barn Savers* (see Chapter 8, Lesson 8.4) by Linda Oatman High (1999) and illustrated by Ted Lewin.

- **Reasoning skills.** Using *Seven Blind Mice* by Ed Young (1992), students apply their own reasoning skills along with the seven blind mice as each one sees only one part of the elephant and, based on that limited information, identifies it incorrectly. Similar skills are used when students explore what is inside a box without looking in the box, modeling how mathematicians and scientists gather data about unknown phenomena.

Imagine the exciting combination of integration possibilities in the areas of mathematics, science, social studies, and literacy using literature. For example, mathematics and science link naturally when both are presented as related processes instead of isolated topics and skills. The American Association for the Advancement of Science (AAAS, 1989) states that proficiency in both the mathematics and science disciplines requires extensive student experience using relevant principles to solve problems, communicate ideas, and connect and generalize concepts.

The current reform documents in mathematics and science education also endorse an interdisciplinary approach, notably between mathematics and science (AAAS, 1989; NCTM, 1989, 1991, 1995, 2000; NRC, 1996). The most common argument for integration is based on the view of science as inquiry and mathematics as problem solving. However, teachers hold diverse views of science as inquiry, including "the process of science, doing hands-on, using kits, or involving students in activities" (Bybee, Ferrini-Mundy, & Loucks-Horsley, 1997, p. 328). Understanding mathematics as problem solving is also often limited to acquiring some problem-solving strategies and developing application abilities with simple word problems (Hiebert et al., 1996; Meier, Hovde, & Meier, 1996). Despite many compelling arguments, the desire for integration remains unfulfilled because mathematics and science usually are taught in an unconnected way in most schools. Classroom instruction emphasizing mathematics–science connections remains an exception rather than a norm (Watanabe & Huntley, 1998, p. 19).

As classroom teachers, we must be cognizant of opportunities to bring science and mathematics together. Scientific investigations present one of the best opportunities for overcoming this problem because children can easily see how the mathematics relate to solving their problem (Benbow & Mably, 2002, p. 225). For example, a thematic unit on weather and the conditions of the lower atmosphere is enhanced with David Wiesner's *Hurricane* (1990; see Chapter 7, Lesson 7.8).

If mathematics and science are natural links using skills and thinking processes, social studies offers overlaps in *content* with other subjects (Sorel, 2005), making it one of the most flexible areas for integration. In fact, the definition of *social studies*, as provided by the National Council for the Social Studies (NCSS), stresses that it provides "coordinated, systematic study drawing upon . . . content from the humanities, mathematics, and the physical sciences" (NCSS, 1994, p. vii). Concepts, topics, themes, and generalizations in the many disciplines within the social studies are fertile grounds to connect mathematics and science knowledge. Imagine any topic in history, geography, economics, or civic education, and think of the many ways you may be able to facilitate mathematics and science learning. For example, interpreting and analyzing polling data for an election in a civics education lesson helps us to project the winner. Geographic knowledge is necessary to plan campaign strategies in specific states, counties, cities, and legislative districts. Historic knowledge of previous elections allows us (or discourages us) to expect a win. Surely, the obvious and subtle connections we can make within content areas using this single concept can go beyond these examples.

An integrated curriculum gives students the tools for lifelong learning and equips them to solve problems as they arise. This type of learning requires imagination as students figure out the inner workings of our world and its myriad connections. Quality children's literature is the ingredient that nurtures imagination and fosters its growth.

Developing Understanding in Mathematics, Science, and Social Studies

eymour Papert (1980), who created the computer language Logo, said, "Children learn by doing *and* by thinking about what they do." For children to learn mathematics, science, and social studies, they have to be actively involved and reflect on their thinking. Key ideas in the construction of this knowledge include the following:

- **Knowledge is constructed by each individual; it is not absorbed passively.** We believe that children's literature is a bridge that helps students make connections to content area concepts that are embedded in a network of interrelated ideas and procedures.

- **Knowledge and understanding are personal matters for each learner.** Ideas are not poured into an empty jug. Children must use what is in their prior knowledge to construct new meanings. Children's literature addresses this personal need by speaking to the heart of the child.

- **Active thinking is an essential learning activity.** Learners must be mentally engaged in constructing new ideas. Making connections to a larger network of ideas is part of the learning process.

- **Teaching is a student-centered activity.** Effective teachers design activities that invite students to learn and always consider what the students will be doing and thinking as they do this.

One of the key concepts the lessons in this book promote is for students to be "active thinkers." In other words, getting them to learn mathematics, science, and social studies by working at forming relationships, making connections, and integrating concepts and procedures. As teachers, we must continually ask ourselves, *How can we structure lessons to invite students to think?*" Following are six guidelines for lessons that promote active thinking (Van deWalle, Karp, & Bay-Williams, 2009):

- Create a problem-solving environment.
- Use models and hands-on materials.
- Encourage interaction and discussion.
- Use cooperative learning groups.
- Require justification of responses.
- Listen actively.

In addition, active thinking through literature naturally involves reading, writing, speaking, listening, viewing, and visually representing as part of the learning process.

CREATE A PROBLEM-SOLVING ENVIRONMENT

Problem solving is seen as a means of acquiring an understanding of mathematics and science. In our classrooms, we help our students *learn* mathematics and science by having them *do* mathematics and science. According to the National Research Council (1996), inquiry is the shifting of emphasis from teachers presenting information to students learning mathematics and science through active involvement.

In the *Math Curse* (see Chapter 9, Lesson 9.4) by Jon Scieszka (1995) and illustrated by Lane Smith, many everyday problems are presented in a humorous manner to help children develop problem-solving strategies, such as "If I want 2 slices of pizza, should I ask for: a. 1/8; b. 2/8; or c. 2 slices of pizza?" This type of question can be solved using a number of different strategies with more than one right answer. Another idea for sharing this book is to present a problem each day for the students to respond to individually in a journal entry; then, discuss possible solutions as a class.

In the science classroom, students may have a problem that requires them to conduct an inquiry search. In this situation, the students may be using more than one piece of literature while doing their research. For example, *Oceans* by Seymour

Simon (2006) is filled with magnificent photographs, diagrams, charts, and statistics. Pair that book with another informational book *The Magic School Bus on the Ocean Floor* by Joanna Cole and Bruce Degen (1992). Both selections will provide answers to students' research questions, but from different perspectives.

USE MODELS AND HANDS-ON MATERIALS

Models are concrete materials to reason with and talk about when referring to abstract relationships. Also, they provide a means of testing conjectures and can be used as props for articulating explanations. It is difficult for students of all ages to talk about and test out abstract relationships using words alone. Models give the learners something to think about, explore with, talk about, and reason with (Van deWalle et al., 2009).

As *Fish Eyes: A Book You Can Count On* (see Chapter 6, Lesson 6.1) by Lois Ehlert (2001) is read aloud, the students can actively model the concept of "one more than,"

an essential addition concept, with counters, beans, macaroni, or chips. "Three smiling fish—3 smiling fish plus me makes 4" portrays three colorful fish with one small black fish that is discretely detached on the two-page spread so that the students are always adding "one more than" to the quantity of brightly colored fish. As we guide the instruction, we can ask, "If you have three fish and add one more fish, how many fish do you have in all?" The students in PreK–1 respond aloud and show the quantity in their workspace with hands-on materials.

After reading *The Sun, the Wind and the Rain* by Lisa Westberg Peters (1988), students can investigate rock erosion by filling a small plastic jar half full of rock chips consisting mostly of sandstone, limestone, or shale. Then, have students take turns shaking the jar vigorously for several minutes. Observe carefully the remaining chips under a magnifying glass. Inspect the water and the bottom of the jar for any deposits. Relate these observations to the passage "The small streams rushed together to become a raging river. The river gouged a deep valley. It ground the earth mountain's rough rocks into smooth pebbles."

Primary documents such as photographs, artifacts, letters, diaries, and government documents may be used as catalysts for meaningful social studies learning. Our lesson with *Sweet Music in Harlem* (Taylor, 2004) (see Chapter 9, Lesson 9.13) includes jazz music as an artifact. For those students in grades 6–8 with limited background knowledge in jazz, the actual experiences of listening to music will not only build the necessary prior knowledge but also serve as a motivating and engaging anticipatory set.

ENCOURAGE INTERACTION AND DISCUSSION

Learning to communicate in content area subjects fosters the interaction and exploration of ideas. Classrooms should be active and verbal environments. Talking, writing, describing, illustrating, and explaining are important to understanding mathematics, science, and social studies concepts. The Communication strand in the NCTM Standards (2000) indicates how this kind of expression is part of the process of thinking about mathematics (see Chapter 4).

Sweet Clara and the Freedom Quilt by Deborah Hopkinson (1993) and illustrated by James Ransome is an excellent springboard for students to create their own map or quilt pattern. This hands-on activity leads to spoken and written descriptions of their maps and quilt patterns. Writing and listening force students to assimilate new ideas into their own personal schemas; both are important forms of interaction and communication.

USE COOPERATIVE LEARNING GROUPS

Arranging the classroom in groups of three or four students encourages and increases the amount of interaction and discussion. Students are more willing to speak out, pose arguments, and share their ideas within a small group than in front of the entire class. Working in cooperative groups is not something that happens instantly in the classroom. Students must be taught how to work productively and collaboratively with their classmates. These skills, like other skills, are improved with practice.

Although teachers often have students working in small groups, to qualify as cooperative learning certain criteria must be met (Lasley, Matczynski, & Rowley, 2002) including:

- Students must be able to work together in a positive way (positive independence).
- Each student is still assessed individually on what he or she knows (individual accountability).
- Specific social skills are emphasized during group work (social skills development).
- Students work together on specific tasks to accomplish particular goals (goal-oriented tasks).

Grandfather Tang's Story by Ann Tompert (1990) and illustrated by Robert Andrew Parker is a story within a story that is embellished with black ink drawings of a tangram, a seven-piece Chinese puzzle. Students in cooperative groups can replicate the characters in the book using the seven standard pieces in the tangram set and then create new characters of their own. In their cooperative groups, the students can create their own stories and illustrate the characters with rearranged pieces of the tangram puzzle.

REQUIRE JUSTIFICATION OF RESPONSES

Justifying their responses has a positive effect on how students view mathematics, science, and social studies and their own abilities within these disciplines. Explaining "why?" requires reflective thinking and diminishes guesses or responses based on rote memorization. The ability to talk about their thinking with confidence is clearly promoted.

In *12 Ways to Get to 11* (see Chapter 7, Lesson 7.1) by Eve Merriam (1993) and illustrated by Bernie Karlin, 12 different combinations that add up to 11 are presented using ordinary experiences. For example, at the circus, six peanut shells and five pieces of popcorn added together make 11, or three sets of triplets and one set of twins make 11. After the read-aloud experience, the students can create their own combinations with popcorn, macaroni, or beans and explain their combinations to the rest of the class, orally and in writing.

In our lesson using *Weslandia* (see Chapter 9, Lesson 9.14), by Paul Fleischman (2002), students are asked to decide which of three cereal brands is the healthiest option for breakfast using the nutritional information. Then they are asked to justify their choice. The answer will be based on not only the facts (i.e., percentage of daily recommended intake for specific nutrients), but also on who is consuming the cereal. Is it a young child, a teenager, or a mature adult?

LISTEN ACTIVELY

Part of listening actively is to uncover misconceptions and to design questions to uncover what children know and understand, as well as how they know and understand it. This information is necessary to design experiences that address student misconceptions.

Active listening is also important because promoting active thinking requires that we place the attention on the children's thoughts instead of ours. We want our children to do more thinking and search for relationships, patterns, and connections—that is, understanding. In the classroom, we can extend our students' responses with wait-time and by asking them to elaborate. Simply asking, "why?" permits the child and others to continue their thinking. "Tell me more . . ." and "Why do you think that?" are standard questions that encourage children to share their thinking. This kind of questioning promotes listening to peers and encourages learning from each other. Getting students to ask each other "why?" is an essential step toward a learning community.

After reading *In the Small, Small Pond* (see Chapter 6, Lesson 6.9) by Denise Fleming (1993), a story about the activities of animals that live near a pond as spring progresses to autumn, question the students about the animals' behaviors and say, "Tell me more about that." The discussion can continue with stories of their own about animals they have observed living near a pond and how the animals' behaviors may change as fall approaches. It is important to remember to be accepting and nonevaluative of all responses, which in turn encourages children to respond more often and to elaborate on their explanations.

Conclusion

We all live in a world that increasingly depends on knowledge in mathematics, science, and social studies. We want students to acquire the conceptual understanding and problem-solving skills they will need to function effectively as workers and citizens in today's world. Children's literature, along with inquiry-based learning, provides excellent opportunities to humanize the concepts, to link related issues, and to bring life to seemingly isolated and abstract ideas.

REFERENCES

Adams, P. (Ed.). (1970). *Overview: MINNEMAST.* Minneapolis, MN: MINNEMAST.

American Association for the Advancement of Science. (1989). *Science for all Americans: Project 2061.* Washington, DC: Author.

Benbow, A., & Mably, C. (2002). *Science education for elementary teachers: An investigation-based approach.* Belmont, CA: Wadsworth/Thomson Learning.

Berlin, D. F. (1994). The integration of science and mathematics education from the NSF/SSMA Wingspread conference plenary papers. *School Science and Mathematics, 94*(1), 32–35.

Berlin, D. F., & White, A. L. (1992). Report from the NSF/SSMA Wingspread conference: A network for integrated science and mathematics for teaching and learning. *School Science and Mathematics, 92*(6), 340–342.

Bybee, R. W., Ferrini-Mundy, J., & Loucks-Horsley, S. (1997). National standards and school science and mathematics. *School Science and Mathematics, 97*(7), 325–334.

Charnitski, D. W., & Harvey, F. A. (1999, February 10). *Integrating science and mathematics curricula using computer mediated communications: A Vygotskian perspective.* A paper presented at the National Convention of the Association for Educational Communications and Technology (AECT). Retrieved September 26, 2001, from INFOTRAC database.

Czerniak, C. M., Weber Jr., W. B., Sandmann, A., & Ahern, J. (1999). A literature review of science and mathematics integration [electronic version]. *School Science and Mathematics, 99,* 421–431.

Freeman, E. B., & Person, D. G. (1998). *Connecting informational children's books with content area learning.* Boston: Allyn & Bacon.

Hamston, J., & Murdoch, K. (1996). *Integrating socially: Planning integrated units of work for social education.* Portsmouth, NH: Heinemann.

Hiebert, J., Carpenter, T. P., Fennema, E., Fuson, K., Human, P., Murray, H., et al. (1996). Problem solving as a basis for reform in curriculum and instruction: The case of mathematics. *Educational Researcher, 25*(4), 12–21.

Isaacs, A., Wagreich, P., & Gartzman, M. (1997). The quest for integration: School mathematics and science. (Reforming the third R: Changing the school mathematics curriculum) [electronic version]. *American Journal of Education, 106,* 179–228.

Kearns, D., & Harvey, J. (2000). *A legacy of learning.* Washington, DC: Brookings Institution Press.

Lasley, T. J., II, Matczynski, T. J., & Rowley, J B. (2002). *Instructional models: Strategies for teaching in a diverse society* (2nd ed.). Belmont, CA: Wadsworth/Thomson Learning.

Lawrence, P. R., Hope, J., Small, M., & Martin, M. (1996). *Windows on math.* Warren, NJ: Optical Data Corporation.

Meier, S. L., Hovde, R. L., & Meier, R. L. (1996). Problem solving: Teachers' perceptions, content area models, and interdisciplinary connections. *School Science and Mathematics, 96*(5), 230–237.

National Council for the Social Studies. (1994). *Expectations of excellence: Curriculum standards for social studies.* Washington, DC: Author.

National Council of Teachers of Mathematics. (1989). *Curriculum and evaluation standards for school mathematics.* Reston, VA: Author.

National Council of Teachers of Mathematics. (1991). *Professional standards for teaching mathematics.* Reston, VA: Author.

National Council of Teachers of Mathematics. (1995). *Assessment standards for school mathematics.* Reston, VA: Author.

National Council of Teachers of Mathematics. (2000). *Principles and standards for school mathematics.* Reston, VA: Author.

National Research Council. (1989). *Everybody counts: A report to the nation on the future of mathematics education.* Washington, DC: National Academy Press.

National Research Council. (1996). *National science education standards.* Washington, DC: National Academy Press.

Pang, J., & Good, R. (2000). A review of the integration of science and mathematics: Implications for further research. *School Science and Mathematics, 100,* 73–93. Retrieved October 18, 2001, from INFOTRAC.

Papert, S. (1980). *Mindstorms: Children, computers, and powerful ideas.* New York: Basic Books.

Sorel, K. (2005). The integrated curriculum. *Science and Children, 46,* 21–25.

Spann, M. B. (1992). *Literature-based multicultural activities: An integrated approach.* New York: Scholastic Professional Books.

Tunnell, M. O., & Jacobs, J. S. (2007). *Children's literature briefly* (4th ed.). Upper Saddle River, NJ: Prentice Hall.

U.S. Department of Education. (2000). *The national commission on mathematics and science teaching for the 21st century.* Jessup, MD: Education Publications Center.

Van deWalle, J. A., Karp, K S., & Bay-Williams, J. M. B. (2009). *Elementary and middle school mathematics: Teaching developmentally* (7th ed.). Boston: Allyn & Bacon.

Watanabe, T., & Huntley, M. A. (1998). Connecting mathematics and science in undergraduate teacher education programs: Faculty voices from the Maryland collaborative for teacher preparation. *School Science and Mathematics, 98*(1), 19–25.

CHILDREN'S LITERATURE

Brumbeau, J. (2000). *The quiltmaker's gift* (G. de Marcken, Illus.). Duluth, MN: Pfeiffer-Hamilton.

Cherry, L. (1990). *The great kapok tree: A tale of the Amazon rain forest.* New York: Harcourt Brace.

Cole, J., & Degen, B. (1992). *The magic school bus on the ocean floor.* New York: Scholastic Trade.

Ehlert, L. (2001). *Fish eyes: A book you can count on.* New York: Harcourt Brace.

Fleischman, P. (2002). *Weslandia* (K. Hawkes, Illus.). Cambridge, MA: Candlewick Press.

Fleming, D. (1993). *In the small, small pond.* New York: Holt.

High, L. O. (1999). *Barn savers* (T. Lewin, Illus.). Honesdale, PA: Boyds Mills Press.

Hoban, T. (1987). *Dots, spots, speckles, and stripes.* New York: Greenwillow.

Hopkinson, D. (1993). *Sweet Clara and the freedom quilt* (J. Ransome, Illus.). New York: Knopf.

Hutchins, P. (1986). *The doorbell rang.* New York: Morrow.

Jackson, E. (2001). *The summer solstice* (J. D. Ellis, Illus.). Brookfield, CT: The Millbrook Press.

Levine, E. (2007). *Henry's freedom box: A true story from the Underground Railroad* (K. Nelson, Illus.). New York: Scholastic.

MacDonald, S. (1994). *Sea shapes.* New York: Harcourt Brace.

Martin, J. B. (1998). *Snowflake Bentley* (M. Azarian, Illus.). New York: Houghton Mifflin.

Merriam, E. (1993). *12 ways to get to 11* (B. Karlin, Illus.). New York: Simon & Schuster.

Miller, D. S. (2002). *The great serum race: Blazing the Iditarod trail* (J. V. Zyle, Illus.). New York: Walker.

O'Brien, P. (2000). *The Hindenburg.* New York: Holt.

Peters, L. W. (1988). *The sun, the wind and the rain* (T. Rand, Illus.). New York: Holt.

Rand, G. (1992). *Prince William* (T. Rand, Illus.). New York: Holt.

Rathmann, P. (1995). *Officer Buckle and Gloria.* New York: Putnam.

Scieszka, J. (1995). *Math curse* (L. Smith, Illus.). New York: Viking.

Simon, S. (2006). *Oceans.* New York: HarperCollins.

Taylor, D. A. (2004). *Sweet music in Harlem* (F. Morrison, Illus.). New York: Lee & Low Books.

Tompert, A. (1990). *Grandfather Tang's story* (R. A. Parker, Illus.). New York: Random House.

Wick, W. (1997). *A drop of water: A book of science and wonder.* New York: Scholastic.

Wiesner, D. (1990). *Hurricane.* New York: Houghton Mifflin.

Wiesner, D. (2006). *Flotsam.* New York: Clarion Books.

Young, E. (1992). *Seven blind mice.* New York: Philomel.

3

Making Literacy
Connections

helves at bookstores and libraries are filled with books written especially for children. Literally thousands of new books are published each year to add to the massive collection already in existence. So, how do consumers—parents, teachers, librarians, and the children themselves—make their selection of *good* books? Some may return to authors they know and love; some may choose based on the visual appeal of the book; some may look for professional validations such as awards or reviews; and some may select books based on content or genre. No matter *how* a book is chosen, there are reasons for the selection. In this chapter, we share some of the qualities we considered as the selection criteria for the children's books presented here.

Selection Criteria: Qualities of a Good Book

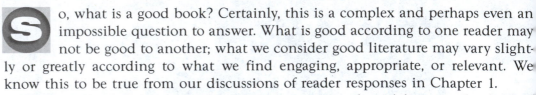

o, what is a good book? Certainly, this is a complex and perhaps even an impossible question to answer. What is good according to one reader may not be good to another; what we consider good literature may vary slightly or greatly according to what we find engaging, appropriate, or relevant. We know this to be true from our discussions of reader responses in Chapter 1.

However, as a framework we can use some general guidelines in the field of children's literature that have been set by the experts. Typically, the selection criteria for children's literature vary according to the genre; each genre has its own particular qualities that make a book a good representative of that particular category. For example, a good informational book should have compelling details as well as an attractive format and design (Tunnell & Jacobs, 2007). When we consider picture books, the criteria for the selection change. According to Norton (2006), questions about illustrations such as "Are the illustrations accurate, and do they correspond to the content of the story?" and "Do the illustrations complement the setting, plot, and mood of the story?" are two of several that the audience should ask when selecting picture books. The criteria for selecting books in particular genres are usually available in children's literature textbooks.

Another way to rely on professional opinions as we select good books is to use the guidelines drafted by experts in various professional organizations in a given field. For example, the criteria for selecting trade books for science instruction, according to Donovan and Smolkin (2002), is published by the International Reading Association in its journal *The Reading Teacher*. Likewise, Hellwig, Monroe, and Jacobs (2000) have an article in *Teaching Children Mathematics*, published by the National Council of Teachers of Mathematics, about selecting trade books for mathematics instruction. The National Council for the Social Studies publishes its annual list of "Notable Tradebooks for Young People" in its professional journal, *Social Education*. This list has become a trusty resource for teachers looking to deliver a range of social studies concepts through quality children's literature. Certainly, these and other professional insights into the selection process are important and useful to consider.

In this chapter, we include *our* list of selection criteria, presented as a set of questions. The questions are based on (1) our own individual experiences and engagement with children's books; (2) our collective and extensive conversations about trade books and their role in students' learning; and (3) careful reading and consideration of experts' opinions. The four questions that guide our selection are:

1. Is the book engaging to the reader?

2. Is the book age appropriate?

3. Does the book contribute to the balance of our collection?

4. Does the book include meaningful and relevant mathematics, science, and/or social studies concepts?

Consider these as overarching principles that we sought to meet in the collection included in this text. With the selection of each children's book, we asked these questions in order to ensure the quality, appropriateness, and relevance—in other words, a justification—for its inclusion.

GUIDING QUESTION 1: IS THE BOOK ENGAGING TO THE READER?

Whether a book is written to provide pleasure or to inform, or to do both, a *good* book always allows readers to make connections from themselves to the words and pictures in the book. And undoubtedly, the first and foremost goal for using literature in the classroom is to elicit students' aesthetic responses and foster a love of books. However, the aesthetic appeal of a book is a difficult criterion for us to judge. Refer back to our discussion of reader response theory in Chapter 1; readers' responses to books depend on *who* they are as readers. For example, age, gender, reading ability, prior knowledge, cultural background, and interest are just a few ways that each reader is different from another, hence making their responses to a particular book just as varied. An education professor would have a very different understanding and response to an article in a medical journal than a doctor. Conversely, a medical doctor may find a book chapter on selecting good children's books uninteresting and irrelevant. Children, too, have various responses to books based on what they themselves bring to the reading.

Experts know some things about how these reader variations change readers' responses to books. For example, studies found that girls tend to like series books more than boys, and girls might venture into books containing boys' topics whereas boys tend to shy away from "girls' books." However, such studies still cannot predict a reader's unique responses to a particular book. Similarly, although we have committed ourselves to include a wide range of books that would engage children of different ages, genders, backgrounds, and reading abilities, only the children who encounter our recommended books can personally judge their appeal.

GUIDING QUESTION 2: IS THE BOOK AGE APPROPRIATE?

Content, language, format, and style all contribute to the appropriateness of a book for a target audience. Books for young children should have appropriate content with effective language and attractive illustrations to make concepts come alive without underestimating children's knowledge about the world. Books for older students should portray the multidimensional and complex nature of a concept and show the interconnectedness that exists among concepts. The content should challenge and expand the views of the students, invoking meaningful questions and resulting in application such as participation in social action or inquiring deeper into the issue. When there is a good match between a book and a reader, the possibilities for learning are boundless. Because we have divided our lesson chapters (Chapters 6 through 9) based on grade levels, this question regarding age appropriateness was particularly crucial. The books presented in Chapters 6 through 9 were considered carefully using the characteristics of appropriateness based on readers' age and grade level.

GUIDING QUESTION 3: DOES THE BOOK CONTRIBUTE TO THE BALANCE OF OUR COLLECTION?

Good teaching using literature includes books of various genres, structures, formats, and perspectives. In order to present a concept fully, one text is probably not enough. Books of both expository and narrative structures representing many genres in children's literature with a number of different perspectives should be shared with the students in order to accurately portray the complexity of *any* topic or concept. For example, historical fiction should accompany informational books; textbook chapters should be supplemented with primary source documents; fiction should be paired with biographies; and a diversity of cultural, racial, and ethnic perspectives should be included. Connections should be made between books and between concepts; after all, no concept is ever in isolation.

In this text, we present a collection of children's literature that represents a balance. We use both expository and narrative texts that capture various perspectives of a concept. As a collection, our books should represent complex and multidimensional views of that concept.

GUIDING QUESTION 4: DOES THE BOOK INCLUDE MEANINGFUL AND RELEVANT MATHEMATICS, SCIENCE, AND/OR SOCIAL STUDIES CONCEPTS?

Perhaps most important, a book worthy of inclusion in our collection should contain a relevant mathematics, science, or social studies concept with the potential to make learning meaningful and powerful. Obviously, the book should be able to achieve *beyond* what would have been possible *without* it. The concept should be presented in ways that allow the students to draw connections to their own lives, learn more about other related concepts, and apply the concept in other contexts.

We believe books that are content explicit, content implicit, and content invisible are all potentially valuable tools for learning. As such, we have included books of all three types in the lessons. Content explicit, content implicit, and content invisible books are discussed in the section "Distinguishing by Content" later in this chapter.

Categories of Books

The thousands of children's books on the market today can be categorized in many different ways. Considering categories ensures the presentation of a balanced collection, representing books with a variety of purposes, audiences, text structures, and content. Because this text attempts to provide a list of quality books for grades PreK–8 that contain meaningful and relevant mathematics, science, or social studies concepts, examining the selection categories is a logical place to start. Following are some of the categories that we used to explore different books.

DISTINGUISHING BY PURPOSE:
TO ENTERTAIN OR TO INFORM

Some books are written to provide pleasure and to elicit children's aesthetic responses; some are written to inform. Surely, many do both simultaneously, with or without the intention of the author.

Dr. Seuss's lyrical and tongue-twisting verses allow readers of all ages to enter into the world of silliness and make-believe. Though many of his books are great tools to foster children's sense of rhyme and provide phonemic awareness training, they usually do not contain information intended to teach content area concepts. Dr. Seuss's books are examples of some of the many beautifully written and illustrated books that purely entertain readers, without any intention to inform or teach.

On the other hand, David Macaulay's intricate and sophisticated ink sketches of architectural structures and the accompanying text (e.g., *Cathedral: The Story of Its Construction*, 1973; *Pyramid*, 1975; *Underground*, 1976; *Castle*, 1977; *Unbuilding*, 1980; *Mill*, 1983) make him one of the most notable authors of children's informational books. Macaulay uses unexpected angles and perspectives to present the structures—from above or even from the ground up—and highlight their forms, details, complexity, and beauty. He also places people, objects, or even other structures in the illustrations to show size, proportion, and function. Although his books are written mainly to inform according to the genre, many readers are mesmerized by the amazing details in both the illustrations and the text.

Russell Freedman's biographies (e.g., *The Wright Brothers: How they Invented the Airplane*, 1991; *Eleanor Roosevelt: A Life of Discovery*, 1993; *The Life and Death of Crazy Horse*, 1996) are other examples of books that inform. However, many readers get engaged in his books as they read about the details of these and other famous people. Freedman's unique ways of presenting the subject from unexpected sources are known to draw the readers into his books. For example, in *Lincoln: A Photobiography* (1987), Freedman describes the contents in Abraham Lincoln's pocket at the time of his death. Among other things, Lincoln's leather wallet with purple silk lining contained "a Confederate five-dollar bill bearing the likeness of Jefferson Davis and eight newspaper clippings that Lincoln had cut out and saved" (p. 130). As a president who was often criticized and ridiculed, he must have found comfort in articles that praised him. Freedman's ability to make biographies come alive has been recognized with numerous prestigious awards, including the Newbery Medal. Consider the very first lines in *Lincoln: A Photobiography*:

> Abraham Lincoln wasn't the sort of man who could lose himself in a crowd. After all, he stood six feet four inches tall, and to top it off, he wore a high silk hat. His height was mostly in his long bony legs. When he sat in a chair, he seemed no taller than anyone else. It was only when he stood up that he towered above other men. (p. 1)

You can almost picture a young reader pulling the book closer to read on. Indeed, adding interesting and compelling details to what we already know about Abraham Lincoln makes this text an engaging one.

DISTINGUISHING BY AUDIENCE:
FOR YOUNGER AND OLDER READERS

Some books are written for young, emerging readers; some are written for older, independent readers. Denise Fleming, Lois Ehlert, and Eric Carle are just a few of the authors whose audience is distinctively the young reader. Their illustrations are colorful and bold; their words are rhythmic and precise, but not necessarily simplified. They all introduce concepts that are appropriate for young children. However, within the seemingly simple concepts, sometimes there are intricate expansions of those concepts, making them amazingly and surprisingly rich and sophisticated in content.

For example, in Ehlert's *Eating the Alphabet: Fruits and Vegetables from A to Z* (1989), illustrations of various fruits and vegetables fill the pages dedicated to each letter of the alphabet. Among some of the less commonly known to young children are currant, date, endive, fig, kumquat, jicama, and quince, all beautifully depicted to suggest their texture, size, and appearance. The glossary at the end of the book chronicles the origins and other facts about each of the fruits and vegetables included. Did you know that radicchio is the Italian name for chicory, and sometimes it is referred to as red chicory? How about the fact that the grapefruit is relatively a new fruit, originating in the West Indies around the 1700s? Compare it to some of the ancient fruits and vegetables such as corn, which has been used as food for almost 10,000 years, or cabbage, which existed in prehistoric times in Europe and Asia. Consider the range of opportunity that Ehlert provides the young reader, most likely with a parent or a teacher, to expand the concepts including climate, geography, and history. The surprising complexity is refreshing from a book that seems simple and direct at first glance.

Then, there are books specifically written for older, more independent readers. Lois Lowry's treatment of the Holocaust in *Number the Stars* (1989) and Mildred Taylor's depiction of the conditions of "freed" African Americans in rural Mississippi in *Roll of Thunder, Hear My Cry* (1976) are specifically and explicitly written for upper elementary students and young adults both in content and language. These books and others written for older readers present topics honestly, preserving the essence and integrity of the core issues. Some are, undeniably, difficult concepts to discuss with students no matter their age. However, the authors' ability to treat the topics accurately and humanely, without diluting the topics' potency, makes their books good biographies, informational books, or historical and realistic fiction.

We should note here that many notable books intended for older readers are in picture book format. Some of these picture books, unexpectedly sophisticated in language and concept, are much better suited for readers with more extensive prior knowledge and understanding of the world than those possessed by young children. For example, Graeme Base's *The Eleventh Hour: A Curious Mystery* (1989) (see Chapter 9, Lesson 9.3) calls for readers with deduction skills and an ability to tune into minute details in order to solve the mystery that unfolds in the plot. Readers are asked to find clues of many types—pictures, numbers, words, and sentences—embedded in the illustrations as well as the text. They are also asked to keep track of the characters in their costumes, perhaps to account for their whereabouts during the various events in the story.

To further the argument, some picture books are not only less suitable for young children; they are *intended* for older readers and adults. There are many examples of such picture books. Tom Feelings in *The Middle Passage: White Ships/Black Cargo* (1995) records the transatlantic slave trade, depicting the suffering of African slaves. Both the illustrations and the content of Feelings' book show the brutal truths about the treatment of slaves. Similarly, Tatsuharu Kodama's *Shin's Tricycle* (1995) and Laurence Yep's *Hiroshima* (1995) both document the horrors of the atomic bomb and its devastating impact on human life. It almost feels counterintuitive or even contradictory to use picture books with older students. However, due to the sensitivity of the content and the painfully honest portrayals of events, some pictures books are *not* intended for young children.

DISTINGUISHING BY STRUCTURE

Children's books are also categorized by genres—picture books, informational books, historical fiction, poetry, biographies, contemporary realistic fiction, and traditional and modern fantasies. Many experts in the field also include multicultural and international books as a type of children's books. Although these genres and how they are defined may vary slightly from one expert to another, genre is still a useful tool of classification due to its general acceptability in the field. In most textbooks for children's literature courses, the presentation and discussions of children's books are organized by genres (Darigan, Tunnell, & Jacobs, 2002; Huck & Kiefer, 2003; Norton, 2006). As teachers, understanding the genres in terms of their content and structure is important, especially as we attempt to use children's literature that represents a wide variety of works to teach content area concepts and topics. However, we leave further discussion about genres to the general children's literature textbooks.

In order to highlight picture books to teach content area concepts, we categorize books in two broad and recognizable ways: narrative and expository.

To tell: Narrative structure

"Once upon a time . . ." begins many stories we know intimately. Narratives *tell* stories—whether they are purely factual (e.g., biographies) or purely fictional (e.g., contemporary realistic fiction) or even fictionalized facts (e.g., historical fiction). Narratives usually have a beginning, a middle, and an ending, often presenting the plot in a sequential manner. And as is commonly known, many narratives have characters, settings, problems, events, and the resolution of problems, though we should add that narrative structures in many cultures are drastically different. As researchers in education, anthropology, linguistics, and cultural studies have learned, some of these narratives rooted in other cultures are told in cyclical, episodic, or collaborative ways (Au, 1980; Michaels, 1986).

To explain: Expository structure

Expository text differs from narrative text in that its primary purpose is to explain. There are various ways to explain, and expository texts vary by *what* and *why* the information is presented. There are five frequently used patterns in expository texts: description, sequence, comparison, cause and effect, and problem and solution (Meyer & Freedle, 1984). A particular pattern is used based on the type and purpose of the text. Readers often tune into key words that signal the incorporation of a pattern, such as "first, second, next, and finally" for sequence. Many informational books use one identifiable pattern. However, within an expository text, one or more patterns may be used.

Some experts claim that students generally have more difficulty with expository texts than narrative texts mainly because of a lack of experience with them (Cooper, 2006). Such claims prompted scholars in the field to study how best to facilitate students' understanding of expository texts. The consensus in the field regarding the best method is to make the expository structure explicit to the students; provide knowledge of the structure to the students for them to recognize and use in the construction of meaning (Tompkins, 2008). Graphic organizers, for instance, have emerged as one of the most popular ways to make the expository structure explicit to children at all levels. Flow charts, semantic feature analysis grids, K-W-L charts, classification maps, and Venn diagrams are just some examples of frequently used graphic organizers, many of which are used in the lessons in Chapters 6 through 9 as a way to promote conceptual learning.

We include some exceptional and selective expository books for children in the lessons. Good expository texts ensure the teaching of the structure, as well as the content, while engaging the readers. Some of Gail Gibbons' books (e.g., *Monarch Butterfly*, 1989; *Penguins!*, 1998) are wonderful examples of expository books for young readers. She uses direct and accurate language to describe and explain the concepts. The accompanying illustrations are simple, almost minimalistic; however, they are relatable to children. Gibbons uses captions, labels, glossaries, and other tools in order to make the text more accessible to young children.

The Tree in the Ancient Forest by Carol Reed-Jones (1995) is another example of expository text that can be used with young readers. The vividness of the Douglas fir tree in both the illustrations and the language depicts not only the tree itself, but also the other animals and plants that mutually exist with the ancient tree. Told in a cumulative tale form, the text is quite unique to the expository structure; however, it effectively presents the concept of interdependence in this ecosystem.

DISTINGUISHING BY CONTENT

Books of all genres and structures may contain and present concepts that match those we are expected to include in our curriculum (see our discussion of standards in Chapter 4) or even those that children *want* to learn more about. For this reason, we now focus our discussion on the different ways *content* is presented in children's books in regard to content area concepts. We can distinguish books by the degree to which concepts are presented and visible in their content.

Content explicit

Some books convey the content of mathematics, science, and social studies concepts explicitly. In many cases, these books were written to inform and to teach the concepts presented in the book. We call this type *content explicit*.

All expository books fall under this type. Seymour Simon's books on various animals, planets, body parts, and natural disasters are well known to children of all ages (e.g., *Saturn*, 1985; *Wolves*, 1993; *The Brain: Our Nervous System*, 1997; *Lightning*, 1997). His expository books, mostly in the informational book format, present facts explicitly. There is little doubt as to the intention of the author; he writes to inform. Simon uses many writing strategies to inform with flair and pizzazz. He often presents interesting facts with comparisons that children can relate to: "The humpback whale is longer than a big bus and heavier than a trailer truck. Some great whales are even larger. Just the tongue of a blue whale weighs as much as an elephant" (*Whales*, 1989, p. 1). The amazing full-page photographs typical of Simon's style lend themselves well to the text and undoubtedly capture the interest of children.

Some narratives are content explicit as well. *The Great Kapok Tree: A Tale of the Amazon Rain Forest* (see Chapter 8, Lesson 8.11) by Lynne Cherry (1990) presents the rain forest as a habitat essential for the survival of the animals in the Amazon rain forest. Their pleas are whispered to a sleeping man who intends to cut down a tree. "Dear Readers, I wrote *The Great Kapok Tree* to let the world know what happens to the rain forest creatures and to the entire planet when rain forests are destroyed," writes Cherry in the epilogue.

One Grain of Rice: A Mathematical Folktale (see Chapter 9, Lesson 9.2) by Demi (1997) is another example of a content explicit narrative story. In this beautifully told and illustrated Indian folktale, a wise young character named Rani is granted a wish. Her wish is to receive one grain of rice, which then doubles each day for 30 days. As the number of rice grains increases exponentially to more than one billion, Demi illustrates this mathematics concept through a magnificent four-page pictorial representation and a chart documenting how much rice Rani receives in all.

Content implicit

Some narratives are *content implicit*, meaning the mathematical, scientific, or social studies concepts included in the book are not central to the story. Rather, the concepts are implicit in the story, subtly and cleverly presenting opportunities for the reader to make the connection to the concepts. *The Quiltmaker's Gift* (2000) by Jeff Brumbeau is a wonderful example of a concept implicit narrative. Through the many quilt patterns scattered throughout the book, the opportunities to highlight various geometry concepts, including patterns and tessellations, are masterfully presented.

Inch by Inch, a Caldecott Honor book by Leo Lionni (1960), presents a similar potential for mathematics learning by young children. The clever inchworm uses his talent to measure things in order to outwit his predators. When challenged with the impossible task to measure a song, he tricks the hungry nightingale in order to escape. Although measurement as a mathematics concept is not explicitly presented, the story of the inchworm can be extended to many hands-on experiences in measurement, in both standard and nonstandard units, and estimation.

365 Penguins (see Chapter 6, Lesson 6.14) by Jean-Luc Fromental (2006) is a whimsical story of a family receiving a penguin a day for a whole year, which causes practical dilemmas, as anyone can imagine. The story subtly implies the problem of global warming, which has resulted in the loss of habitat for penguins in Antarctica. The message of conservation is not presented in obvious ways in this humorous story; it is just too apparent to ignore.

Content invisible

The last type of book is referred to as *content invisible* because it may not have any visible or apparent connection to content area concepts. However, in the hands of a creative teacher with the vision to integrate literature into teaching content area subjects, these books possess marvelous potential as a tool to teach these concepts. We do not advocate a forced or unnatural insertion of concepts, however. Meaningful and relevant connections to mathematics, science, and social studies concepts should derive from children's responses to and discussions about the story. Perhaps the book can be used as an inspiration or a springboard to inquire deeper into a topic. Or the book can serve as an invitation to introduce other books and resources about the topic in order to construct a fuller, more complete understanding of the concepts.

Tuesday (see Chapter 8, Lesson 8.2) by David Wiesner (1991) may be a great example of a content invisible book. The reading of this book can be extended to a paper-folding activity that presents many geometry concepts, followed by an activity in which students make their paper frogs leap. Measuring distances, recording data, representing results using various types of graphs, and analyzing data (e.g., finding mean, mode, and median) can all be included in the follow-up activity using this book. Effective teachers, those who are aware of what literature can offer, can make these connections visible in their teaching.

Our discussion of the categories of children's books may have seemed lengthy. Yes, Seymour Simon's *Whales* (1989) is an informational book with expository text structure written to inform intermediate grade students with an explicit presentation of science concepts. However, all of these features—purpose, audience, genre, text structure, and content—are necessary to judge the appropriateness of a book's selection. Considering these categories allows us to think about the possibilities, about the balance of representation, and about ensuring a variety in our collection.

Teaching Literacy Strategies in an Integrated Classroom

Mathematics, science, and social studies learning often requires extensive reading, writing, speaking, listening, and visual skills. Because we are using books to promote learning, the lessons in Chapters 6 through 9 teach and support students' growth in the language arts. Each lesson includes reading, speaking, and listening components. A focal point for each is the teacher's reading of a specific picture book or students reading it on their own, preceded and followed by class or small group discussions about key elements of the book. While all lessons include reading, speaking, and listening, they also include a variety of other specific language arts experiences. To make these experiences explicit, we have listed the relevant ones for each lesson under the heading *Language Arts Experiences*.

The lessons also include a focus on strategies that promote comprehension advocated by literacy experts and scholars (Harvey & Goudvis, 2007; Keene & Zimmermann, 2007; McEwan, 2004; McLaughlin & Allen, 2002; Oczkus, 2004). From one expert to another, the lists of essential comprehension strategies vary; we have chosen to present and use the list most appropriate for learning in the content areas. The list of "Super 6" comprehension strategies (Oczkus, 2004) and a brief description of each strategy is presented below. We highly recommend that you con-

Super 6 Comprehension Strategies

From Oczkus, 2004

1. *Connecting.* Readers must make text-to-self, other text, and world connections before, during, and after reading (Keene & Zimmermann, 1997, 2007). This is a way to activate and use prior knowledge, which is one of the essential ways to comprehend.

2. *Predicting/Inferring.* Inferences occur as readers merge their prior knowledge and the text. Inferences allow readers to make predictions as they read and set purposes in reading.

3. *Questioning.* Questions, both literal and inferential, help readers guide and monitor their comprehension and interact with the text.

4. *Monitoring.* Good readers assess their comprehension as they read and use fix-up strategies if their comprehension fails.

5. *Summarizing/Synthesizing.* Readers recall details about the text and then determine what is important in the text. Articulating key points and main ideas through this process is a difficult task for many readers.

6. *Evaluating.* Readers make judgments before, during, and after reading about many aspects of the text, including content, text structure, author's craft, and their responses to the text.

sult the references listed at the end of the chapter for more complete and detailed discussions of the strategies and examples of effective instructional activities.

Many effective research-based instructional strategies teach, promote, and facilitate those strategies that readers use to comprehend. Some of these instructional activities are presented in Chapters 6 through 9 as a way to promote mathematics, science, and social studies learning using picture books. Modifications were made in some cases to tailor the strategy to the book in order to ensure the students' understanding of the text and the concept. In addition, the instructional activities presented in the lessons involve many modes of learning, including writing, researching, critical thinking, problem solving, drawing, summarizing, and more. And although using instructional activities in the lessons is a great way to promote and teach literacy strategies, their primary purpose is to *support* the students' learning the key concepts in the lesson.

Conclusion

In our definition of meaningful and effective learning, children learn to read and they read to learn. Great literature can be, and should be, used to inspire learning and promote important concepts. Using the quality books that we have carefully and intentionally selected to promote student learning in various content areas, we hope you not only experience the inherent joy of teaching and learning, but also the joy of experiencing books.

REFERENCES

Au, K. H. (1980). Participation structures in a reading lesson with Hawaiian children: Analysis of a culturally appropriate instructional event. *Anthropology and Education Quarterly, 11*(2), 91–115.

Cooper, J. D., & Kiger, N. D. (2006). *Literacy: Helping children construct meaning* (6th ed.). New York: Houghton Mifflin.

Darigan, D. L., Tunnell, M. O., & Jacobs, J. S. (2002). *Children's literature: Engaging teachers and children in good books.* Upper Saddle River, NJ: Merrill Prentice Hall.

Donovan, C. A., & Smolkin, L. B. (2002). Considering genre, content, and visual features in the selection of trade books for science instruction. *The Reading Teacher, 55*(6), 502–520.

Harvey, S., & Goudvis, A. (2007). *Strategies that work: Teaching comprehension to enhance understanding* (2nd ed.). Portland, ME: Stenhouse.

Hellwig, S. J., Monroe, E. E., & Jacobs, J. S. (2000). Making informed choices: Selecting children's trade books for mathematics instruction. *Teaching Children Mathematics, 7*(3), 138.

Huck, C. S., & Kiefer, B. Z. (2003). *Children's literature in the elementary school* (8th ed.). New York: McGraw-Hill.

Keene, E. O., & Zimmermann, S. (1997). *Mosaic of thought: Teaching comprehension in a reader's workshop.* Portsmouth, NH: Heinemann.

Keene, E. O., & Zimmermann, S. (2007). *Mosaic of thought: The power of comprehension strategy instruction* (2nd ed.). Portsmouth, NH: Heinemann.

McEwan, E. K. (2004). *7 strategies of highly effective readers: Using cognitive research to boost K–8 achievement.* Thousand Oaks, CA: Corwin Press.

McLaughlin, M., & Allen, M. B. (2002). *Guided comprehension: A teaching model for grades 3–8.* Newark, DE: International Reading Association.

Meyer, B. J., & Freedle, R. O. (1984). Effects of discourse type on recall. *American Educational Research Journal, 21,* 121–143.

Michaels, S. (1986). Narrative presentations: An oral preparation for literacy. In J. Cook-Gumperz (Ed.), *The social construction of literacy* (pp. 94–116). Cambridge, MA: Cambridge University Press.

Norton, D. E. (2006). *Through the eyes of a child: An introduction to children's literature* (7th ed.). Upper Saddle River, NJ: Prentice Hall.

Oczkus, L. (2004). *Super 6 comprehension strategies: 35 lessons and more for reading success.* Norwood, MA: Christopher-Gordon.

Tompkins, G. E. (2008). *Language arts: Patterns of practice* (7th ed.). Upper Saddle River, NJ: Merrill Prentice Hall.

Tunnell, M. O., & Jacobs, J. S. (2007). *Children's literature, briefly* (4th ed.). Upper Saddle River, NJ: Prentice Hall.

Base, G. (1989). *The eleventh hour*. New York: Abrams.

Brumbeau, J. (2000). *The quiltmaker's gift* (G. de Marcken, Illus.). New York: Pfeifer-Hamilton.

Cherry, L. (1990). *The great kapok tree: A tale of the Amazon rain forest*. New York: Harcourt Brace.

Demi. (1997). *One grain of rice: A mathematical folktale*. New York: Scholastic.

Ehlert, L. (1989). *Eating the alphabet: Fruits and vegetables from A to Z*. New York: Harcourt Brace.

Feelings, T. (1995). *The middle passage: White ships/black cargo*. New York: Dial.

Freedman, R. (1987). *Lincoln: A photobiography*. New York: Clarion.

Freedman, R. (1991). *The Wright brothers: How they invented the airplane*. New York: Holiday.

Freedman, R. (1993). *Eleanor Roosevelt: A life of discovery*. New York: Clarion.

Freedman, R. (1996). *The life and death of Crazy Horse*. New York: Holiday.

Fromental, J. (2006). *365 penguins* (J. Jolivet, Illus.). New York: Abrams.

Gibbons, G. (1989). *Monarch butterfly*. New York: Holiday.

Gibbons, G. (1998). *Penguins!* New York: Holiday.

Kodama, T. (1995). *Shin's tricycle* (K. Hokuman-Jones, Trans.; N. Ando, Illus.). New York: Walker.

Lionni, L. (1960). *Inch by inch*. New York: Obolensky.

Lowry, L. (1989). *Number the stars*. Boston: Houghton Mifflin.

Macaulay, D. (1973). *Cathedral: The story of its construction*. Boston: Houghton Mifflin.

Macaulay, D. (1975). *Pyramid*. Boston: Houghton Mifflin.

Macaulay, D. (1976). *Underground*. Boston: Houghton Mifflin.

Macaulay, D. (1977). *Castle*. Boston: Houghton Mifflin.

Macaulay, D. (1980). *Unbuilding*. Boston: Houghton Mifflin.

Macaulay, D. (1983). *Mill*. Boston: Houghton Mifflin.

Reed-Jones, C. (1995). *The tree in the ancient forest* (C. Canyon, Illus.). San Diego, CA: Dawn.

Simon, S. (1985). *Saturn*. New York: Morrow.

Simon, S. (1989). *Whales*. New York: Scholastic.

Simon, S. (1993). *Wolves*. New York: HarperCollins.

Simon, S. (1997). *The brain: Our nervous system*. New York: Morrow.

Simon, S. (1997). *Lightning*. New York: Morrow.

Taylor, M. D. (1976). *Roll of thunder, hear my cry* (J. Pinkney, Illus.). New York: Dial.

Wiesner, D. (1991). *Tuesday*. New York: Clarion.

Yep, L. (1995). *Hiroshima*. New York: Scholastic.

4

*Meeting Mathematics,
Science, Social Studies,
and Language Arts
Standards*

n this age of accountability and high-stakes testing, discussions about academic standards seem especially timely. By the end of 2000, most major national professional organizations had established school achievement standards in their various fields. Most states have also developed standards for school performance and student achievement. Notwithstanding the debates surrounding the formulation of standards during the past few decades, these professional and state standards have received wide recognition in the field of education. Teacher education programs, for example, present and discuss academic standards in their foundation courses, as well as in specific content methods courses. States require their schools to administer annual standardized tests based on state academic standards. Many school districts use these state academic standards as well as state-sponsored tests as a way to set goals and objectives. Many educators are concerned with how often educational resource and funding decisions are made based on test scores. Many also worry that teachers are "teaching to the test" in order to show improvement in their students' test scores. In this chapter, we briefly explore how academic standards have influenced the realities of schools during the past few decades and how they impact teaching and learning content area subjects.

Professional Standards Developed by National Organizations

Several national organizations have led the way in developing and introducing standards in specific content areas. It must be emphasized that these are not "federally" mandated standards. Rather, the standards presented in this section are created by national professional organizations in the fields of mathematics, science, social studies, and English education (and are referred to as "professional" standards throughout this text). These professional organizations serve as tremendous resources to teachers and offer expert guidance that many teachers use as a valuable part of their professional development. Although states do not mandate that these standards be implemented, it is fair to say that many states use them to shape and inform their own state academic standards. Of particular interest in this text are the academic standards developed by the following national organizations:

National Council of Teachers of Mathematics (NCTM), www.nctm.org

The National Research Council (NRC) of the National Academy of Sciences (NAS), the National Academy of Engineering (NAE), and the Institute of Medicine (IOM), www.nationalacademies.org/nrc

National Council for the Social Studies (NCSS), www.socialstudies.org

International Reading Association, www.reading.org

National Council of Teachers of English, www.ncte.org

STANDARDS FOR MATHEMATICS EDUCATION

The mathematics standards have been available since 1989 as *The Curriculum and Evaluation Standards for School Mathematics* (NCTM, 1989) and were revised in 2000 as the *Principles and Standards for School Mathematics* (NCTM, 2000). The standards for grades PreK–12 (available at www.nctm.org/standards) were designed to ensure that students become mathematically fluent and are able to demonstrate competence in the following 10 areas of mathematics (strands 1–5 are content standards and strands 6–10 are process standards):

1. Numbers and Operations
2. Algebra
3. Geometry
4. Measurement
5. Data Analysis and Probability
6. Problem Solving
7. Reasoning and Proof
8. Communication
9. Connections
10. Representation

These 10 strands in the NCTM standards are to be used across grade levels PreK–12. Each strand varies in breadth and depth according to the grade level. For example, geometry in a PreK classroom may encompass such topics as shapes and classification. In a sixth grade classroom, geometry may mean measuring angles in triangles, an expansion of the foundation started in earlier grades.

Our lessons address specific content strands from these mathematics professional standards. Using *Counting on Frank* (Clement, 1991) (see Chapter 7, Lesson 7.3), a humorous look at counting things around one's neighborhood, we provide a lesson on estimation for second and third grade students that applies the Numbers and Operations strand. The Data Analysis and Probability strand is addressed using *Flight: The Journey of Charles Lindbergh* (Burleigh, 1991) (see Chapter 8, Lesson 8.6), a lesson for fourth and fifth grade students. In this lesson, the students learn that data may be represented in a variety of ways, and they gain experience in the use of one method as they learn to plot coordinates on a grid.

The NCTM standards also emphasize problem solving and reasoning, while de-emphasizing rote memorization and computational skills that are divorced from real life. Therefore, books like *Math Man* (Daniels, 2001), *Sir Cumference and the Dragon of Pi* (Neuschwander, 1999) (see Chapter 9, Lesson 9.8), and *The Grapes of Math* (Tang, 2001) provide excellent opportunities to introduce and expand mathematics concepts in realistic and entertaining ways.

STANDARDS FOR SCIENCE EDUCATION

The science standards were developed by the National Research Council (NRC) of the National Academy of Science, the prestigious group that influenced the development of the mathematics standards, and were published as the *National Science Education Standards* (NRC, 1996). The NRC provides an extensive listing of standards (available at www.nap.edu/openbook.php?record_id=4962) in six categories: (1) teaching standards; (2) professional development standards; (3) assessment standards; (4) education program standards; (5) education system standards; and (6)

content standards. Classroom teachers are most concerned about the content standards, which are divided into eight categories and include broad content areas and processes of inquiry. In much summarized form, those eight categories are as follows:

1. Unifying Concepts and Processes in Science
2. Science as Inquiry
3. Physical Science
4. Life Science
5. Earth and Space Science
6. Science and Technology
7. Science in Personal and Social Perspectives
8. History and Nature of Science

Our lessons reflect specific concepts from these professional science standards. For example, using *Growing Vegetable Soup* (Ehlert, 1987) (see Chapter 6, Lesson 6.10), we address the life science standard by developing a lesson on the characteristics of organisms. *The Dandelion Seed* (Anthony, 1997) (see Chapter 7, Lesson 7.12) and *They Came from the Bronx* (Waldman, 2001) accurately present life science concepts using plant and animal life examples.

Another major aspect of the science standards is to develop inquiry and "scientific thinking." Technology and its application to the study and analysis of information are a major focus of the content standards. According to Steen (1994), many similarities exist between the *Standards for School Mathematics* (NCTM, 1989) and the *National Science Education Standards* (NRC, 1996). Five similarities are shared below:

- Both advocate a significant shift away from the "filter" model of education by raising expectations of student learning.
- Both argue for more depth, understanding, and thinking and less memorization, mechanics, and mimicry.
- Both advocate active learning, increased collaboration, discussion, exploration, and "student talk" and less rote learning.
- There is a greater reliance on performance-based instruments that are coordinated with the curriculum and embedded in instruction and viewed as a recursive and reflective process.
- Both advocate full use of technology as a means and a goal of instruction.

Chapter 2 offers various examples of how an integrated curriculum translates into classroom practices. As well, many lessons in Chapters 6 through 9 exemplify the text-to-self, text-to-text, and text-to-world connections that are found naturally in content area topics.

STANDARDS FOR SOCIAL STUDIES EDUCATION

The National Council for the Social Studies (NCSS) published its curriculum standards, *Expectations of Excellence: Curriculum Standards for Social Studies*, in 1994 to serve as a "curriculum alignment and development tool." Currently, the NCSS standards (available at www.socialstudies.org/standards) present ten interdisciplinary thematic strands in social studies for grades PreK–12:

1. Culture
2. Time, Continuity, and Change
3. People, Places, and Environment
4. Individual Development and Identity
5. Individuals, Groups, and Institutions
6. Power, Authority, and Governance
7. Production, Distribution, and Consumption
8. Science, Technology, and Society
9. Global Connections
10. Civic Ideals and Practices

These ten themes derive from the formal definition of social studies adopted by the NCSS:

> Social studies is the integrated study of the social sciences and humanities to promote civic competence. Within the school program, social studies provides coordinated, systematic study drawing upon such disciplines as anthropology, archaeology, economics, geography, history, law, philosophy, political science, psychology, religion, and sociology, as well as appropriate content from the humanities, mathematics, and natural sciences. The primary purpose of social studies is to help young people develop the ability to make informed and reasoned decisions for the public good as citizens of a culturally diverse, democratic society in an interdependent world. (NCSS, 1994, p. vii)

One of the NCSS themes highlighted in our book is People, Places, and Environment. Many beautiful books present environmental concepts in both implicit and explicit ways; thus, integrating the nature and consequences of human actions in the environment is a connection that is made effortlessly. *365 Penguins* (Fromental, 2006) (see Chapter 6, Lesson 6.14) and *Flotsam* (Wiesner, 2006) (see Chapter 9, Lesson 9.15) are two of the many books that stress the importance of conservation.

Time, Continuity, and Change as a historical perspective is another theme deserving of inclusion in the book. Using this theme, some of the lessons integrate social studies and mathematics. For example, *The Keeping Quilt* (Polacco, 1998) (see Chapter 7, Lesson 7.6) beautifully weaves the patterns in mathematics with the history of the Polacco family.

STANDARDS FOR THE ENGLISH LANGUAGE ARTS

Joint efforts by the IRA and the NCTE produced the *Standards for the English Language Arts*, which were adopted by both organizations. These standards broadly address oral and written communications and more specifically, reading, writing, speaking, and listening. The 12 standards (available at www.ncte.org/standards) are presented in Exhibit 4.1.

These English Language Arts standards are general, but thorough. They cover areas believed to be crucial to the study of the English language by students at every grade level. The lessons in this text help students meet the NCTE/IRA standards in three ways. First, they expose the students to the quality literature

EXHIBIT **4.1** NCTE/IRA Standards for the English Language Arts (1996).

1. Students read a wide range of print and nonprint texts to build an understanding of texts, of themselves, and of the cultures of the United States and the world; to acquire new information; to respond to the needs and demands of society and the workplace; and for personal fulfillment. Among these texts are fiction and nonfiction, classic and contemporary works.

2. Students read a wide range of literature from many periods and many genres to build an understanding of the many dimensions (e.g., philosophical, ethical, aesthetic) of human experience.

3. Students apply a wide range of strategies to comprehend, interpret, evaluate, and appreciate texts. They draw on their prior experience, their interactions with other readers and writers, their knowledge of word meanings and of other texts, their word identification strategies, and their understanding of textual features (e.g., sound–letter correspondence, sentence structure, context, graphics).

4. Students adjust their use of spoken, written, and visual language (e.g., conventions, style, vocabulary) to communicate effectively with a variety of audiences and for different purposes.

5. Students employ a wide range of strategies as they write and use different writing process elements appropriately to communicate with different audiences for a variety of purposes.

6. Students apply knowledge of language structure, language conventions (e.g., spelling and punctuation), media techniques, figurative language, and genre to create, critique, and discuss print and nonprint texts.

7. Students conduct research on issues and interests by generating ideas and questions, and by posing problems. They gather, evaluate, and synthesize data from a variety of sources (e.g., print and nonprint texts, artifacts, people) to communicate their discoveries in ways that suit their purpose and audience.

8. Students use a variety of technological and informational resources (e.g., libraries, databases, computer networks, video) to gather and synthesize information and to create and communicate knowledge.

9. Students develop an understanding of and respect for diversity in language use, patterns, and dialects across cultures, ethnic groups, geographic regions, and social roles.

10. Students whose first language is not English make use of their first language to develop competency in the English language arts and to develop understanding of content across the curriculum.

11. Students participate as knowledgeable, reflective, creative, and critical members of a variety of literacy communities.

12. Students use spoken, written, and visual language to accomplish their own purposes (e.g., for learning, enjoyment, persuasion, and the exchange of information).

necessary to develop the literacy skills described in the standards. Second, they include experiences in reading, writing, speaking, listening, viewing, and visually representing as outlined in standards 1–6 and 12. These language arts experiences help the students learn the mathematics, science, and social studies concepts. Third, the lessons will help students apply a wide range of comprehension strategies (standard 3) as discussed in Chapter 3. For example, Lesson 7.2 in Chapter 7 involves reading *The Water Hole* (Base, 2001), a delightful book about the importance of water to living things. Not only does this lesson teach both science and mathematics concepts, it also provides opportunities for reading, speaking, listening, writing, and visually representing as students read and discuss the book and then write and illustrate their own story about a habitat. Others like *Snowflake Bentley* (Martin, 1998) (see Chapter 7, Lesson 7.5), and *Starry Messenger* (Sis, 1996) (see Chapter 8, Lesson 8.7) provide opportunities for learning the structure of the language, for vocabulary development, for character study, or for enjoyment.

STATE AND LOCAL STANDARDS

A look at state and local standards reveals an enormous variety in specificity. Some identify the month, week, and day a teacher is supposed to address a particular standard. Some are stated broadly and leave most of the instructional planning (topic, placement in the curriculum, etc.) to the teacher. To see the extensive variety of standards available, use any of the Internet search tools and search for information on "mathematics standards," "science standards," "social studies standards," or "English/language arts standards." Among the millions of results, you will find thousands of relevant websites about standards. All states and many school districts provide an explicit listing of their standards for your evaluation.

Conclusion

Standards are a guide that enables you (1) to set goals and objectives for learning and (2) to determine if you have accomplished what you set out to teach. If you examine the professional standards developed by the major national organizations, you will note that the standards—while specifically dealing with the language arts, mathematics, science, or social studies—are also stated rather broadly. The categories provided in the standards (e.g., physical science, life science, or social science) appear reasonable and represent the domains of knowledge that both educated laypersons and scientists support. Therefore, in this text, our lessons follow the specific categories used in the professional standards.

If teachers need to address specific standards in mathematics, science, and social studies, children's books are available to help them do so. Literally thousands of such books are available and hundreds more are published each month, covering a wide range of topics. Match the children's book with the standard you wish to address, and you will achieve a level of interest from your students that will surprise you if you have previously restricted your instructional activities to grade-level textbooks. Using high-quality children's literature with specific themes tied to appropriate standards—the standards addressed by the curriculum—capitalizes on what we know about the interests and motivation of students.

REFERENCES

National Commission on Excellence in Education. (1983). *A nation at risk: The imperative for educational reform.* Washington, DC: U.S. Government Printing Office.

National Council for the Social Studies. (1994). *Expectations of excellence: Curriculum standards for social studies.* Washington, DC: Author.

National Council of Teachers of English and the International Reading Association. (1996). *Standards for the English language arts.* Urbana, IL & Newark, DE: Author.

National Council of Teachers of Mathematics. (1989). *Curriculum and evaluation standards for school mathematics.* Reston, VA: Author.

National Council of Teachers of Mathematics. (2000). *Principles and standards for school mathematics.* Reston, VA: Author.

National Research Council. (1996). *National science education standards.* Washington, DC: National Academy Press.

Roeber, E., Bond, L., & Connealy, S. (1997). *Annual survey of state student assessment programs: Data on 1996–1997 statewide student assessment programs.* Washington, DC: Council of Chief State School Officers.

Steen, L. A. (1994). Integrating school science and mathematics: Fad or folly? In D. Berlin (Ed.), *NSF/SSMA Wingspread conference: A network for integrated science and mathematics for teaching and learning—Conference plenary papers. School science and mathematics association topics for teachers, series 7.* Columbus, OH: National Center for Science Teaching and Learning.

CHILDREN'S LITERATURE

Anthony, J. (1997). *The dandelion seed* (C. Arbo, Illus.). Nevada City, CA: Dawn.

Base, G. (2001). *The water hole.* New York: Abrams.

Burleigh, R. (1991). *Flight: The journey of Charles Lindbergh* (M. Wimmer, Illus.). New York: Philomel.

Clement, R. (1991). *Counting on Frank.* Milwaukee, WI: Gareth Stevens.

Daniels, T. (2001). *Math man* (T. Bush, Illus.). New York: Orchard Books.

Ehlert, L. (1987). *Growing vegetable soup.* New York: Voyager Books.

Fromental, J. (2006). *365 penguins* (J. Jolivet, Illus.). New York: Abrams.

Martin, J. (1998). *Snowflake Bentley* (M. Azarian, Illus.). New York: Houghton Mifflin.

Neuschwander, C. (1999). *Sir Cumference and the dragon of Pi: A math adventure* (W. Geehan, Illus.). Watertown, MA: Charlesbridge.

Polacco, P. (1998). *The keeping quilt.* New York: Simon & Schuster.

Sis, P. (1996). *Starry messenger.* New York: Farrar, Straus & Giroux.

Tang, G. (2001). *The grapes of math* (H. Briggs, Illus.). New York: Scholastic.

Waldman, N. (2001). *They came from the Bronx: How the buffalo were saved from extinction.* Honesdale, PA: Boyds Mills Press.

Wiesner, D. (2006). *Flotsam.* New York: Clarion.

CHAPTER

5

Getting Started
in Your Classroom

T he universal appeal of children's literature makes it a powerful tool for teachers at the PreK–8 grade levels. Involving children with books in a variety of ways serves to connect concepts to reality and make learning a personal experience. Appropriate selections provide the opportunity to extend the concepts into the child's world. This is one of the most inviting ways to engage students in actively doing mathematics, science, and social studies.

Matching Concepts to Books to Children

O n our text, we selected stories from children's literature to develop and extend content area concepts for students in PreK–8 grades. Quality and variety were the main criteria when selecting genres, authors, and topics. In addition, professional standards for mathematics, science, social studies, and the English language arts were taken into consideration. Because there are many standards for these content areas and literally thousands of quality books that meet those standards, we narrowed our scope to the professional academic standards developed by national organizations.

The picture books were chosen for the connections that could be made to teach the important mathematics, science, or social studies concepts. Think of our text as an inspiration that can take you on the journey of using children's books to teach any subject matter or concept in engaging and powerful ways. Next, we provide you with a good model on *how* to use books as a teaching and learning tool.

KNOWING CONCEPTS

Content area subjects are not composed of isolated rules, formulas, and lists of dates and events. Children's literature can play a significant role in integrating content area concepts into real-world applications. For example, *The Doorbell Rang* (Hutchins, 1986) and *Gator Pie* (Mathews, 1979) create a real-life need to know division when sharing cookies and pie. This kind of learning context takes children away from rules, formulas, and lists and encourages them to explore ideas in a more natural and informal manner, to discover connections and interrelationships among content and concepts. The way children explore concepts in authentic and natural contexts brings many surprises.

KNOWING BOOKS

As discussed in Chapter 3, children's books can be categorized in numerous ways. Our categories for exploration include purpose, audience, genre and text structure, and content. Using these categories, the question "Are they *good* children's books?" is challenging to answer. The best children's books offer readers enjoyment, memorable characters and situations, and valuable insights into real-life situations. For example, such characters as Henry and his dog Frank in *Counting on Frank* (Clement, 1994) (see Chapter 7, Lesson 7.3), Alexander in *Alexander, Who Used to Be Rich Last Sunday* (Viorst, 1980), or Bartholomew in *The 500 Hats of Bartholomew Cubbins* (Seuss, 1976) help make these books of permanent value.

The most important personal gain that good books provide is simply enjoyment. All of us have wonderful memories from our childhood of stories that were so funny we laughed out loud or scary stories that caused our hearts to beat rapidly. Good books open the doors of our imaginations and allow us as readers to explore uncharted realms of thought; that, in itself, is valuable.

KNOWING CHILDREN

Through education, experience, and reflection we get to know and understand children. Through understanding the contexts of teaching and effective interactions, we provide students with meaningful experiences. Whatever the context, it helps if we know how children change so we can encourage what they are good at and what they enjoy. There is no substitute for knowing the children.

In classrooms, effective teachers use strategies to differentiate instruction as they acknowledge the different and unique backgrounds that children bring to the learning community. In differentiated classrooms, "teachers provide specific ways for each individual to learn as deeply as possible and as quickly as possible, without assuming one student's road map for learning is identical to anyone else's" (Tomlinson, 1999, p. 2). Typically, differentiation is done by varying the content (what is taught), the process (how it is taught), and/or the product (how it is assessed) within a given lesson or a unit. Cornett (2009) suggests the following questions for shaping differentiated instruction:

- What is special about this student?
- What is the student's background (sociocultural, economic, linguistic, etc.)?
- What values does the learner hold (e.g., cultural and religious)?
- What does the learner already know and what can he or she do?
- What are the learner's strengths and general developmental needs?

For obvious reasons, the lessons in this book do not provide *all* possible options for differentiation. By using the lessons as models, we hope that you, the teacher, will adapt responsive learning situations based on your intimate knowledge of students' interests, backgrounds, and needs.

Student interests and experiences

The best teachers are aware of their students' interests, home environments, cultural factors, social activities, friends, skills, hobbies, and reading abilities. Because books have been on almost every topic, it is not difficult to match a child to the right book. For a child mesmerized by floating dandelion fluff, *The Dandelion Seed* (Anthony, 1997) (see Chapter 7, Lesson 7.12) is the right selection; for a child fascinated by falling snow, consider *Snowflake Bentley* (Martin, 1998) (see Chapter 7, Lesson 7.5); for a child who moved and left family behind, *The Keeping Quilt* (Polacco, 1998) (see Chapter 7, Lesson 7.6) is an excellent option. Teachers who know both the student and the books make these connections effortlessly. As we continue to expand our students' range of interests and knowledge by introducing them to new topics and titles, reference tools are available to help find books (e.g., IRA's Children's Choices).

Developmental stages

Cognitive, social, emotional, and physical aspects of a child's development are pertinent to the decisions made about the books used with them at different stages in their lives. The greater our knowledge about children and their stages of development, the better we make decisions about meaningful ways of bringing books and children together. From child development courses, we recall Piaget's stages of cognitive development—sensorimotor, preoperational, concrete operational, and formal operational—and Erickson's eight stages that unfold throughout our life cycle (Santrock, 2007). As teachers, we must be mindful of the complexity of children's intellectual and behavioral development that might influence the choice of a book.

Implementation

Guided by our knowledge of children's literature; mathematics, science, and social studies concepts; and stages of child development, we can bring children and books together in ways that will make the relationship a lasting one. Chapters 6 through 9 contain lesson plans with detailed activities that can be implemented: (1) step-by-step; (2) with selected excerpts; or (3) as a springboard for other ideas. Each lesson contains a brief summary of the book, a grade-level focus, the standards addressed, language arts experiences, objectives, key concepts, materials needed, procedures, assessment, and ways to make connections to other concepts, books, and websites.

Exhibit 5.1 is a sample of a lesson included in Chapter 7. We will walk through this lesson and discuss the component parts.

PART A

Part A provides a summary of each book. The summary captures the essence, mood, tone, and style of the book, as well as the content. Because we focus on picture books, we include appropriate comments about the illustrations. You may use these summaries to decide whether you will use a particular book in your classroom, but you may want to examine the book itself before making a final decision.

PART B

Part B includes information on the lesson's academic standards, language arts experiences, objectives, key concepts, and necessary materials. You may select a lesson to support state and/or local standards, literacy skills, content objectives, or concepts that have to be developed in your classroom. In our book, the focus is on the professional standards in mathematics, science, and social studies, with an awareness that teachers should link to their state and local standards. Literacy and art connections and language arts experiences are also explicitly addressed in this section. The *Objectives* and *Key Concepts* derive from the content of the story and our own creative connections to the content and illustrations. The materials should be prepared in advance in order to develop the objectives and transition smoothly between the different components of the lesson plan.

PART C

Part C presents ways to introduce and share the book with children. Depending on the book, the concepts to be taught, and the students, there are many ways to share a book. Use the steps in *Sharing the Book* as a guide or an inspiration or even as an example.

EXHIBIT | **5.1** | Sample lesson.

7.1

LESSON

12 Ways to Get to 11

Eve Merriam • **Bernie Karlin, Illus.**

Part A

Where's eleven? Is it missing? 12 Ways to Get to 11 is a whimsical romp about 12 creative ways to get to 11. Each double-page spread consists of brightly colored cutouts of objects such as "Three sets of triplets in baby carriages and a pair of twins in the stroller" and "In the mailbox: seven letters, two packages, a mail-order catalog, and a picture postcard" that are combinations that total 11. The readers must supply the numbers for the addition sentence and add them up for a total. The sum is always 11. Some combinations are more challenging than others for an amusing counting adventure.

Part B

GRADE LEVELS: **2–3**

MATHEMATICS STANDARD ADDRESSED: numbers and operations—meaning of operations

LANGUAGE ARTS EXPERIENCE: narrative writing

ARTS CONNECTION: drawing

OBJECTIVES: to recognize that the order of the addends does not change the sum (associative property), to use a variety of addends to total 11, to express numbers using a variety of equations

KEY CONCEPTS: number sense, numeration, whole number operations

MATERIALS: counters, unifix or multilink cubes, paper (two sheets per student), crayons

Part C

Procedure

SHARING THE BOOK

1. After reading the book, go back and have the students express aloud the number sentence for the objects on each two-page spread. Then, ask them if they notice a pattern.

2. Ask the students what the total number of objects is on each page, and what happens if they add the objects in a different order? Model several different combinations, such as "9 pinecones and 2 acorns make 11" and "2 acorns and 9 pinecones make 11."

3. Then, have the students represent the number sentences with cubes or counters in their workspace. Have them make a written record of their number sentences. Have them rewrite the sentences to add the objects in a different order and explain what happens.

4. Now, have them create their own number sentences using counters or cubes: If they were going on a field trip, what are some items they would need? Ask each student to share a number sentence aloud.

5. Record on the board the number sentences that are shared, and ask what happens when the number sentence is added in a different order.

Part D

PROMOTING CONCEPTS

1. Have 2, 3, and 6 students come to the front of the room in three separate groups. Ask the groups of 2 and 3 to come together and have a volunteer tell

(continued)

EXHIBIT **5.1** Continued.

EXHIBIT **7.1** Unifix® cube and multilink cubes.

Uniflex® cube   Multilink cubes

the class how many students are in the combined group. Next, have the group of 6 join the others. Let a volunteer tell the class how many there are in all. Next, have the students move back into their separate groups. Have the students make different combinations of the three groups, and ask whether the new combinations add up to a different number of students.

2. Students can also use cubes, as shown in Figure 7.1, and counters. Have them show different combinations of 11 using 3 addends. After several combinations, have the students record their combinations in a vertical format. Then, ask them if they add up or down, is the sum the same.

3. Next, have the students use cubes or counters to show different combinations of 11 using 4 addends, then 5 addends.

4. Have the students create number stories aloud similar to *12 Ways to Get to 11*. Some students may use a situation such as a field trip or class party to create their number sentence. Encourage them to use three addends or more, and model them with counters or cubes in their workspace. State the number sentence aloud.

5. Have the students record one of their number stories using numbers and words on one piece of paper and then illustrate their number sentence on another piece of paper.

6. Extend the lesson to other number combinations such as 12, 13, 14, etc.

Assessment

1. *Observation:* Have students create combinations of 11 in their workspace using counters or cubes.

2. *Performance:* Have the students draw pictures and write number sentences for other number stories they shared aloud. Encourage them to use more than two addends.

3. Use the rubric in Exhibits 5.3 or 5.4 to evaluate students' knowledge of using a variety of addends to make 11.

Making Connections

OTHER CONCEPTS

Using counting on, making a 10, doubles, and doubles plus one to recall addition facts; counting by 2s, 3s, and 4s; practice basic facts; fact families.

OTHER BOOKS

Anno's Counting House, Mitsumasa Anno (1982)
Fish Eyes: A Book You Can Count On, Lois Ehlert (1990)
What Comes in 2's, 3's, and 4's? Suzanne Aker (1990)

WEBSITES

http://funBrain.com/math/index.html
www.matematiko.com
www.scienceacademy.com/BI/add.htm
www.teachervision.com

Book introductions get the children ready to learn and allow you to share your enthusiasm for both the book and the topic. Of course, practice reading the selection aloud before sharing it with your students to ensure the fluency of the reading heightens the students' enjoyment of the book. "Read it again!" is the confirmation of the joy and pleasure that comes from literature shared aloud. There is power in the meaning and rhythm of the words and in the striking and stunning illustrations. Sharing books with children shows them how effectively language can be used and what delight it can bring. Reading aloud is a critical component of any literature curriculum; it is just as important in the development of readers at the intermediate level as it is in kindergarten (Lynch-Brown & Tomlinson, 1993). Although all lessons provide suggestions you can use to introduce a book to your students, the intention is not that you should necessarily read the book aloud to them. Instead you should consider your students' needs as well as your goals for the lesson. Cornett (2010) offers the guidelines in Exhibit 5.2 for reading aloud to students.

EXHIBIT 5.2   Guidelines for reading aloud to students (Cornett, 2010).

1. Set up the physical space. Consider gathering students on a rug with the teacher on a low chair. Make sure you can make eye contact with every student and that they have a clear view.

2. Introduce the text. Considerations and choices include:
   - Change lighting, play background music (mood set).
   - Show the book title and give information about the author and/or illustrator; use objects/pictures (attention get).
   - Describe what to listen for. Cue to upcoming response expected at the end (purpose set).
   - Relate to other texts, activate or build student background, and connect to content units.
   - Introduce key words and concepts.
   - Explicitly teach a comprehension strategy or text characteristic.
   - Review audience etiquette including active listening.

3. Using a picture book, hold the book at the bottom center with your nondominant hand so you can track print and point with your dominant hand.

4. Read expressively. Change the pitch (high–low), tone (gentle–rough), and volume (soft–loud) of your voice to show different characters or create a mood. Vary pace and use pauses to create suspense. Let your voice reflect the mood. Pay special attention to verbs. Be careful with dialect and names.

5. Use facial expressions and make eye contact. Use your face to show your responses to the content.

6. Use your body and arm gestures to convey the message, but don't overdo it.

7. Encourage active participation. Invite students to repeat refrains and use oral cloze, which asks for students to supply missing words when you pause. You may stop and interview students who pretend to be characters; ask them, "What happened?" Use a plastic mike. Use signals such as thumbs-up and thumbs-down. Insert vocabulary discussions, as needed, for comprehension.

8. After reading, return to the purposes. Ask good questions—not "Did you like it?" but "What did you learn? What did you notice? What was it really about? How did it make you feel? What did the author or artist do that worked? How?" Engage students in writing and arts-based responses.

Troubleshooting:
- Prevent problems by explicitly teaching students how to attend, concentrate, and do active listening.
- If students say they have already heard the book, tell them to listen for new ideas.
- Lower volume and pause to retrieve attention. Stop and wait, if necessary, for attention.
- Sit students who need extra supervision near you.

Used with permission.

Teachers create opportunities for students to share their individual insights into a shared book experience in different ways. Perhaps the most used means of eliciting students' responses is through whole class discussion. A good class discussion encourages students to share how they feel about the book, its characters, its events, and its outcome. In this type of class discussion, the teacher plays a key role as discussion leader by providing an opportunity for as many students as possible to express their viewpoints.

Part C also includes questions to focus the students' attention on the mathematical, science, and social studies concepts embedded in the story. In Exhibit 5.1, the children are asked, "What is the total number of objects on each page? What happens if they add the objects in a different order?" These questions are designed to encourage thinking, actively engage the children, promote discussion, and activate or build on prior knowledge.

PART D

Part D, *Promoting Concepts*, presents specific instructions for developing the *Key Concepts* and *Objectives*. This part presents a wide range of experiences, including observing and recording, talking through an idea, arguing a viewpoint, dramatizing, drawing, collecting data, making a hypothesis, drawing conclusions, and listening to others as some of the many ways of teaching and testing emerging ideas.

In addition, *Promoting Concepts* provides suggestions for extending, differentiating, reteaching, or reviewing to meet the needs of a range of ability levels in the classroom. Those students who consistently exhibit either competence or protracted difficulty in learning the concepts require modifications to the teaching strategies to meet their specific needs. Students who show the potential to excel should be given additional opportunities to problem solve and engage in extended activities. Special-needs learners often benefit from additional experiences and the use of manipulative models. These opportunities are provided in this section. For example, in Exhibit 5.1, if a student is unable to represent objects with the correct number of cubes, then counting by 2s, 3s, and 4s, or practicing basic facts may provide success in the lesson. For students who have demonstrated a complete understanding of the mathematical concepts and processes, the lesson can be extended to creating number combinations for 12, 13, 14, and so on.

PART E

Part E presents ideas for assessment. In the age of high-stakes assessment and accountability, authentic ways to assess and evaluate students that *inform* instruction in the classroom are even more crucial. Using a compilation of scholarly work in educational assessment and evaluation (Clarke, 1992; Rhodes & Shanklin, 1993; Valencia & Pearson, 1987), we offer the following principles as guidelines for authentic assessment:

- *Assessment should be meaningful.* Assessment should inform teachers about students' strengths and weaknesses so that decisions can be made about instruction. The aim is for better, more appropriate assessment, not simply more assessment.

- *Assessment should be multimodal.* Many assessment tools are available (e.g., performance assessment, portfolios, logs, projects, interviews/conferences, anecdotal records, journals, checklists, rubrics, inventories/surveys); a combination of these tools should be used to fully indicate whether students have met learning goals.

- *Assessment should be ongoing.* Assessment should occur frequently so that a complete and accurate picture of progress is documented.
- *Assessment should occur in authentic contexts.* As much as possible, assessment should mirror the instruction and the learning activities.

When teachers assess *for learning*, the assessment process should provide for a continuous flow of information about student achievement in order to advance student learning (Stiggens, 2002). In addition to writing, the following assessment tools are used in Part E of the lessons:

Questioning

Observation

Performance

Rubrics

Learning logs

Expanded examples of these assessment tools are presented in the following lessons:

Questioning and learning log example in *Henry's Freedom Box* in Chapter 8, Lesson 8.14 (grades 4–5)

Observation example in *Jump, Frog, Jump* in Chapter 6, Lesson 6.7 (grades preK–1)

Performance example in *The Keeping Quilt* in Chapter 7, Lesson 7.6 (grades 2–3)

Rubrics example in *Spaghetti and Meatballs for All!* in Chapter 8, Lesson 8.3 (grades 4–5)

Questioning

Most teachers find it difficult to communicate without asking questions. Effective questioning allows teachers to check for understanding, obtain information, and provide indirect cues (Columba, 2001). Can you imagine teaching an entire lesson and not asking any questions? The clear and consistent message from research on teacher questioning is that no teacher should underestimate the value of good questioning techniques. Questioning provides one of the most effortless methods to monitor student progress on a continuous basis and a means to detect problems at the earliest stage possible (Berliner, 1989). Good questions, prepared before a lesson, will help a teacher determine whether students use varied approaches to a problem and how well students can explain their own thinking. This process complements observation. Specifically, **probing questions** are a teaching/assessment strategy that provides insight into the mental processes students use by engaging them in conversation about the subject. The goal of the questions is to deepen students' understanding of the content.

In the *Procedure* section of the lessons, we provide many questions for the classroom assessment of student performance based on the specific content. In Exhibit 5.1, after sharing the book, some of the suggested questions include the following: "Do they notice a pattern? What is the total number of objects on each page? What happens if they add the objects in a different order?" These questions encourage student participation in the interactive discussion and provide the teacher with insight into which students are grasping the concepts and which students may need further challenges or remediation.

Observation

By observing how students undertake practice activities, teachers learn a great deal about student progress and potential problems. These elicitations are teacher guided, organized, and directed. Quality practice provides learners the opportunity to encounter challenges and to see progress in a variety of examples and situations.

As we formalize the student observations, we should develop systematic methods of recording. Some teachers keep journals, while others prefer to complete forms or use 3 x 5 cards. Note cards are a good way to record anecdotal information about almost any aspect of a student's performance. One or two observations—focusing on student behaviors such as reasoning, metacognitive processes, or affective considerations—are sufficient. Periodically, select one or two aspects of a lesson for which to be looking and write them down on your lesson plan so you will be reminded to look for these items and make notes. The note-card approach is also convenient for putting comments in student folders to use later in conference with the student or parent (Nitko & Brookhart, 2006).

The Observation Checklist and the Daily Observation Sheet, examples of which are shown in Exhibit 5.3, are tools to help the teacher keep observational records of students engaged in open-ended tasks in the classroom. They can be used in conjunction with the lesson's Assessment section (Part E in Exhibit 5.1). Observation checklists are lists of criteria a teacher has determined are important. Next to each criterion, the teacher makes a notation as to whether she has observed that particular criterion in a particular student at a particular time. You can use checklists to record the presence or absence of knowledge, skills, learning processes, or attitudes.

The Daily Observation Sheet is used to gather information as the students are working. Keep in mind that not every performance task must be scored.

Performance

Performance assessment is a broad term. It evaluates students' learning behaviors or products by their demonstration of knowledge and skills through such activities as writing, oral reports, dramatizations, simulations, experiments, portfolios, and projects. These activities enable the teacher to get a full picture of whether students have grasped a concept, put skills to work, generalized, used a variety of reasoning skills, and so forth. The characteristics of performance assessment include:

- Asking students to perform, create, produce, or do something.
- Tapping higher-level thinking and problem-solving skills.
- Using tasks that represent meaningful instructional activities.
- Invoking real-world applications.
- Scoring using human judgment.

Advantages of performance assessment include the potential to assess "doing" and the integration of knowledge, skills, and abilities (Nitko & Brookhart, 2006). The performance assessments provided in these lessons link with the teaching activities and assess students' use of processes as well as products.

Rubrics

New instructional methods of teaching require a new assessment tool—the rubric. A rubric is a coherent set of rules used to assess the quality of a student's performance. A rating scale is one component of a rubric. Rubrics help guide our

EXHIBIT **5.3** Sample observational records.

Student Names

OBSERVATION CHECKLIST	Keith	Isabella	Milo	Mira
Processes				
Justifies answers				
Listens carefully to others				
Explains choices				
Knowledge				
Explains procedures				
Uses models appropriately				
Applies mathematical concepts				
Participation				
Willing to try problems				
Demonstrates self-confidence				
Perseveres				

DAILY OBSERVATION SHEET

Name	Date	Activity	Observations	Suggestions

judgment and ensure that we apply it consistently from one student to the next. Other characteristics of a rubric include:

- It is a scoring guide or tool based on a full range of criteria ("What counts").
- It is an authentic assessment tool used to measure students' work (gradations of quality).
- It is a working guide for students and teachers that is usually given to students before the assignment begins.
- It enhances the quality of direct instruction.
- It can be created for any content.
- It can be shared with students before the lesson so they know the assessment criteria.

We believe that rubrics improve students' end products and therefore increase learning. When these tools are made available for students to use, they provide the scaffolding necessary to improve the quality of the students' work. Rubrics are a fundamental component of our planning, not an additional commitment to preparation. Once a rubric is created, it can be used for a variety of activities. Exhibits 5.4 and 5.5 are sample rubrics that can be used with the lesson in Exhibit 5.1.

EXHIBIT 5.4 Sample rubric with numeric descriptors.

12 WAYS TO GET TO 11

Name: Date:

CRITERIA	4	3	2	1	POINTS
Explanation	Explains how to represent object with the same number of cubes. Constructs different combinations of 11 using 3, 4, and 5 addends. A complete response with details.	Explains how to represent object with the same number of cubes. Constructs different combinations of 11 using 3, 4, and 5 addends. A solid response with details.	Explains how to represent object with the same number of cubes. Explanation is unclear.	Unable to represent objects with the correct number of cubes. Explanation is missing key points.	
Drawings	Clear and detailed sketch or diagram.	Clear sketch or diagram.	Inappropriate or unclear drawings.	No drawings.	
Understanding the Problem/ Concept	Shows complete understanding of the mathematical concepts and processes.	Shows substantial understanding of the concepts and processes.	Shows some understanding of the concepts and processes.	Shows a complete lack of understanding of the concepts and processes.	
Computations	No mathematics errors or flaws in reasoning.	No major mathematical errors or serious flaws in reasoning.	Minor computational errors or flaws in reasoning.	Major mathematical errors and serious flaws in reasoning.	
				Total	

EXHIBIT 5.5 Sample rubric with qualitative descriptors.

12 WAYS TO GET TO 11

Name: Date:

PERFORMANCE DESCRIPTORS	QUALITY			STUDENT'S LEVEL
	ADVANCED	**PROFICIENT**	**BASIC**	
Understanding/ Connecting Concepts	Indicates a comprehensive understanding of concepts with connections throughout.	Indicates a broad understanding of some concepts with connections.	Indicates a basic understanding of concepts.	
Reasoning	Uses perceptive, creative, and complex mathematical reasoning.	Uses perceptive mathematical reasoning.	Uses mathematical reasoning.	
Performance	Recognizes patterns in the objects. Represents the objects with the same number of cubes. Constructs different combinations of 11 using 3, 4, and 5 addends. Records number sentences for the different combinations. Relates the task of making combinations to the task of illustrating a number sentence.	Recognizes patterns in the objects. Represents the objects with the same number of cubes. Constructs different combinations of 11 using 3, 4, and 5 addends. Records number sentences for the different combinations.	Recognizes patterns in the objects. Represents the objects with the same number of cubes. Constructs different combinations of 11 using 3, 4, and 5 addends.	
Explanation of Process or Strategy	Clearly describes the process used to combine different combinations of cubes (addends) to form 11 and states the number sentence. Creates number combinations with sums beyond 11.	Clearly describes the process used to combine different combinations of cubes (addends) to form 11 and states the number sentence.	Creates combinations of cubes (addends) to form 11 with guidance.	

Rubrics allow you to assess several dimensions of performance, as well as how the student integrates those dimensions when performing a task. Rubrics can be also used to review, reconceptualize, and revisit the same concepts from different angles.

Constructing rubrics requires a scale that reflects the quality levels of performance, gradations, specific description, and criteria for each dimension. Each level of quality may be represented numerically (Exhibit 5.3) or with a qualitative description such as *advanced, proficient,* and *basic* (Exhibit 5.4).

Contemporary assessment recognizes the inadequacy of the "Assessment as Measurement" metaphor. Our goal is now "Assessment as Portrayal." Put simply, good daily assessment is good instruction because it is carefully aligned with what is taught and how it is taught. Skillful teachers have known for years that good teaching and effective assessment are often difficult to distinguish (Columba, 2001).

Learning logs

Learning logs can help students crystallize their thinking and understanding of content area concepts. Immediately after a content area lesson, students can respond to the lesson in their learning logs. These responses can vary and include:

- A summary of a concept or example that demonstrates an understanding of the lesson.
- A summary or an example of what they didn't understand.
- Questions about concepts they didn't understand.
- A personal response to the reading.

Teachers can then respond to the students' logs, answering questions and directing them to other sources of information to clarify concepts. Exhibit 5.6 presents examples from a math lesson with the teacher's responses on the right.

PART F

Part F of Exhibit 5.1 presents various ways to make connections to other concepts, other books, and relevant websites for additional research.

Other concepts

This section is used to introduce related concepts to further support the interrelationship and connections between and among concepts. In Exhibit 5.1, "counting on," "making a 10," "doubles," and "doubles plus one" are thinking strategies that are used to recall basic facts and reinforce the development of number sense, numeration, and numerical operations.

EXHIBIT	5.6	Examples from a third grader's math learning log, with the teacher's responses (Cecil, 2007).

How is multiplication like addition?	You are adding, but you're doing it much more quickly.
How do I know when to divide?	Look for the word "each."
What problems should I watch out for when I am borrowing?	Be sure to cross out the old number and put in the new one so you're not confused.
Why do I need to know the times tables when I have a calculator?	You may not always have one with you!

Other books

This section provides a list of books with similar topics and concepts. Teachers know the individual interests of their students, so we provide a variety of books for you to share and to help you match the student with the right book. For example, *Fish Eyes: A Book You Can Count On* (Ehlert, 1990) (see Chapter 6, Lesson 6.1), a stunningly illustrated book of fish, provides additional fun practicing basic facts with the pattern of "one more than" throughout the book. This is another resource to help you meet the needs of a range of learners, including students who are learning disabled or gifted, or for whom English is a second language.

Websites

The websites will help you prepare to teach the relevant concepts. Effective teachers have *content familiarity*. They research and prepare for concepts that may confuse students. Use this section to enhance your lesson plans or provide clarity for difficult concepts. Also, these websites provide additional activities for students who need reinforcement or further challenges (www.funBrain.com/math/index.html provides puzzles, problems, and practice for all ability levels).

Conclusion

Children's literature provides a powerful opportunity to share the world of knowledge and foster unique learning experiences. By knowing concepts, children, and books, we as teachers can match the child with the right book. Thoughtful book selection encourages children to explore topics of interest and satisfy their natural curiosity.

As we create the environment for learning, it is our responsibility to make sure that when children and books come together the experience is enjoyable and thought provoking. In Chapters 6 through 9, we share quality books and meaningful lessons to provide powerful learning experiences for students.

Enjoy sharing books with your students; in turn, the students will have the opportunity to respond authentically and naturally to those various experiences. These selections and activities will enrich the lives and imaginations of the young mathematicians, scientists, and social scientists in our classrooms.

REFERENCES

Berliner, D. C. (1989). The teaching profession. *Equity and Excellence, 24,* 4–19.

Cecil, N. L. (2007). *Striking a balance: Best practices for early literacy* (3rd ed.). Scottsdale, AZ: Holcomb Hathaway.

Clarke, D. J. (1992). Activating assessment alternatives in mathematics. *Arithmetic Teacher, 40,* 24–29.

Clarke, D. J., Clarke, D. M., & Lovitt, C. J. (1990). Changes in mathematics teaching call for assessment alternatives. In T. J. Cooney & C. R. Hirsch (Eds.), *Teaching and learning mathematics in the 1990's: Yearbook 1990* (pp. 118–129). Reston, VA: The National Council of Teachers of Mathematics.

Columba, L. (2001). Daily classroom assessment. *Education, 122,* 372–374.

Cornett, C. (2010). *Comprehension first.* Scottsdale, AZ: Holcomb Hathaway.

Countryman, J. (1992). *Writing to learn mathematics: Strategies that work, K–12.* Portsmouth, NH: Heinemann.

Dolgos, K. A., & Columba, L. (1993). Alternative assessment: The mathematics portfolio. In M. K. Heid & G. W. Blume (Eds.), *Alternative assessment in mathematics, 1993 yearbook* (pp. 23–28). University Park, PA: Pennsylvania Council of Teachers of Mathematics Yearbook.

Freeman, E. B., & Person, D. G. (1998). *Connecting informational children's books with content area learning.* Boston: Allyn & Bacon.

Lesh, R., & Lamon, S. J. (Eds.). (1992). *Assessment of authentic performance in school mathematics.* Washington, DC: American Association for the Advancement of Science.

Lynch-Brown, C., & Tomlinson, C. M. (1993). *Essentials of children's literature.* Boston: Allyn & Bacon.

Nitko, A. J., & Brookhart, S. M. (2006). *Educational assessment of students* (5th ed.). Upper Saddle River, NJ: Prentice Hall.

Rhodes, L. K., & Shanklin, N. L. (1993). *Windows into literacy: Assessing learners K–8.* Portsmouth, NH: Heinemann.

Santrock, J. W. (2007). *Children* (10th ed.). New York: McGraw-Hill.

Stiggens, R. J. (2002). Assessment crisis: The absence of assessment for learning. *Phi Delta Kappan, 83*(10), 758–765.

Tomlinson, C. A. (1999). *The differentiated classroom: Responding to the needs of all learners.* Alexandria, VA: ASCD.

Valencia, S., & Pearson, P. D. (1987). Reading assessment: Time for change. *The Reading Teacher, 40*(8), 726–733.

Webb, N. L., & Coxford, A. F. (Eds.). (1993). *Assessment in the mathematics classroom.* Reston, VA: The National Council of Teachers of Mathematics.

CHILDREN'S LITERATURE

Anthony, J. (1997). *The dandelion seed* (C. Arbo, Illus.). Nevada City, CA: Dawn.

Clement, R. (1994). *Counting on Frank.* New York: Houghton Mifflin.

Ehlert, L. (1990). *Fish eyes: A book you can count on.* New York: Harcourt Brace.

Hutchins, P. (1986). *The doorbell rang.* New York: Morrow.

Martin, J. B. (1998). *Snowflake Bentley* (M. Azarian, Illus.). New York: Houghton Mifflin.

Mathews, L. (1979). *Gator pie.* New York: Dodd, Mead.

Merriam, E. (1993). *12 ways to get to 11* (B. Karlin, Illus.). New York: Simon & Schuster.

Polacco, P. (1998). *The keeping quilt.* New York: Simon & Schuster.

Seuss, Dr. (1976). *The 500 hats of Bartholomew Cubbins.* New York: Random House.

Viorst, J. (1980). *Alexander, who used to be rich last Sunday* (R. Cruz, Illus.). New York: Simon & Schuster.

CHAPTER

6

Discovering Mathematics, Science, and Social Studies

Grades PreK-1

T he cognitive, language, and social development of young children requires interactive discussions where learners share experiences under the guidance of knowledgeable and sensitive adults. The research of Piaget (1963) informs us of the importance of appropriate sensory experiences and concrete learning activities, and the work of Vygotsky (1978) shows us how the skillful teacher can use these experiences and activities to stretch a young child's cognitive abilities.

Wise teachers also work to develop positive dispositions toward learning (Bruner, 1996). Dispositions are attitudes or feelings that influence how learners respond to certain experiences. The best example of how a disposition has an impact on learning is the child's feelings about reading. Because we know that the skills involved in reading are improved by reading, it is important that the "disposition" to be a reader and to read is nurtured by teachers, parents, and caregivers. We believe that this is equally true when teaching and learning mathematics, science, and social studies.

Because of our constructivist position—that knowledge is actively constructed by the individual—we support active and lively learning. Learning is not a passive activity. Young children must be engaged. They must discover. They must manipulate. They must talk and discuss among themselves. For young children, the process of learning takes place when they attempt to make sense of the world around them. Constructivism emphasizes the role of others in the learning process (Harris & Graham, 1994). Furthermore, knowledge is developmentally organized, and learning has a social component in which the learners' interaction with their environment and other learners is critical.

For the reasons we discussed in Chapter 1, children's literature provides the springboard to engage learning by helping the young learner to make connections. In the early levels of development, using in-class activities or life experiences helps the child make text-to-self connections. At this level, informed teachers read and discuss books like *Will You Be My Friend?* (Tafuri, 2000), *David Goes to School* (Shannon, 1999), *Brown Bear, Brown Bear What Do You See?* (Martin, 1995), or *Chicka Chicka, Boom Boom* (Martin & Archambault, 1989). These books allow children to relate to the story characters, the settings, the problems, and the rhythm of the language. As children become more familiar with the conventions of text, teachers should share stories that require them to make text-to-text connections and text-to-world connections (Fountas & Pinnell, 2001).

Helm, Beneke, and Steinheimer (1998, pp. 153–156) share an excellent example of how the reading of one book, *A Letter to Amy* (Keats, 1968), led to a series of learning activities. The teacher of a class of three- and four-year-old children learns that her students are curious about what happens after Peter, the main character, mails a letter to Amy because, when they next see the letter, Amy is taking it out of her mailbox. The students wanted to know what happens after a letter is mailed. Through a number of activities including constructing mailboxes, mailbags, and flow charts; making and selling stamps; investigating; and ultimately developing a pen pal system for their school, the teacher stated that she "was amazed by the nature of her students' growth [as learners, as knowers, as language users]." These learning experiences were not hurried, however; this project ran for about four weeks.

This type of teaching and learning experience represents the best of practices in the lives of young children. Therefore, in Appendix A.1 we have provided a list of the principles of child development and learning that offer guidance for such instruction. These principles, developed by the National Association for the Education of Young Children (Bredekamp & Copple, 1996), are widely accepted by teachers of young children throughout the country.

In this chapter, we provide lessons to use to teach science, mathematics, and social studies to young children ages 4 to 6. Using children's books such as *In the Small, Small Pond* (Fleming, 1993), *Officer Buckle and Gloria* (Rathmann, 1995), and *Growing Vegetable Soup* (Ehlert, 1987), we devised lessons to help young learners develop an understanding about environments, growing things, and the essentials for life. Similarly, using other books—such as *A Three Hat Day* (Geringer, 1985), *Fish Eyes: A Book You Can Count On* (Ehlert, 1990), *Over in the Garden* (Ward, 2002), *That Pesky Rat* (Child, 2002), *Time for Bed* (Fox, 1993), and *365 Penguins* (Fromental & Jolivet, 2006)—we introduce mathematics concepts that are essential to being able to make sense of numbers at all levels. *365 Penguins* can also be used to teach a social studies lesson about the environment and conservation.

These lessons use books that represent outstanding examples of children's literature that will develop positive dispositions for learning mathematics, science, and social studies (and also, quite frankly, beginning reading). We have built these lessons around the professional mathematics standards (NCTM, 2000) that promote the understanding of (1) numbers and operations and (2) data analysis and probability. The science lessons were written to correspond to the professional standards (NRC, 1996) that address (1) life science and (2) science in personal and social perspectives. The social studies lessons focus on the professional standards involving the thematic strands of people, places, and environments; culture; and production, distribution, and consumption.

The lessons provided are just a few of the many that can be created using the books introduced here. Creative teachers will use the books discussed here in many other ways, and they will find hundreds of other superb children's books around which they will create their own lessons.

Fish Eyes: A Book You Can Count On

Lois Ehlert

This rhyming and counting book is illustrated with brilliantly and vividly colored fish on a dark blue background. The narrow rectangular shape of the book accentuates the depictions of fish that extend onto two-page spreads. One green fish, two jumping fish, three smiling fish . . . keep the count going. Also, the vibrant fish have cutout circle eyes that draw the reader into the journey through rivers and seas. A small, dark fish flits playfully across the pages saying, "Follow me" to create the "one more than" concept of addition. This is an eye-catching and fun read for counting and adding "one more than" in typical Ehlert fashion.

GRADE LEVELS:	**PreK–1**
MATHEMATICS STANDARD ADDRESSED:	numbers and operations—ways of representing numbers
LANGUAGE ARTS EXPERIENCE:	visual representation
OBJECTIVES:	to use the mental mathematics strategy of counting on 1 to find sums
KEY CONCEPT:	"one more than" counting patterns
MATERIALS:	Counting on 1 Exploration sheet (Appendix A.2; or have students create their own ocean watercolor), fish crackers (construction paper fish or counters—tiles, beads, beans, etc.), Number Cards 1–12 (Appendix A.3), paper, crayons, water colors

Procedure

SHARING THE BOOK

1. Before reading the book, ask the students if they have ever been fishing. Ask if any of them have fish at home. Ask if they have ever been to an aquarium. Share other experiences with fish. Many pictures are available at http://animals. nationalgeographic.com/animals/fish.html.

2. After reading, ask what helps fish to breathe underwater. Describe or act out how fish swim. Ask what else students notice about the fish in the book. Ask which fish they liked and how they would describe it.

3. Have students look closely at an illustration in the book. Ask if they can see one more fish. Return to the beginning of the book and have students count one more fish on each page.

4. Ask students to describe the kind of fish they would like to be: what color, stripes, long or short, narrow or wide, color eyes, kind of fins. Have students create the kind of fish they would like to be.

PROMOTING CONCEPTS

1. Place the Counting on 1 Exploration sheet on the students' workspace. (The students can create their own ocean environment using the Exploration sheet or an ocean watercolor.)

2. Say the number "one" and have each student put one fish (or counter) on the Exploration page and say, "One plus me [pointing to the fish on the worksheet] makes two."

3. Repeat this format for the numbers 2–10 (or 11–20 depending on the students' ability level).

4. Working in pairs, have the students draw from a deck of number cards (Appendix A.3) labeled 1 to 12 and place that number of fish (or counters) on their Counting on 1 Exploration sheet or ocean watercolor. Then, state aloud the number of fish represented "plus me makes ___" as they point to the fish on the Exploration sheet or their own ocean watercolor.

5. Some students may be ready to extend these two activities to "counting on 2 or 3."

Assessment

1. *Performance:* Have the students draw and color a fish with crayons. When you say a number from 1 to 10, have them hold up their fish and say "plus me makes ___."

2. *Performance:* Ask students to place number cards from 1 to 10 face down in their workspace. As they randomly flip the cards over, ask students to say, "___ plus one more makes ___."

3. *Performance:* Have students create a watercolor wash of their own ocean using colors and designs that are their favorites (in place of the Exploration sheet provided). Then repeat steps 2 and 3 in Promoting Concepts.

Making Connections

OTHER CONCEPTS

Counting on 2 and 3; zero property; mental math strategies for counting on 1, 2, or 3; "counting on" using turnaround facts; writing the number before, after, or between; counting by 2s and 5s; introducing the addition symbol (+) for the plus language.

OTHER BOOKS

Color Zoo, Lois Ehlert (1997)

Eating the Alphabet: Fruits & Vegetables from A to Z, Lois Ehlert (1989)

One Hungry Monster, Susan Heyboer O'Keefe, Lynn Munsinger (Illus.) (1989)

1, 2, 3 to the Zoo, Eric Carle (1968)

Rosie's Walk, Pat Hutchins (1971)

Ten, Nine, Eight, Molly Bang (1983)

WEBSITES

http://animals.nationalgeographic.com/animals/fish.html

www.fishlinkcentral.com/

www.fws.gov/

www.infomath.com/oltutor/math1/demo/mt1_demo.asp

6.2
LESSON

Ten, Nine, Eight
Molly Bang

A father prepares his little girl for bed with a rhyming countdown from 10 to 1. The story begins with "10 small toes all washed and warm" and concludes with "one big girl all ready for bed" as she is tucked into bed. The numerals are on the left-hand side, and brightly colored illustrations of the quantity from the little girl's bedroom are on the right-hand side. This delightful counting book portrays a warm and loving family with an element of diversity added through Bang's beautiful illustrations.

GRADE LEVELS: PreK–1

MATHEMATICS STANDARD ADDRESSED: numbers and operations—ways of representing numbers

LANGUAGE ARTS EXPERIENCE: visual representation

OBJECTIVES: to count backward from 10

KEY CONCEPTS: numbers before and after, counting order, counting patterns

MATERIALS: masking tape; Number Cards 1–10 (Appendix A.4); calendar; markers; number cubes with numbers 1, 2, and 3; Counting Chain 10–1 (Appendix A.5)

Procedure

SHARING THE BOOK

1. Before reading the book, ask the students about getting ready for bed at night. Tell the students what you do to prepare for bedtime, such as brushing your teeth, reading a story, putting on your pajamas, and so on. Ask the students who helps them get ready for bed at night. Ask them if they have a special story they like to hear.

2. Read the book aloud.

3. Ask the students who helped this little girl get ready for bed. Also ask how their routine varies from the character's in the story.

4. Say to the students, let's go back and count together the items that are in her bedroom. Then, count in unison or call on individuals (e.g., "7 empty shoes in a short straight row").

5. Then, read the book aloud a second time and have the students hold up 10 fingers, then 9, then 8, and so forth as the story progresses.

PROMOTING CONCEPTS

1. Ask 10 children to line up in front of the class. Have the tenth child begin by saying "10" and sitting down. The ninth child then says "9" and sits down. Continue the sequence until all students are seated.

2. Tell the students to pretend that they can travel backward in time. Have them read the numbers on the calendar with you as you point to each one, beginning with 10 and counting back to 1.

3. Have the students cut out number cards from 1 to 10 and arrange them on their workspace from 10 to 1. (Alternatively, you can cut them yourself and set them out for students.)

4. As a class, create a masking-tape number line on the floor using the number cards 1–10. Have the students gather around the number line. Ask a student to start at 10 and walk backward 1 step for each number. Have the class count along with the student who is doing the stepping.

5. Ask a student to begin at 7 and walk backward 3 steps. Have another student start at 5 and walk back 3 steps. Continue until each student has had a turn.

6. Line up 10 chairs in the classroom. Have the students count back from 10 as they take chairs away one by one.

Assessment

1. *Performance:* Use a number cube with numbers 1, 2, and 3 on it and a Counting Chain (Appendix A.5) with numbers 1–10 (or create a zigzag number line from 1–10 of your own) and have the students work in pairs. Have them roll a number cube and then move their marker back the number of spaces on the cube from 10 on the number line. The goal is to arrive at the number 1 first.

2. *Performance:* Have the students illustrate their own preparation for bed by counting items in their bedroom, starting with 10 and counting down to 1.

Making Connections

OTHER CONCEPTS

Numbers from 20–1; patterns in whole number counting; counting backward by two; counting back using pennies, nickels, and dimes; one less than; mental mathematics counting back 1, 2, or 3 to find differences; counting on 1, 2, or 3; subtract a 1-digit from a 2-digit number by counting back by ones.

OTHER BOOKS

Big Fat Hen, Keith Baker (1997)

Blueberries for Sal, Robert McCloskey (1976)

Brown Bear, Brown Bear, What Do You See? Bill Martin, Eric Carle (Illus.) (1995)

The Carrot Seed, Ruth Krauss (1945)

Have You Seen My Duckling? Nancy Tafuri (1984)

Rosie's Walk, Pat Hutchins (1971)

The Snowy Day by Ezra, Jack Keats, Linda Terheyden (Illus.) (1963)

Ten in a Bed, Mary Rees (1988)

WEBSITE

www.apples4theteacher.com/math.html

Time for Bed

Mem Fox • **Jane Dyer, Illus.**

In rhyming couplets, this bedtime lullaby gives an eye-level view of mothers from the animal kingdom preparing their babies for bed. A few of the animal pairs are bees, snakes, birds, and horses that endearingly tell their young it is time for sleep. Each two-page layout is warmly and gently illustrated in large-scale watercolors with a mother and newborn on the right-hand side and the rhyme on the left-hand side. The last baby to be put to bed is a human baby with the mother saying, "Sweet dreams, my darling . . . good night!"

GRADE LEVELS: PreK–1

MATHEMATICS STANDARD ADDRESSED: numbers and operations—ways of representing numbers

LANGUAGE ARTS EXPERIENCES: poetry, shared writing experience

OBJECTIVES: to count by twos, to observe patterns

KEY CONCEPTS: patterns, even numbers, continuing a counting pattern

MATERIALS: cubes, crayons, Hundreds Chart (Appendix A.6), calculators

Procedure

SHARING THE BOOK

1. After reading the book aloud, discuss with the students the relationship of this book to *Ten, Nine, Eight* (Lesson 6.2) as appropriate. Create a Venn diagram representing similarities and differences.

2. Ask the students what they notice on each page, what is happening, and what time it is in each illustration.

3. Ask the students who puts them to bed. Have each student share what happens at bedtime at his or her house. Ask the students if they have a favorite bedtime story.

4. Have students think of other animals that can be added to this story.

5. Ask the students whether they notice the pattern for the number of animals on each page.

6. Finally, have the students count by twos for each pair of animals as the pages are turned.

PROMOTING CONCEPTS

1. Have the students use cubes to represent the number pattern that they have been counting aloud. Tell them to place two cubes (a pair of cubes) in their workspace for the mother and baby mice, two cubes for the mother and baby geese, etc.

2. Now, have them count by two for each pair of cubes: "2, 4, 6, 8, . . ." Ask what is the name of this pattern. *Skip counting by twos* or *counting by twos*.

3. Pass out the Hundreds Chart and tell them to color the pattern as it is said aloud. Ask what do they call this pattern. *Skip counting by twos* or *counting by twos*.

4. Now, tell the students to key "2 + 2 =" into their calculator, and ask what do they get. *4*. Have them press = again, and ask what do they get. *6*. Repeat the process.

5. Ask them what pattern they see. *2, 4, 6, 8, . . .* Ask what is the name for this pattern. *Skip counting by twos* or *counting by twos*.

6. Have the students provide another name for this pattern. *Even numbers*.

7. Ask them if this is the same pattern they colored on their Hundreds Chart. Then, ask them if they can make this same pattern with other materials, such as tiles, beads, and counters.

Assessment

1. *Performance:* The students will color in the pattern for counting by twos on the Hundreds Chart as they count aloud.

2. *Performance:* The students will draw a picture of "what comes in 2s" in their environment, such as 2 eyes, 2 ears, 2 arms, 2 hands, 2 legs, 2 feet, 2 pieces of bread on a sandwich, 2 seats on a seesaw, 2 wings on a bird, etc.

3. *Performance:* Create an illustration of a mother and newborn that is not in the book. Compose as a class a rhyming couplet to go with the illustration, such as a mother hen and baby chick: "It's time for bed, little chick, little chick. Lie close under my wing, come quick."

Making Connections

OTHER CONCEPTS

Ordinal numbers; counting by 5s; counting on; counting back; multiplication by 2; the relationship between multiplication and repeated addition; relationship between counting, multiplying, and adding.

OTHER BOOKS

Brown Bear, Brown Bear, What Do You See? Eric Carle, Bill Martin (Illus.) (1995)

Goodnight, Gorilla, Peggy Rathmann (1996)

Goodnight, Moon, Margaret Brown Wise, Clement Hurd (Illus.) (1991)

Guess How Much I Love You, Sam McBratney (1994)

I Love You as Much, Laura Krauss Melmed, Henri Sorensen (Illus.) (1998)

Jamberry Board Book, Bruce Degan (1995)

What comes in 2's, 3's, & 4's? Suzanne Aker, Bernie Karlin (Illus.) (1990)

WEBSITES

http://standards.nctm.org/document/chapter4/index.htm
www.fi.edu/pieces/knox/skipsong.htm
www.eduplace.com/math/mthexp/

Somewhere in the Ocean

Jennifer Ward and T. J. Marsh • Kenneth J. Spengler, Illus.

In this excellent counting book, Ward and Marsh share 10 creatures of the ocean with 10 counting rhymes, a musical score, and hidden numbers. Manatees, whales, otters, sharks, and hermit crabs are among the collection of marine life shown in Spengler's vivid illustrations, in two-page spreads of realistic color. For teachers (and advanced readers), five pages of expository information on the ocean creatures are depicted in the story. Through singing and counting, reading and rhyming, five- and six-year-olds will enjoy this book in many ways.

GRADE LEVELS:	**PreK–1**
MATHEMATICS STANDARDS ADDRESSED:	numbers and operations—counting
SCIENCE STANDARDS ADDRESSED:	life science—organisms and environments
SOCIAL STUDIES STANDARDS ADDRESSED:	people, places, and environments—geographic perspectives of the world
LANGUAGE ARTS EXPERIENCES:	vocabulary study, visual representation, listening to poetry
OBJECTIVES:	to count from 1 to 10; to identify numerals 1–10; to write numerals 1–10; to identify organisms found in the ocean; to talk about the Earth's surface; to discover that oceans cover most of our world
KEY CONCEPTS:	quantity, numerals, ecosystem, living things
MATERIALS:	Number Cards 1–10 (Appendix A.4), counters (tiles, beads, beans, etc.), box lids or tin pie pans, sand or salt, globe or world map, paper, watercolors

Procedure

SHARING THE BOOK

1. Discuss the pictured sea creatures on the cover of the book and ask the students to identify them if they can. Tell the students that all of these living things are found somewhere in the ocean. Read the title of the book.

2. Read the story following the rhythm of the verse. Allow the students to observe the illustrations. After the first reading, discuss some of the words that the students may not know.

3. Discuss all of the living things illustrated in the story. Guide the students in observing that the oceans are filled with living things, large and small.

4. Point out land mass and water on the globe or world map. Ask the students if they know whether most of the Earth's surface is land or water. How much of the world is covered by land? How much of the world is covered by ocean?

PROMOTING CONCEPTS

1. Reread the book using the rhythmic style of the verse. Assign a number from 1 to 10 to each child and give them the corresponding number card (from Appendix A.4). As each assigned number is read, have the student stand and hold up the number card. This may require several readings.

2. Using the structure of the book, assign each student a number and a sea creature: manatees are number 1, whales are 2, etc. Sharing the information from the "Fun Facts" section of the book together with the illustrations, have the students draw their assigned animal.

Assessment

1. *Performance:* Using the Number Cards 1–10 and counters, have the students place the appropriate quantity of counters to match the number card and each number you read in another reading of the book. For example, if "three" is read, the student places 3 counters on the number 3 card.

2. *Performance:* Have students create a seascape with their own sea creatures in a watercolor wash or on blue construction paper. Ask them to count and label the number of creatures in their seascape.

3. *Performance:* Cover the bottom of a box lid or tin pie pan with sand or salt. Let the children practice writing numbers in the sand. Gently shake to erase and begin again.

Making Connections

OTHER CONCEPTS

Other ecosystems, counting back from 10 to 1, counting from 11 to 20, writing numbers, matching sets, greater than and less than.

OTHER BOOKS

Annie and the Wild Animals, Jan Brett (1998)

Come to the Ocean's Edge, Laurence Pringle, Michael Chesworth (Illus.) (2003)

How Big Is a Foot, Rolf Myller (1991)

Pigs Will Be Pigs: Fun with Math and Money, Amy Axelrod, Sharon McGinly-Nally (1997)

Sea Shapes, Suse MacDonald (1994)

A Swim Through the Sea, Kristin Joy Pratt (1994)

WEBSITES

http://home.earthlink.net/~cmalumphy/countinggame.html

www.abc.net.au/oceans/alive.htm

www.abc.net.au/science/ocean/default.htm

6.5

LESSON

Over in the Garden

Jennifer Ward • **Kenneth J. Spengler, Illus.**

The book begins "Over in the garden in the early morning sun lived a mother praying mantis and her little mantis one." Then, on to more counting with two little beetles, a mother dragonfly and her little dragons three, and, finally, on to 10 little beetles. This counting book introduces garden creatures through a musical score, rhythmic language, and vibrant illustrations. Each number and corresponding garden creature is introduced on a two-page color spread. For example, with the introduction of the number four, students will see four little snails pictured. And in each illustration, children will discover a hidden number among the colorful insects.

GRADE LEVELS:	**PreK–1**

MATHEMATICS STANDARDS ADDRESSED: numbers and operations—ways of representing numbers

SCIENCE STANDARDS ADDRESSED: life science—organisms and environments

LANGUAGE ARTS EXPERIENCES: visual representation, rhyming, listening to poetry, vocabulary study

OBJECTIVES:	to match the quantities 1–10 with the numbers 1–10; to count from 1 to 10
KEY CONCEPTS:	quantity, numerals, grouping
MATERIALS:	10 counters (buttons, beads, beans, etc.) for each child, Number Cards 1–10 (Appendix A.4), construction paper

Procedure

SHARING THE BOOK

1. Share the cover of the book and discuss the insects pictured. Also discuss the kinds of creatures the students might find in a garden.

2. Discuss numbers and counting. Ask who can count to 10. Discuss the meaning of numbers such as 1, 2, 3, etc. Represent the quantity for each number discussed.

3. Read the first page as a rhyme and have the students view the illustrations. Ask the students if they can find the number the artist has drawn on the page. Continue to read each page and ask the students to look for the hidden number.

PROMOTING CONCEPTS

1. Count up to 10 in a rhythmic fashion. Add clapping, finger snaps, turning around, or any other movement as the count goes up.

2. On construction paper, write the numbers (1–10) large enough for the students to hold easily. Assign numbers so that each has one number. Tell the students that you will reread the story and, as they hear their number, they are to hold it up in the air. This may be done several times and in several ways. For example, have the students stand in numbered order in two or more lines of 10 students.

3. Have the students create that quantity with counters in their workspace as the story is being read. Then, match that quantity with the Number Cards.

Assessment

1. *Performance:* Count up and back between two numbers. Place the Number Cards in a stack facedown. Have the students draw a card and count forward and backward from that number. For example, start with 5 and count to 10 and back to 5.

2. *Performance:* Create dot cards to match the Number Cards. For example, a card with one dot to match the numeral 1, two dots to match the numeral 2, etc. Stack the dot cards facedown in a pile. Have the students choose a dot card, use counters to produce a set with that quantity, and match it to a Number Card.

3. *Performance:* Have students create their own bright and bold garden creatures— spider, insect, snail, etc. Using green bulletin board paper, create a class garden filled with their giant garden creatures. Count the creatures.

Making Connections

OTHER CONCEPTS

Recognizing spatial patterns for numbers 1–10; one and two more, one and two less; counting back in a rhythmic fashion; counting sets.

OTHER BOOKS

Over in the Meadow, Ezra Jack Keats (1999)

Over in the Meadow, Jane Cabrera (2000)

Over in the Meadow: A Counting Rhyme, Olive A. Wadsworth and Anna Vojtech (2002)

Rabbit's Pajama Party, Stuart J. Murphy, Frank Remkiewicz (Illus.) (1999)

Ten Black Dots, Donald Crews (1995)

Ten Old Pails, Nicholas Heller, Yossi Abolafia (Illus.) (1994)

Way Out in the Desert, T. J. Marsh and Jennifer Ward, Kenneth J. Spengler (Illus.) (2001)

WEBSITES

http://insected.arizona.edu/uli.htm

www.educationworld.com/a_special/bugs.shtml

www.learningplanet.com/stu/kids1.asp

www.nbii.gov/

www.uen.org/themepark/insects/index.shtml

A Three Hat Day

Laura Geringer • **Arnold Lobel, Illus.**

His father collected canes. His mother collected umbrellas. R. R. Pottle the Third was a collector of hats. For all collectors, this whimsical story provides humor at a variety of levels; with a little help, first grade students will delight in the silliness of R. R. Pottle and his unusual experiences. "Sometimes when he was feeling sad, he chose two and wore them, one on top of the other." One day, however, he felt so sad that he wore three hats. All readers will delight in how the day—and the story—progresses and how the book ends. Lobel's illustrations portray the characters and the hats with colorful reality. Several of his illustrations show pairs of objects and creatures that make this a good book for counting and organizing by two.

GRADE LEVELS: **PreK–1**

MATHEMATICS STANDARDS ADDRESSED: numbers and operations—ways of representing numbers, recognize "how many" in sets of objects; data analysis and probability—sorting and counting to organize information

LANGUAGE ARTS EXPERIENCES: creating and interpreting graphic elements, character study, visual representation

OBJECTIVES: to match written numerals to sets, to sort by attributes

KEY CONCEPTS: quantities, numerals, groups

MATERIALS: counters (beans, tiles, cubes, etc.), multiple copies of the book, several hats of different types (or have students wear a hat to school on this particular day), Number Cards 1–10 (Appendix A.4)

Procedure

SHARING THE BOOK

1. Because hats play such an important role in this book, begin with a discussion about hats. Ask students to name different kinds of hats. Share those you have available. Ask students how many different hats they (their father, mother, siblings) have. Which ones do they wear most often, and when?

2. While reading the book, allow the students to see the many hats R. R. Pottle wears.

3. Discuss the title of the book. Ask the students if they know why R. R. Pottle wore three hats on some days?

4. Have the students explain why it is unusual to wear three hats at one time, and when they might wear three hats at once.

5. Ask them why R. R. and Isabel became such good friends so quickly? The events of the story on pages 22–26 provide many reasons to discuss friendship.

PROMOTING CONCEPTS

1. This book provides many opportunities to count and to group objects.

2. Using multiple copies of the book, organize the students (groups of 3–5) so that they can easily see the illustrations in the book. Ask the following questions:

    a. How many hats do you see on page 13?   (3)

b. Can you find any groups of two on page 15?   (*birds, snakes, shoes*)

c. Can you find any groups of three on page 15?   (*hats*)

d. How many frogs are there on page 16?   (2)

e. How many cattails do you see on page 16?   (3)

f. On page 24, how many bells are on Isabel's hat?   (3)

g. On pages 28–29, how many birds, snakes, frogs, and people are there?   (*2 of each*)

3. Page 9 provides opportunities for both counting and grouping. Ask students how many hats are shown on the page. Ask how many groups of three hats they see. Ask how many groups of four hats they see.

4. Have students draw a picture of a hat and share their drawings with a partner. Then, as a class, have them organize and label the different types of hats. Bring in hats for students to further identify, label, and categorize. Create a graph of labeled hats by purpose, season, or type.

5. Ask the students what else comes in groups of three. *Triplets, tricycle (3 wheels), triangle (3 sides), trios, clover, 3 months in each season, leaves of poison oak, a 3-scoop ice cream cone, 3 meals each day, 3 primary colors, 3 lights in a traffic signal, 3 utensils for eating—knife, fork, spoon, etc.*

6. Have each student design a "thinking cap" to wear when special problems are tackled in the classroom.

Assessment

1. *Performance:* On a sheet of paper, have students draw groups of two, three, four, and five hats. Have the students count the hats in all four groups and match each to a Number Card, then write the number for each set.

2. *Performance:* Have the students wear a hat for a special Hat Day. Sort or classify the hats by their attributes: color, style (bonnets, caps, visors, etc.), fabrics, size, etc. Repeat several times for different attributes.

3. *Performance:* Create a graph mat about 8 feet long using plastic or bulletin board paper. Make 3–5 columns with about 12 inches for each square. Have students place hats in the columns to show the number of each.

4. *Performance:* What Doesn't Belong? Select four hats such that three of the hats have some attribute in common that is not an attribute of the fourth. Have the students try to decide which hat is different.

Making Connections

OTHER CONCEPTS

Patterns; counting by twos, threes, etc.; picture graphs; symbolic graphs; collecting data; grade level surveys.

OTHER BOOKS

Caps for Sale: A Tale of a Peddler, Some Monkeys and Their Monkey Business, Esphyr Slobodkina (1987)

The 500 Hats of Bartholomew Cubbins, Dr. Seuss (1938)

Hats Off for the Fourth of July! Harriet Ziefert and Gustaf Miller (2002)

How Many Bugs in a Box? David A. Carter (1988)

Let's Count It Out, Jessie Bear, Nancy White Carlstrom (2001)

WEBSITES

http://intranet.cps.k12.il.us/lessons/

www.educationworld.com/a_curr/voice/voice102.shtml

www.marblesoft.com

www.villagehatshop.com/art_history.html

Jump, Frog, Jump!

Robert Kalan • **Byron Barton, Illus.**

In this repetitive tale, a frog tries to catch a fly without getting caught himself. Each time, he gets away from a snake, a fish, and a turtle. How did the frog get away? The children can join in with the text by saying, "Jump, frog, jump!" The suspense builds each time he gets away. Then, a group of children placed a basket over the frog. How does he get away this time? Read the story for a surprise twist. The simple plot with folk-art illustrations will soon have all the young frogs in your classroom hopping!

GRADE LEVELS: PreK–1

MATHEMATICS STANDARDS ADDRESSED: data and probability—gathering and representing data

SCIENCE STANDARDS ADDRESSED: life science—organisms and environment

LANGUAGE ARTS EXPERIENCES: creating and interpreting graphic elements, visual representation

OBJECTIVES: to make a bar graph, to read data from a bar graph

KEY CONCEPTS: collecting data, using data from a graph, title for a graph, bar graph in vertical form

MATERIALS: adding machine tape, masking tape, space for jumping (gym or playground), sidewalk chalk, scissors for the teacher, cubes, note cards, Observation Checklist (Exhibit 6.1)

Procedure

SHARING THE BOOK

1. Show the students the book cover and read them the title. Then, ask them what they think the title means. Ask them whether they have ever tried to catch a frog and, if so, to describe what happened for the class.
2. Read the book aloud.
3. Have the students explain how the frog escaped from the snake, fish, and turtle.
4. Have a student retell how the frog was caught. Have the students explain how the frog got out from under the basket. Ask them if they could catch a frog with a basket.
5. Ask if there are other animals that eat frogs. See if the students know what frogs eat.
6. Have the students jump like a frog (with sufficient space).

PROMOTING CONCEPTS

1. After the students practice jumping like a frog, see who has the greatest frog jump in the class.
2. Place masking tape on the playground. Pair up the students and have them take turns lining up with their toes on the masking tape. One student jumps like a frog, and the partner uses chalk to mark where he or she lands.
3. Then, give each student a strip of adding machine tape that measures the length of his or her best frog jump.
4. Back in the classroom, have the students write their names on their strips of adding machine tape.

5. Using masking tape, line up the adding machine tapes on a wall or the chalkboard, keeping them level at the bottom. This becomes a graph of all the frog jumps.

6. Have the students suggest a title for the graph they created, and describe how the title explains what the graph is about.

7. Ask the students who has the greatest frog jump, who has the smallest frog jump, and if there are frog jumps that are the same.

8. Ask students what else they can tell from looking at the graph.

Assessment

1. *Performance:* Create a three-dimensional bar graph using cubes. On the chalkboard, write the names of three frogs such as Bullfrog, Cricket frog, and Tree frog, or have the students make their own suggestions. Have students place a cube underneath the name of their favorite frog. The stacks of cubes are to represent the frogs' jump length. Ask the students questions 7 and 8 in the preceding "Promoting Concepts" section.

2. *Performance:* Have students draw their own version of how the frog got away.

3. *Observation:* Observing students as they work and play can provide valuable information about their progress and potential problems. Observation data can be recorded in a number of different way; two examples are observation checklists and 3 x 5 note cards.

   • **Checklists.** In this lesson, the focus is on gathering and representing data, and teacher observation should focus on students' ability to engage in these processes. A checklist such as that shown in Exhibit 6.1 can help the teacher gather data about each student to ensure standards and lesson objectives are met. Make individual copies of a checklist for each student, and use the checklists to record the results of your observations. Checklists may be used to record many behaviors for one student; they

EXHIBIT 6.1   Observation checklist.

Student: **Date:**

LEARNING OBJECTIVE:

DATA COLLECTION	USUALLY	SOMETIMES	SELDOM	NEVER	NOTES
Gathers data					
Represents data					
Creates a title for a graph					
Explains what the graph is about					
Makes observations/comparisons about the data					
Creates a bar graph using cubes					
Interprets/reads data from a graph					
Determines greatest, smallest, and the same on a graph					

may also be used to record one behavior for many students, at any time during the day when they demonstrate the criterion being observed.

- **Note cards.** These are a good way to record anecdotal information about almost any aspect of a student's performance. Teachers can easily make their own note cards using 3 x 5 index cards with labels to organize the recording of information (see Exhibit 6.2). One or two observations per card are sufficient, focusing on student behaviors, reasoning and metacognitive processes, or affective considerations. Periodically, select one or two aspects of the lesson to look for. Record them on your lesson plan to remind yourself to look for these items and make notes. The note card approach is convenient for placing comments into individual student folders and to use later during a conference with the student or the parents (Nitko & Brookhart, 2006).

Making Connections **OTHER CONCEPTS**

Pictographs, using data to solve problems, making a table, tally marks, making number comparisons, bar graph in horizontal form, prey, food chain, amphibians.

EXHIBIT 6.2 Sample 3 x 5 note card for recording anecdotal data.

> Student: Joseph
>
> Date: 10/27/09
>
> Objectives: Demonstrates gathering and representing of data
>
> Observations:
>
> Still has difficulty comparing greater than and less than, but is successful in comparing items that are the same. Proficiently measured his "frog leap" and taped it to the wall. Creative suggestion for the title of the graph.

OTHER BOOKS

Brown Bear, Brown Bear, What Do You See? Bill Martin, Eric Carle (Illus.) (1995)

Chicka Chicka, Boom Boom, Bill Martin and John Archambault, Lois Ehlert (Illus.) (1989)

Frog and Toad Are Friends, Arnold Lobel (1979)

A Frog in the Bog, Karma Wilson and Joan Rankin (2003)

Frogs Jump: A Counting Book, Alan Brooks and Steven Kellogg (1996)

It Looked Like Spilt Milk by Charles, Charles G. Shaw (1988)

I Went Walking, Sue Williams and Julie Vivas, Carolyn Graham (Illus.) (1991)

The Napping House, Audrey Wood, Don Wood (Illus.) (1984)

WEBSITES

http://allaboutfrogs.org/
http://cgee.hamline.edu/frogs/
www.exploratorium.edu/frogs/
www.frogs.org/
www.kiddyhouse.com/Themes/frogs/

6.8
LESSON

That Pesky Rat
Lauren Child

This humorous story is about a brown rat's desperate desire to become someone's pet. The Pesky Rat sees other animals living in the "lap of luxury" as they eat chocolates, sit by the fire doing puzzles, and sit on a soft feather cushion. Although these animals report that they have to put up with equally unpleasant things as pets, the Pesky Rat is determined to find an owner. With a handwritten sign posted at the pet parlor, the Pesky Rat does indeed attract a willing owner, Mr. Fortesque. A humorous twist in the story is revealed as Pesky Rat finds out that vision-challenged Mr. Fortesque thinks that he has found the perfect "cat," not a "rat." Nonetheless, Pesky Rat finds himself having all that he ever wanted, even if he has to say, "I am!" whenever Mr. Fortesque asks, "Well, Tiddles, who's a pretty kittycat?"

GRADE LEVELS: **PreK–1**

MATHEMATICS STANDARD ADDRESSED: data analysis and probability—gathering and representing data

LANGUAGE ARTS EXPERIENCES: vocabulary study, character study, shared writing experience

LITERACY CONNECTIONS: questioning, predicting

OBJECTIVES: to make a bar graph, to read data from a bar graph

KEY CONCEPTS: collecting data; using data from a graph; bar graph in horizontal form; most, least

MATERIALS: poster charts, markers, cubes in different colors, crayons, Bar Graph in Horizontal Form (Appendix A.7), Questions for a Dinner Party (Appendix A.8)

Procedure

SHARING THE BOOK

1. Ask the students what animals make good pets, what are some common pets, and what are some unusual pets. Write the students' responses down on the poster chart as a shared writing experience.

2. Have the children explain how people care for their pets.

3. Introduce the book and the main character, a brown rat who wants to be a pet. Ask the students to predict if the rat will make a good pet.

4. Read the book aloud.

5. Then, ask the students the following questions. What are some funny parts of the book? Did the Pesky Rat, now known as Tiddles, accomplish what he set out to do? How did that happen? Finally, ask if they would like to have Tiddles as a pet. Why or why not?

6. Have the students name some characters in the book. Using the Questions for a Dinner Party (see the example that follows in Exhibit 6.3), generate 1–3 questions for the characters as a shared writing experience. Which characters do the students think are intriguing? Ask the students what they would like to know about them, and what would be a good question to ask to find out.

EXHIBIT **6.3** **Questions at a dinner party chart.**

I would like to ask _____Tiddles_____ (character's name) these questions.
1. Are you happy with your name?
_____

2. What is your favorite part of being a pet?
_____

3. _____
_____

I would like to ask _____Mr. Fortesque_____ (character's name) these questions.
1. Don't you think Tiddles is an unusual cat?
_____

2. What is the best part about owning a pet?
_____

3. _____
_____

I would like to ask _____Mrs. Trill_____ (character's name) these questions.
1. How surprised were you when the Pesky Rat was bought by
Mr. Fortesque?
2. Other than the Pesky Rat, what is the strangest animal that
you sold at your pet store?
3. _____
_____

I would like to ask _____ (character's name) these questions.
1. _____
_____

2. _____
_____

3. _____
_____

From Oczkus, 2004.

PROMOTING CONCEPTS

1. Allow students to discuss the kinds of pets they have at home. Generate a list of pets (dog, cat, bird, fish, hamster) and write them on the poster chart, leaving enough room to document students' responses (as shown in Exhibit 6.4). If they do not have a pet, they can still contribute an answer based on what they would like to have as pets.

2. Optional: Before collecting the data for question 1, students can draw pictures of their pets or write about them.

3. Have each student come up to the chart and color in a box for every pet he or she owns. Each animal can have a designated color for greater visual distinction. The completed graph may look like Exhibit 6.4. Students can also create individual graphs using the Bar Graph in Horizontal Form (Appendix A.7) with either color cubes or crayons.

EXHIBIT **6.4**   Title of graph: *Our pets.*

	1	2	3	4	5	6	7	8	9	10
FISH	▓	▓	▓	▓						
CAT	▓	▓	▓	▓	▓					
BIRD	▓	▓	▓	▓	▓					
DOG	▓	▓	▓	▓	▓	▓	▓	▓	▓	
HAMSTER	▓	▓								
GUINEA PIG	▓									

4. Using the pet count bar graphs created by the class, ask questions such as the following:

- Which animal is the most common pet? Least common?
- How can you tell?
- How many students own dogs as pets? Cats? Birds?
- How many more students own dogs than cats?
- What did you learn about pets by creating this graph?
- What else could you count and graph?

Assessment

1. *Performance:* Students respond to the data analysis questions.
2. *Performance:* Students can conduct simple surveys to collect data (e.g., favorite fruit, favorite game, etc.) and create bar graphs.

Making Connections

OTHER CONCEPTS

Probability, pictographs, bar graph in vertical form.

OTHER BOOKS

The Cookie-Store Cat, Cynthia Rylant (1999)

Hondo and Fabian, Peter McCarty (2002)

Lunch, Denise Fleming (1992)

My Cats Nick & Nora, Isabelle Harper and Barry Moser (1995)

Our New Puppy, Isabelle Harper and Barry Moser (1996)

The Stray Dog: From a True Story by Reiko Sassa, Marc Simont (2001)

The Very Kind Rich Lady and Her One Hundred Dogs, Chin-lun Lee (2003)

Weird Pet Poems, Dilys Evans, Jacqueline Rogers (Illus.) (1997)

WEBSITES

www.avma.org/careforanimals/kidscorner/default.asp

www.fund.org/

www.nwf.org/kids/

www.planet-pets.com/kidscorner.htm

www.worldalmanacforkids.com/

In the Small, Small Pond

Denise Fleming

The beautiful illustrations and the musical language make this an excellent book to read aloud to young children. Through the colorful and vivid pictures and the rhyming prose, the reader learns about the remarkable life in a small pond. Frogs, tadpoles, ducks, turtles, minnows, muskrats, and bugs are among the many living things in this pond. Look for the green frog that hides on every page!

GRADE LEVELS:	**PreK–1**
SCIENCE STANDARD ADDRESSED:	life science—organisms and environments
LANGUAGE ARTS EXPERIENCES:	dramatic expression, shared writing experience, retelling
ARTS CONNECTION:	expressive movement to music
OBJECTIVE:	to identify the many types of living things found in a small pond
KEY CONCEPTS:	ecosystems, living things, animals, plants
MATERIALS:	music CD or tape for dramatization of the movements, index cards, chart paper or white board

Procedure

SHARING THE BOOK

1. Activate the students' prior knowledge with a discussion about ponds. Identify the location of a pond near the school or someplace in the community, and have the students name some things that might be found in the pond.

2. Read the book. Then, during a second reading, have the children act out the movements of the animals as you read. Accompanying music might add to the children's dramatic expression. To highlight the beautiful rhythmic language of the story, read the book so that the rhyme of the words ("Hover, shiver, wings quiver," "Splish, splash, paws flash") is heard.

PROMOTING CONCEPTS

1. Multiple readings of the book will elicit student comments about what they notice on each page. As students identify animals, engage them in a discussion about that animal. As these discussions take place, share interesting and important facts about the animals and ask the following questions: Why is the pond a good place to find animals? What other things might you see in the pond? How does the pond change in the fall or in the winter?

2. Ask the students to retell the story of *In the Small, Small Pond* by recalling the animals they remember from the story. The movements and sounds of the animals may be reproduced to add interest and enhance comprehension.

3. Having the students dictate their knowledge about the animals in the pond can provide a shared writing experience. Record the information on chart paper or a white board. The text later becomes a shared reading or an independent reading tool for the students.

Assessment

1. *Performance:* Using index cards, prepare student response cards on which you have written "YES" on one set and "NO" on another set. Be sure to have a set for each student. Then, ask them to respond to your questions by holding up the appropriate card. This may also be done as a "thumbs up" (for yes) and a "thumbs down" (for no) activity. Questions may vary, but some of the following are appropriate:

   a. Was there a frog in the small, small pond?   YES
   b. Was there a duck in the small, small pond?   YES
   c. Was there a tadpole in the small, small pond?   YES
   d. Was there a bicycle in the small, small pond?   NO
   e. Was there a TV set in the small, small pond?   NO
   f. Was there a horse in the small, small pond?   NO

2. *Performance:* Have students create a collage or picture of a pond with its plants and animals.

Making Connections

OTHER CONCEPTS

Seasons of the year, life cycles of living things, other ecosystems.

OTHER BOOKS

All Eyes on the Pond, Michael Rosen (1995)

Jump, Frog, Jump! Robert Kalan (1989)

Pond Animals, Francine Galko (2002)

Sea Shapes, Suse MacDonald (1998)

What's in the Pond? Anne Hunter (1999)

WEBSITES

http://ccb_themes.tripod.com/themes_pondlife.html

http://teacher.scholastic.com/lessonrepro/k_2theme/tguidemay01.htm

www.alleypond.com/

www.lessonplanspage.com

6.10 Growing Vegetable Soup

LESSON

Lois Ehlert

Ehlert shows us how to grow vegetables for soup and also provides the recipe for those who need one. In a collage of bold illustrations, we see the planting, watering, growing and harvesting. Then, we see how to make vegetable soup. Finally, we see soup in a bowl "It was the best soup ever . . ."

GRADE LEVELS: **PreK–1**

SCIENCE STANDARDS ADDRESSED: life sciences—characteristics of organisms; culture

SOCIAL STUDIES STANDARDS ADDRESSED: production, distribution, and consumption

LANGUAGE ARTS EXPERIENCES: shared and independent writing, visual representation

LITERACY CONNECTION: summarizing/synthesizing

OBJECTIVES: to discover that plants need soil, water, and sunlight in order to live; to describe how to make vegetable soup; to describe foods that are eaten by one's family

KEY CONCEPTS: nourishments essential for life, life cycle, livings things must be able to get what they need to live from their environment

MATERIALS: ingredients and utensils necessary to make vegetable soup, poster chart for a Venn diagram

Procedure

SHARING THE BOOK

1. Begin with questions concerning vegetable soup, such as some of the following: Have you ever eaten vegetable soup? What is vegetable soup? What do you find in vegetable soup? Where do the vegetables in the soup come from? Foster a brief discussion after each question.

2. Discuss the book title and read the first page. Then, ask the students what they think Dad means when he says that "we are going to grow vegetable soup."

3. Read the story and share the illustrations so that everyone can see them.

4. Discuss the students' culture and what kind of vegetables they eat at their house.

5. Discuss the key concepts like vegetables, planting, growing, watering, and weeding.

6. If time permits, follow the directions on the back page of the book and make vegetable soup.

PROMOTING CONCEPTS

1. Promote the conceptual development of living things. Discuss the concept of growth and how seeds need the proper soil (for nourishment) and water to grow and to become edible vegetables.

2. Ask the children what they themselves need to grow. Promote a discussion about the necessities of life.

3. Using a Venn diagram (see Exhibit 6.5) on a large poster chart, list the things that plants and people need to grow. Write down students' responses.

EXHIBIT | **6.5** | Sample Venn diagram.

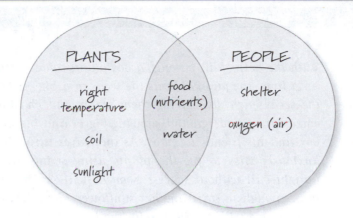

4. Brainstorm a list of ingredients for vegetable soup. Measure ingredients for the soup using cups and spoons.

5. Have students observe how the vegetables change form as they are cooking (or mixing).

Assessment

1. *Performance:* Have students identify several living things, plants or animals. Then identify at least two elements that the plant or animal needs to live.

2. *Performance:* Illustrate and sequence the steps in preparing vegetable soup.

3. *Writing:* Make a class book of "What would you grow in your garden?"

4. *Shared writing:* Compose a class recipe for vegetable soup.

Making Connections

OTHER CONCEPTS

Counting, grouping, and sequencing; nutrition and the value of the vegetables found in soup; setting the table; shopping for food; tools for food preparation; planning a family picnic; food pyramid; cooking with kids; jobs related to cooking and food preparation.

OTHER BOOKS

Chicken Soup with Rice: A Book of Months, Maurice Sendak (1991)

Dog Food, Saxton Freymann and Joost Elffers (2002)

Eating the Alphabet, Lois Ehlert (1996)

Feast for Ten, Cathryn Falwell (1995)

Janice VanCleave's Food and Nutrition for Every Kid: Easy Activities That Make Learning Science Fun, Janice Van-Cleave (1999)

The Little Nut Tree, Sally Gardner (1993)

Mouse Soup, Arnold Lobel (1983)

Seaweed Soup: Level 1, Matching Sets, Stuart J. Murphy and Frank Remkiewicz (2001)

Stone Soup, Marcia Brown (1997)

Waiting for Wings, Lois Ehlert (2001)

WEBSITES

http://seeds.thompson-morgan.com/us/en

www.aodr.com/Home/Cooking/For_Children

www.urbanext.illinois.edu/kids/index.html

6.11 Sunflower House

Eve Bunting • **Kathryn Hewitt, Illus.**

With the help of his parents, a boy plants some sunflower seeds in the soil. Rather than "in a line," the family plants the seeds in a big circle in the yard. The boy takes care of the seeds each day, giving them water and chasing the birds away. The sunflowers emerge from underground, growing bigger and bigger, and create a special room for the boy and his friends to enjoy. As the leaves turn brown and the plants droop, the boy anxiously tries to fix the plants using string, sticks, and even glue to keep them upright—all without success. Soon he realizes that the sunflowers produce seeds, more than enough to start another sunflower house next season. The seeds are picked and even shared with the birds with the hope that the cycle will continue.

GRADE LEVELS: **PreK–1**

SCIENCE STANDARD ADDRESSED: life science—the characteristics of organisms, life cycles of organisms

LANGUAGE ARTS EXPERIENCES: graphic organizers, shared writing experiences

LITERACY CONNECTION: summarizing/synthesizing

ARTS CONNECTION: drawing

OBJECTIVES: to name the basic needs of plants, to describe the life cycle of plants

KEY CONCEPTS: living things, life cycle, plants, seeds, seedlings, stems, leaves, sequencing

MATERIALS: poster chart, markers, Circular Flowchart (Appendix A.9), clip art of plants provided at the end of the lesson (or other pictures drawn or found by students)

Procedure

SHARING THE BOOK

1. Begin with a set of questions to activate the students' prior knowledge: What are plants? What plants do you know? What are some different kinds of plants (e.g., grasses, flowers, shrubs, trees)? What grows in your backyard? Have you seen sunflowers before? Why do you think they are called sunflowers? Ask students to listen for what sunflowers need to grow as the story is read.

2. Read the book aloud. Pause and identify things that plants need to grow as those examples are presented (e.g., soil, water, protection from predators). As students respond, complete a Concept Map (as shown in Exhibit 6.6) representing things that plants need to grow.

3. Ask comprehension questions as the book is read: How do the characters enjoy the sunflower house? Why is the boy trying to fix the sunflower plants? How does he try to fix the sunflower plants? What makes him feel better?

PROMOTING CONCEPTS

1. Ask the students what the boy provided for the sunflowers to grow. (Add light and air to the list of things plants require for survival.) Then, ask them what do people need to grow (air, water, and food). And what are some things that all living things need?

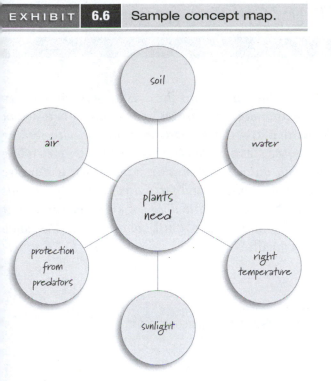

2. Have students use the Circular Flowchart (Appendix A.9) to identify the cycle of the sunflower plants (seed to seedling to plant to seed). On a separate copy of the flowchart or on the same chart, students can write a word or phrase that describes the cycle. This can be a done as a shared writing activity as children dictate the words.

Assessment

1. *Performance:* Make an individual sunflower book or a cycle graphic organizer using plant clip art (see Exhibit 6.7).

2. *Performance:* Fold a piece of drawing paper into four boxes. Draw the life cycle of a flower.

Making Connections

OTHER CONCEPTS

Nonliving things, life cycles of animals, characteristics of animals.

OTHER BOOKS

From Seed to Plant, Gail Gibbons (1993)

Growing Vegetable Soup, Lois Ehlert (1987)

Jack's Garden, Henry Cole (1997)

One Bean, Anne Rockwell, Megan Halsey (Illus.) (1999)

Planting a Rainbow, Lois Ehlert (1992)

Tiny Seed, Eric Carle (1970)

WEBSITES

http://jmgkids.us

www.ars.usda.gov/IS/KIDS/plants/plantsintro.htm

www.kidsgardening.com/primer/primer1049.asp

www.urbanext.illinois.edu/kids

I Will Never NOT EVER Eat a Tomato

Lauren Child

Charlie's little sister Lola is a fussy eater. She claims that she does not eat "peas or carrots or potatoes or mushrooms or spaghetti or eggs or sausages." The items on her "do not eat" list continue on and on. Lola particularly hates tomatoes. Charged with feeding Lola, Charlie tricks her into trying the food items on her "do not eat" list by pretending they are something else and giving them unique and strange names such as "orange twiglets from Jupiter" (for just a carrot). Lola, amused and fascinated, tries a bite of this and a bite of that, liking most of what she tries. Charlie does not know, however, that Lola has been on to him and his clever trick all along, until Lola points to the tomatoes and calls them "moonsquirters, my favorite."

GRADE LEVELS: **PreK–1**

SCIENCE STANDARD ADDRESSED: science in personal and social perspectives—personal health

LANGUAGE ARTS EXPERIENCE: vocabulary study

LITERACY CONNECTIONS: making connections, predicting

OBJECTIVES: to understand that nutrition is essential to health

KEY CONCEPTS: food groups, grains, vegetables, fruits, meats, milk, fat & sweets; sorting and classifying

MATERIALS: pictures of food items brought in by the students, poster charts, glue, markers, words—GRAINS, VEGETABLES, FRUITS, MEATS, MILK, FAT & SWEETS—written on cards, paper plates, Connections Chart (Appendix A.10)

Procedure   SHARING THE BOOK

1. Facilitate a prereading discussion about food with the students by asking them: What are some of your favorite foods? What don't you like to eat? Who prepares meals at home? What kinds of dishes are prepared for breakfast? Lunch? Dinner? Have students cut out pictures of their favorite foods from magazines and bring them to class.

2. Introduce Lola who does not like to eat many, many things. Read the title and have the students predict what Lola will not eat.

3. Read the book.

4. Engage the children in a post-reading discussion by asking such questions as the following: How did Charlie trick Lola to eat? How did Lola trick Charlie? What about all the things that Lola claimed not to eat? Did she really not like them? What makes you think so?

5. Using the Connections Chart, as shown in Exhibit 6.8 and Appendix A.10, document students' connections to self, text, and world by asking: What personal experiences have you had to relate to Lora? To Charlie? What other books, movies, and TV shows have you seen where characters are fussy eaters? What do you know about eating healthy foods? On a large poster chart, write the students' responses in appropriate columns.

EXHIBIT | 6.8 | Use the Connections Chart to document student responses.

TEXT-TO-SELF	TEXT-TO-TEXT	TEXT-TO-WORLD
I have a sister who is a picky eater.	Cookie Monster loves to eat cookies.	Healthy foods are needed for strong bodies.

From Keene and Zimmermann (1997).

PROMOTING CONCEPTS

1. The USDA site http://teamnutrition.usda.gov/kids=pyramid.html, has a printable poster of the food guide pyramid for children ages 2 to 6 and a worksheet that parents can use to log children's intake for a week.

2. Copy the food guide pyramid on a large poster chart with the food groups labeled, or print out on large paper.

3. Point to each food group and discuss the food group we need the most each day, the food group we need the least, and some examples for each group.

4. Collect the students' food pictures. Sort the pictures using the food group words. Discuss the appropriateness of the examples for each food group.

5. Glue the pictures on the food pyramid on the poster chart.

Assessment

1. *Performance:* Record students' examples of appropriate foods.

2. *Performance:* Using the pictures on the pyramid, form small groups to create a menu for either breakfast, lunch, or dinner. Use paper plates to collect and glue food items from the menu.

Making Connections

OTHER CONCEPTS

Servings, healthy snacks, setting the table, planning a family picnic, shopping for food.

OTHER BOOKS

A Bad Case of Stripes, David Shannon (1998)

Dumpling Soup, Jama Kim Rattigan, Lillian Hsu-Flanders (Illus.) (1993)

The Edible Pyramid: Good Eating Every Day, Loreen Leedy (1994)

Mice and Beans, Pam Munoz Ryan, Joe Cepeda (Illus.) (2001)

The Seven Silly Eaters, Mary Ann Hoberman, Marla Frazee (Illus.) (1997)

Too Many Tamales, Gary Soto, Ed Martinez (Illus.) (1993)

WEBSITES

http://nutritionforkids.com/

http://vm.cfsan.fda.gov/~dms/educate.html

www.ext.nodak.edu/food/kidsnutrition/kids-2.htm

www.healthyfridge.org/kidsrec.html

www.kidfood.org/

Officer Buckle and Gloria

Peggy Rathmann

Officer Buckle takes delight in giving safety speeches to the children of Napville. His obsession with safety helps generate endless tips for safety, from perfectly sensible to the utterly bizarre. It is not until Gloria, Napville's new police dog, begins to accompany Officer Buckle that people realize how interesting and important safety tips really are. Shadowing Officer Buckle on stage, Gloria acts out the safety tips, to everyone's amusement. Not knowing it is Gloria who is entertaining the audience, Officer Buckle beams in the spotlight. When Officer Buckle finds out the truth from seeing himself and Gloria on the 10 o'clock news, he realizes that it is Gloria people truly adore. Officer Buckle's refusal to give anymore safety speeches results in the biggest disaster of Napville's history. It becomes a moment for everyone, including Officer Buckle and Gloria, to learn that it is best to "always stick with your buddy, Safe Tip #101." Look for the brilliant and not-so-brilliant safety tips in the ending pages.

GRADE LEVELS:	**PreK–1**
SCIENCE STANDARDS ADDRESSED:	science in personal and social perspectives—types of resources
SOCIAL STUDIES STANDARDS ADDRESSED:	civic ideals and practices—promoting civic competence
LANGUAGE ARTS EXPERIENCES:	shared/individual writing, storytelling, visual representation
LITERACY CONNECTION:	summarizing/synthesizing, predicting/inferring
OBJECTIVES:	to discuss safety tips; to illustrate a safety tip
KEY CONCEPTS:	safety—a nonmaterial resource that humans need; recognizing police officers as important members of our community
MATERIALS:	poster chart, marker, drawing paper, star-shaped figure, Prediction Chart (Appendix A.11), sequence flow chart

Procedure

SHARING THE BOOK

1. Show the book cover to the students and ask them questions to elicit story predictions: Who do you think Officer Buckle is? Who do you think Gloria is? What can you tell about Gloria? How can you tell? Point to the patch on Officer Buckle's sleeve. What do you think that means?

2. As a shared writing experience or an independent writing activity, have the students predict what the story will be about using the Prediction Chart (Appendix A.11).

3. Read the book and the safety tips illustrated in the ending pages.

4. Have the students complete the "The story really was about . . ." column of the Prediction Chart.

5. Using a sequence flowchart, as shown in Exhibit 6.9, have the students retell the story in order. Write their responses on the large flowchart.

TITLE *Officer Buckle and Gloria*

Officer Buckle makes safety speeches to Napville School, but no one is paying attention to them.

Officer Buckle takes Gloria, the police dog, to the school to make the speech.

Without letting Officer Buckle know, Gloria acts out Officer Buckle's safety tips. The audience loves it.

Officer Buckle realizes that Gloria is the reason for their success. He refuses to make any more speeches.

Gloria performs by herself. No one pays attention.

PROMOTING CONCEPTS

1. Ask the students which safety tips they like, which are funny, and which seem really important.

2. As a shared writing activity, have students generate safety tips for the classroom, the school, and the home. Write them down on a poster chart. The safety tips can also be sorted as they are shared (for the classroom, for the school, for the home).

3. Each student can pick a favorite safety tip, write it on a star-shaped figure, and illustrate it as shown in Exhibit 6.10.

EXHIBIT 6.10 Sample safety tip star.

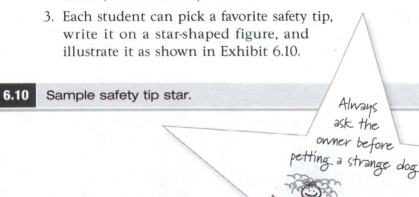

Always ask the owner before petting a strange dog

Assessment

1. *Performance:* Students can choose more safety tips, then write and illustrate them to make a safety book.

2. *Performance:* Have students create a map of the fire escape route from their classroom to the nearest exit of the school.

Making Connections

OTHER CONCEPTS

Bicycle helmets; water, fire, poison, dog, playground safety; wrist guards and knee pads for Rollerblades and skateboards; everyday illnesses; insect bites; smoke detectors; consumer product safety.

OTHER BOOKS

The Berenstain Bears Learn About Strangers, Stan Berenstain (1985)

The Buzy Body Book: A Kid's Guide to Fitness, Lizzy Rockwell (2004)

Mike Hart Was Here, Barbara Park (1995)

WEBSITES

http://kidshealth.org/kid/

www.cpsc.gov/kids/kidsafety/

www.dos.state.ny.us/kidsroom/firesafe/firesafe.html

www.nhtsa.dot.gov/

www.safekids.org/

www.smokeybear.com/

www.sparky.org

www.ufsa.dha.gov/kids/flash.shtm

6.14

LESSON

365 Penguins

Jean-Luc Fromental • **J. Joliet, Illus.**

This oversized picture book integrates math concepts and environmental concerns into a witty and whimsical tale. On New Year's Day a box containing one penguin arrives with a note attached that says, "I'm number 1. Feed me when I'm hungry." A family of four continues to be puzzled as, one by one, day by day, penguins continue to arrive and fill the house for one full year. As they arrive, readers must recall the number of days in each month. At first the penguins are cute, but with every passing day the family is concerned about the food budget and the storage issue and cleaning up after all these penguins. And who is sending these penguins and why? The text provides endless opportunities to develop word problems and units on penguins and global warming. The illustrations are in black, blue, and orange, which gives the book a retro feel.

GRADE LEVELS:	**PreK–1**
MATHEMATICS STANDARDS ADDRESSED:	measurement—measures of time in a real context
SOCIAL STUDIES STANDARDS ADDRESSED:	people, places, and environment—conservation
LANGUAGE ARTS EXPERIENCE:	shared writing
LITERACY CONNECTION:	predicting
OBJECTIVES:	to read a calendar; to identify patterns on a calendar; to introduce global warming and endangered species
KEY CONCEPTS:	names of the days of the week, how many days are in a month, patterns in the numbers in a calendar, ecology, global warming, endangered species
MATERIALS:	a large calendar for the current month, a blank calendar for the month (Appendix A.12), a calendar for the year (available at www.timeanddate.com/calendar), a map or globe of the world, chart paper, the Clocks vs. Calendars Exploration sheet (Appendix A.13)

Procedure

SHARING THE BOOK

1. Before reading the book, ask students if they have ever seen a penguin at the zoo or if anyone has seen the movies *Happy Feet* or *March of the Penguins?*
   a. Then ask the students to share what they know about penguins. (*flightless birds with black and white feathers who live together in colonies, they walk with a funny waddle, they look like they are wearing a tuxedo*)
   b. Ask students where do penguins live? (*Antarctica*) Locate Antarctica on a map or globe. Have the students describe where Antarctica is located. (*South Pole*) Where do we live in relationship to the South Pole?
2. Have the students predict what *365 Penguins* might be about. Ask if they know anything else that has 365 items in it. During the read-aloud, encourage the students to look closely at the illustrations for a penguin that looks different from the others.

3. After reading the book, ask the students to describe how many penguins were in the story. Ask students to imagine and describe the problems they would have if 365 penguins lived in their house. How did this family go about solving some of these problems? Describe some of the ways the father organized the penguins. Ask students how they would organize the penguins.

4. Ask: "Who was sending the penguins? Why? What is an ecologist?" (*a scientist who studies the relationships between living organisms and their environment*)

5. Then ask the students if they noticed a penguin that was different from all the others?

    a. How was he different? (*His feet are blue.*)

    b. What was the penguin's name? (*Chilly*)

6. At the end of the story, what happened to all the penguins, including Chilly? What was the next package that arrived?

PROMOTING CONCEPTS

1. How many penguins arrived in all? (365) How many penguins did Uncle Victor send each day? (*One a day during the year or 182 couples for 364 penguins plus Chilly to make 365 penguins*) If one penguin arrived for each day in the year, how many days are there in a year?

2. Review the names of the days of the week. Songs, poems, and rhymes to reinforce the days of the week can be found at www.canteach.ca/elementary/songspoems4.html

3. Display last month's calendar and ask the students how many days are in a week? Days in the month? Saturdays in the month? The date of the second Monday? The fourth Wednesday? If we needed to know how many Tuesdays were in the month, how could we find out?

4. Next, focus students' attention on the Calendar Exploration page (Appendix A.12). Ask: Why do the rows in a calendar have seven boxes? What is the last day of the week? What day comes next? How can there be another day after the last day of the week? (*The days of the week are in a repeating pattern.*)

5. Have students complete a calendar for the current month onto the blank calendar. Then ask:

    a. What is the first day of the month?

    b. What is today's date?

    c. What date is the third Monday?

    d. How many school days are in this month?

    e. How many days are in the month?

    f. What are the numbers for all the Thursdays?

    g. What are the numbers for all the Tuesdays?

6. Review even and odd numbers. Have the students color the squares with odd numbers green and the squares with even numbers orange. Are there more odd or even days? Describe any other patterns you see.

7. Then, provide a calendar of the current year (available at www.timeanddate .com/calendar). Have each student find the month and day of their birthday and circle it. Locate other significant dates such as President's Day, Mother's Day, Thanksgiving, and so on. How does each month begin? After that, reread *365 Penguins* and have students follow along with their calendar of the current

year. Locate the following dates and ask how many penguins had arrived by that date: January 1: 1 penguin; January 31: 31 penguins; February 28: 31 + 28 penguins; April 10 (the 100th day of the year): 100 penguins; May 24: 144 penguins (also 12 boxes of 12); August 4: 216 penguins (also a cube, 9 x 9 x 9); December 31: 365 penguins. Challenge: Ask "How many penguins had arrived by your birthday?"

8. When summer arrived there was a new complication for the family and the penguins. Ask: What was the new complication? Why? What type of environment do penguins live in?

9. Ask: Why did Uncle Victor send his family the penguins? (*He was trying to keep or protect or conserve the penguins*) What is an endangered species? (*Plant and animal species that are in danger of extinction—dying out*) What is happening to the ice caps in the South Pole? (*They are melting*) What is global warming? (*An increase in the world's temperature*)

Assessment

1. *Performance:* Have students complete the calendar for the current month. Call out various dates and ask for volunteers to give the day of the week.

2. *Exploration:* Use the Exploration sheet on clocks and calendars (Appendix A.13) to discover how a clock and a calendar are used for measurement. Have students draw/write how a clock and a calendar are alike and how they are different. Hint: What do they measure? Ask: Can you think of anything else that measures time? *Watch (digital and analog), cuckoo clock, sundial, hour glass, etc.*

3. *Performance:* Create 12 cooperative groups. Provide each group with a copy of the blank calendar for the month (Appendix A.12). Assign each group a month of the year. Guide the students in completing their month. Then place the students' calendars in order on a bulletin board or on chart paper. Encourage students to talk about the patterns they observe from month to month.

4. *Shared Writing:* Have the class work together to create their own version of the story using polar bears instead of penguins, with each student contributing a sentence aloud as you record them on chart paper.

Making Connections

OTHER CONCEPTS

Counting on and counting back; elapsed time; time on both standard and digital clocks; seasons; Earth Day; other endangered species; ecosystem; adaptation; extinct

OTHER BOOKS	WEBSITES
And Tango Makes Three, Peter Parnell and Justin Richardson (2005)	http://kids.nationalgeographic.com/Animals/CreatureFeature/Emperor-penguin
These Birds Can't Fly, Allan Fowler (1999)	http://science.howstuffworks.com/question473.htm
The Emperor's Egg: Read and Wonder, Martin Jenkins, Jane Chapman (Illus.) (2002)	www.fws.gov/endangered/
Penguin (Watch Me Grow), DK Publishing (2004)	www.nrdc.org/globalwarming/qthinice.asp
Penguin Chick (Let's Read About Science), Betty Tatham, Helen K. Davie (Illus.) (2001)	www.seaworld.org/infobooks/Penguins/home.html
	www.siec.k12.in.us/west/proj/penguins/main.html
	www.worldwildlife.org/species/index.html

REFERENCES

Bredekamp, S., & Copple, C. (Eds.). (1996). *Developmentally appropriate practices in early childhood programs serving children from birth through age 8* (Rev. ed.). Washington, DC: National Association for the Education of Young Children.

Bruner, J. (1996). *The culture of education.* Cambridge, MA: Harvard University Press.

Fountas, I. C., & Pinnell, G. S. (2001). *Guiding readers and writers, grades 3–6. Teaching Comprehension, Genre, and Content Literacy.* Portsmouth, NH: Heinemann.

Harris, K. R., & Graham, S. (1994). Constructivism: Principles, paradigms, and integration. *The Journal of Special Education. 28,* 233–247.

Helm, J. H., Beneke, S., & Steinheimer, K. (1998). *Windows on learning: Documenting young children's work.* New York: Teachers College Press.

Keene, E. O., & Zimmermann, S. (1997). *Mosaic of thought: Teaching comprehension in a reader's workshop.* Portsmouth, NH: Heinemann.

National Council of Teachers of Mathematics. (2000). *Principles and standards for school mathematics.* Reston, VA: Author.

National Research Council. (1996). *National science education standards.* Washington, DC: National Academy Press.

Nitko, A. J., & Brookhart, S. M. (2006). *Educational assessment of students* (5th ed.). Upper Saddle River, NJ: Prentice Hall.

Oczkus, L. (2004). *Super 6 comprehension strategies: 35 lessons and more for reading success.* Norwood, MA: Christopher-Gordon.

Piaget, J. (1963). *The origins of intelligence in children.* New York: Norton.

Vygotsky, L. S. (1978). *Mind in society.* Cambridge, MA: Harvard University Press.

CHILDREN'S LITERATURE

Bang, M. (1983). *Ten, nine, eight.* New York: Mulberry Books.

Bunting, E. (1996). *Sunflower house* (K. Hewitt, Illus.). New York: Scholastic.

Child, L. (2000). *I will never NOT EVER eat a tomato.* Cambridge, MA: Candlewick Press.

Child, L. (2002). *That pesky rat.* Cambridge, MA: Candlewick Press.

Ehlert, L. (1987). *Growing vegetable soup.* New York: Voyager Books.

Ehlert, L. (1990). *Fish eyes: A book you can count on.* New York: Harcourt Brace.

Fleming, D. (1993). *In the small, small pond.* New York: Holt.

Fox, M. (1993). *Time for bed* (J. Dyer, Illus.). New York: Harcourt Brace.

Fromental, J. (2006). *365 Penguins* (J. Joliet, Illus.). New York: Abrams.

Geringer, L. (1985). *A three hat day* (A. Lobel, Illus.). New York: Harper & Row.

Kalan, R. (1981). *Jump, frog, jump!* (B. Barton, Illus.). New York: Mulberry Books.

Keats, E. J. (1968). *A letter to Amy.* New York: Harper & Row.

Martin Jr., B. (1995). *Brown bear, brown bear, what do you see?* (E. Carle, Illus.). New York: Holt, Rinehart & Winston.

Martin Jr., B., & Archambault, J. (1989). *Chicka chicka, boom boom* (L. Ehlert, Illus.). New York: Simon & Schuster.

Rathmann, P. (1995). *Officer Buckle and Gloria.* New York: Putnam.

Shannon, D. (1999). *David goes to school.* New York: Blue Sky Press.

Tafuri, N. (2000). *Will you be my friend?* New York: Scholastic.

Ward, J. (2002). *Over in the garden* (K. J. Spengler, Illus.). Flagstaff, AZ: Rising Moon.

Ward, J., & Marsh, T. J. (2000). *Somewhere in the Ocean* (K. J. Spengler, Illus.) Flagstaff, Az: Rising Moon.

7

Exploring Mathematics,
Science, and
Social Studies

Grades 2-3

his chapter focuses on two primary mathematics standards: *Numbers and Operations* and *Geometry* (NCTM, 2000). Numbers and operations continue to be our emphasis in Grades 2–3. Building from the concepts presented in the lessons for Grades PreK–1—representation of numbers in counting concepts, understanding meanings of whole number operations— this chapter introduces such concepts as place-value structure of the base-10 number system and properties of operations.

For example, *Counting on Frank* (Clement, 1991), a whimsical counting tale, develops numbers and operations by emphasizing computational fluency and estimation. In this lesson, the students estimate quantities less than 100 and round to the nearest 10 using different materials.

The promotion of geometry concepts at this level includes exploring patterns and symmetry. Students predict, experiment, and confirm their predictions based on their exploration. We used their attraction to *exploring* at this age to design lessons that are active and hands on (Wood, 1997). For example, in *Snowflake Bentley* (Martin, 1998), students use pictures of beautiful ice crystals with all of their geometric splendors to explore both the symmetry and the properties of two-dimensional shapes, especially the formation of hexagonal shapes. Geometry explorations are continued in *Round Trip* by Ann Jonas (1983) in which the students analyze the attributes of the two-dimensional shapes in our natural environments such as circles, squares, and rectangles. Investigating patterns and developing a spatial sense as part of geometry continue with *The Keeping Quilt* (Polacco, 1998) as students explore two-dimensional shapes to create their own quilt patches.

Students' sense of exploration is again used in the science lessons. Using two strands in the science standards (NRC, 1996)—*Science as Inquiry* and *Earth and Space Science*—the science lessons are designed to highlight the scientific inquiry process in order to question, observe, reflect, and learn about different environments and the organisms within those environments. Rather than simply reading about the concepts as a means of learning, students are predicting and speculating, observing and describing, discussing and sharing in order to develop concepts in science.

The daily, and even hourly, changes in the environment are the focus of the lessons that address concepts in earth and space science. Perhaps these are changes that students took little notice of prior to the lessons, such as the location of the sun throughout the day. Perhaps the changes were noticed before, but not quite in the sense that requires careful observations and the recording of data. Surely, students have observed clouds in the sky many times. But as they try to predict whether there is a correlation between the clouds today and the weather tomorrow, students are challenged to examine data and confirm or adjust their predictions. Either way, the science lessons prompt students to use a different framework, a more scientific framework, to understand their world.

A lesson without at least some degree of inquiry is unimaginable in a constructivist classroom. Concepts ought to be presented using students' natural wonderment and curiosities about the world. Most of our lessons have modes of inquiry, no matter the specific standard connection. However, the lessons that are part of the science-as-inquiry strand focus on making the inquiry process *explicit* to the students. Although all of the lessons present science concepts, the *process* is the primary goal. The modes of inquiry should be and are processes that students can apply in other exploration situations.

The lessons with social studies connections also appeal to students' sense of exploration as they are invited to explore the environments. For example, in Lesson 7.2 on *The Water Hole* (Base, 2001), students are invited not only to explore the organism and environment of a habitat from a scientist's perspective but also to consider the differences between their habitat and the one in the book from a social scientist's perspective.

Across all lessons, students share and debate ideas, observe to speculate and hypothesize solutions, and write to collect and record data. The interrelated processes of reading, writing, speaking, listening, and viewing are used to foster students' exploration of various experiences. For example, in *Hurricane* (Wiesner, 1990), students write to record both their prior knowledge and new concepts in a K-W-L chart, as well as write about how they can protect themselves in a hurricane. Students gather and record data as they track the position of the sun and the lengths of shadows using *Sun Up, Sun Down* (Gibbons, 1983). In *The Keeping Quilt* (Polacco, 1998), they discuss family traditions and beliefs as they make connections with their personal history.

As we regularly draw our students' attention to thoughtful connections between literature and the content areas, they grow to understand the richness of these interactions. The advantage of these curricular links is that they provide students with a meaningful context within which to enhance their understanding of these relationships.

In order to represent a balance in our collection of books, we include a variety of genres, styles, and reading levels. From expository to narratives, from content explicit to content invisible, the books range greatly. And again, we kept in mind our selection criteria for quality literature as we chose the books.

7.1

12 Ways to Get to 11

LESSON   **Eve Merriam** • **Bernie Karlin, Illus.**

Where's 11? Is it missing? 12 Ways to Get to 11 is a whimsical romp about 12 creative ways to get to 11. Each double-page spread consists of brightly colored cutouts of objects such as "Three sets of triplets in baby carriages and a pair of twins in the stroller" and "In the mailbox: seven letters, two packages, a mail-order catalog, and a picture post-card" that are combinations that total 11. The readers must supply the numbers for the addition sentence and add them up for a total. The sum is always 11. Some combinations are more challenging than others for an amusing counting adventure.

GRADE LEVELS:	**2–3**
MATHEMATICS STANDARD ADDRESSED:	numbers and operations—meaning of operations
LANGUAGE ARTS EXPERIENCE:	narrative writing
ARTS CONNECTION:	drawing
OBJECTIVES:	to recognize that the order of the addends does not change the sum (associative property), to use a variety of addends to total 11, to express numbers using a variety of equations
KEY CONCEPTS:	number sense, numeration, whole number operations
MATERIALS:	counters, unifix or multilink cubes, paper (two sheets per student), crayons

Procedure

SHARING THE BOOK

1. After reading the book, go back and have the students express aloud the number sentence for the objects on each two-page spread. Then, ask them if they notice a pattern.

2. Ask the students what the total number of objects is on each page, and what happens if they add the objects in a different order? Model several different combinations, such as "9 pinecones and 2 acorns make 11" and "2 acorns and 9 pinecones make 11."

3. Then, have the students represent the number sentences with cubes or counters in their workspace. Have them make a written record of their number sentences. Have them rewrite the sentences to add the objects in a different order and explain what happens.

4. Now, have them create their own number sentences using counters or cubes: If they were going on a field trip, what are some items they would need? Ask each student to share a number sentence aloud.

5. Record on the board the number sentences that are shared, and ask what happens when the number sentence is added in a different order.

PROMOTING CONCEPTS

1. Have 2, 3, and 6 students come to the front of the room in three separate groups. Ask the groups of 2 and 3 to come together and have a volunteer tell

EXHIBIT 7.1 Unifix® cube and multilink cubes.

Uniflex® cube

Multilink cubes

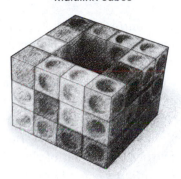

the class how many students are in the combined group. Next, have the group of 6 join the others. Let a volunteer tell the class how many there are in all. Next, have the students move back into their separate groups. Have the students make different combinations of the three groups, and ask whether the new combinations add up to a different number of students.

2. Students can also use cubes, as shown in Figure 7.1, and counters. Have them show different combinations of 11 using 3 addends. After several combinations, have the students record their combinations in a vertical format. Then, ask them if they add up or down, is the sum the same.

3. Next, have the students use cubes or counters to show different combinations of 11 using 4 addends, then 5 addends.

4. Have the students create number stories aloud similar to *12 Ways to Get to 11*. Some students may use a situation such as a field trip or class party to create their number sentence. Encourage them to use three addends or more, and model them with counters or cubes in their workspace. State the number sentence aloud.

5. Have the students record one of their number stories using numbers and words on one piece of paper and then illustrate their number sentence on another piece of paper.

6. Extend the lesson to other number combinations such as 12, 13, 14, etc.

Assessment

1. *Observation:* Have students create combinations of 11 in their workspace using counters or cubes.

2. *Performance:* Have the students draw pictures and write number sentences for other number stories they shared aloud. Encourage them to use more than two addends.

3. Use the rubric in Exhibits 5.3 or 5.4 to evaluate students' knowledge of using a variety of addends to make 11.

Making Connections

OTHER CONCEPTS

Using counting on, making a 10, doubles, and doubles plus one to recall addition facts; counting by 2s, 3s, and 4s; practice basic facts; fact families.

OTHER BOOKS

Anno's Counting House, Mitsumasa Anno (1982)

Fish Eyes: A Book You Can Count On, Lois Ehlert (1990)

What Comes in 2's, 3's, and 4's? Suzanne Aker (1990)

WEBSITES

http://funBrain.com/math/index.html

www.matematiko.com

www.scienceacademy.com/BI/add.htm

www.teachervision.com

The Water Hole
Graeme Base

In The Water Hole, *animals from all continents and habitats gather at the secret water hole to drink. First to appear is one rhino, then two tigers. As their numbers swell to 10 kangaroos, look closely because something is happening to the secret water hole. The water hole, which is a concentric die-cut oval, is beginning to diminish. Also, there is a cast of frogs on each landscape and their number is decreasing. And look even closer still and you will see other animals hiding in the landscape and in the borders. Each gathering of animals depicts a different continent's habitat, from the plains of Africa to the deserts of outback Australia. During the season of drought, all the animals go away. But after a great rain, all of the animals come back!*

GRADE LEVELS: 2–3

MATHEMATICS STANDARDS ADDRESSED: number and operations—computational fluency

---

SCIENCE STANDARDS ADDRESSED: life science—organisms and environments and the life cycles of organisms

---

SOCIAL STUDIES STANDARDS ADDRESSED: geography—environmental questions and issues

---

LANGUAGE ARTS EXPERIENCES: writing (learning log and story), vocabulary use, viewing

---

LITERACY CONNECTION: evaluating

OBJECTIVES: to group numbers to 100 by 10s, to explain the need of water for survival, to describe different habitats, to describe the physical characteristics of the Earth's surface and the reshaping of the surface by physical processes

---

KEY CONCEPTS: place value, counting by 10s, grouping sets of 10s and 1s, adapting for survival, importance of water, habitats, countries and their wildlife

---

MATERIALS: craft sticks or base-10 materials (other groupable materials—paper clips, unifix cubes, or counters), crayons or markers, rubber bands, paper, crayons, Inquiry Chart (Appendix A.14), Hundreds Chart (Appendix A.6), learning log, world map or globe

---

Procedure

SHARING THE BOOK

1. While sharing the book, encourage the students to look closely. The animals around the water hole stand out and are most obvious, but there are many more animals on the page and even in the borders. Encourage the students to look closely for all of the animals on the page by asking such questions as: How many animals are in the border? How many animals are around the water hole? How many frogs are on each page? How many animals are camouflaged on the page?

2. Encourage the students to look closely at the habitats and describe what they notice. Encourage them to use vivid and colorful language to describe what is similar or different from where they live.

3. Ask the students why the water hole is getting smaller. Have they noticed what is happening to the number of frogs, and do they know why? Have the students explain what they think the author is trying to say.

4. Reread the book, then ask the students what they noticed this time. Have them point out the things they did not see the first time.

PROMOTING CONCEPTS

1. On each two-page spread, have the students locate animals in the border that are indigenous to that ecosystem until they have a group of 10. They can represent this group of 10 with a long (10-stick) or 10 craft sticks and put a rubber band around them. Continue this process for each two-page landscape in the book until each student has 10 groups of 10 or 100 represented by 10 longs or 10 groups of craft sticks. A flat is equivalent to 10 longs (100) and a grouping of 10 bundles of craft sticks (100). (Students working in pairs will facilitate the use of the materials.)

2. Practice counting aloud by groups of 10 beginning at zero and counting to 100. Then, reverse the order and count from 100 to zero.

3. Using a Hundreds Chart (Appendix A.6), have the students color in the numbers that they counted aloud and make observations about the pattern. Have them look at the numbers that end in zero and describe the skip-counting pattern they see.

4. Ask the children to identify the number of animals gathered around the water hole and represent them with cubes (base-10 materials) or single craft sticks. For example, on the first panoramic view, 10 animals in the border plus 1 rhino equal "11," represented by one long and one cube or by one bundle of craft sticks and a single craft stick. Then, have them show in their workspace three groups of 10 plus three single sticks and count the number of toucans for "33," and so on.

5. Have the students represent a variety of combinations such as three 10s and five 1s, one 10 and six 1s, or two 10s and four 1s. With each representation stated aloud, have the students show the number with materials and write the number.

6. Using the last page of the book, ask students to identify the different continents and locate them on a world map or globe. Then, have the students illustrate one of the habitats described in *The Water Hole* to use for their work mat, such as Rivers and Streams or Galapagos Islands.

7. Using an Inquiry Chart (Appendix A.14), generate questions about these habitats. Provide print resources and/or Internet resources to help the students locate answers to their questions. Websites such as http://library.thinkquest.org/J0112126/habitats.htm and www.fi.edu/tfi/units/life/habitat/habitat.html are great sources of information about habitats and ecosystems.

8. Have the students make up an animal number story about the habitat they illustrated using a number from 39 to 100. Have the class show that number in their workspace. For example, there are eight 10s and five 1s of kangaroos at the water hole in the Australia habitat. Another example: there are six 10s and three 1s of tortoises at the water hole in the Galapagos habitat. Say to the students, if one group of 10 leaves, how many tortoises are at the water hole? Answer in terms of 10s and 1s.

Assessment

1. *Performance:* Using base-10 materials, ask the students to show 16 in their workspace. Write 16 on the board only (do not say "16" aloud). Then, ask to see "6" by underlining it. And then, ask to see "1" by circling it. Check to see if the students show a long (representing a 10) or a cube (representing a 1) for the 1 in the 10s place.

2. *Observation:* Make anecdotal observations about the students' ability to manipulate the place-value materials fluently.

3. *Performance:* Create a drawing of a habitat from a different part of the world (10 are listed on the last page of the book).

4. *Performance:* Have the students describe the physical characteristics of the habitat they drew and point out how it is different from the habitat where they live.

5. *Writing:* Create a learning log entry reflecting on the need of water by all living things for survival.

Making Connections

OTHER CONCEPTS

Compare numbers to 100; identify even and odd numbers; count by 2s, 3s, and 5s; identify the number that is before, after, or between given numbers; camouflage; evaporation (water disappearing from the chalkboard); water cycle.

OTHER BOOKS

One Hundred Hungry Ants, Elinor J. Pinczes, Bonnie MacKain (Illus.) (1993)

A Remainder of One, Elinor J. Pinczes, Bonnie MacKain (Illus.) (1995)

A River Ran Wild, Lynne Cherry (1992)

WEBSITES

www.abcteach.com/directory/basics/math

http://library.thinkquest.org/J0112126/habitats.htm

www.fi.edu/tfi/units/life/habitat/habitat.html

Counting on Frank

Rod Clement

Frank's owner, Henry, narrates Counting on Frank, *a humorous and silly adventure in measuring and counting everything of significance in his neighborhood, including his dog. From peas that have fallen on the floor to the number of Franks it would take to fill up his bedroom, Henry observes his environment in factual and mathematical detail. This counting tale takes you on a comparing and estimating spree that makes mathematics fun. Using his brain, Henry estimates the number of jellybeans in a jar in order to win a trip to Hawaii. (Other counting problems are provided in the book's appendix.)*

GRADE LEVELS: **2–3**

MATHEMATICS STANDARD ADDRESSED: numbers and operations—computational fluency, estimation

LANGUAGE ARTS EXPERIENCE: writing (learning log)

OBJECTIVES: to estimate quantities (less than 100), to estimate length, to estimate capacity

KEY CONCEPTS: number sense, capacity, length, quantity

MATERIALS: 30-gallon garbage bag; paper plates; note cards; counters; cubes; tiles, buttons, beads, beans, toothpicks, or jelly beans, other objects in the classroom; Estimation Recording Sheet I (Appendix A.15); learning log

Procedure

SHARING THE BOOK

1. Henry's dad says, "You have a brain. Use it!" Ask the students to explain how Henry used his brain and to describe one of Henry's counting adventures.

2. Ask the students what estimating is and when they might use it.

3. Following are some questions to ask the students so they can practice estimating:

   a. Did you know how long a line an average ballpoint pen draws? What if we drew a line 7,000 feet long? Starting at our classroom (or on the playground or in the gymnasium), how far do you think the line would be?

   b. Show students a 30-gallon garbage bag. Then ask them, "If we filled a 30-gallon garbage bag full of crayons, how many crayons would it take to fill the bag?"

   c. How many Franks would fit in our classroom? In the school? How many humpback whales would fit in the school?

   d. About how many peas are in an average serving? About how many peas would it take to fill an entire plate? If 15 peas fell off Henry's plate each night for a month, how many peas would that be? Two months, etc.

   e. In the story, the local club had a competition. What was it? How many jellybeans were in the jar? What was the prize?

4. Ask the students to pretend they are a measuring maniac like Henry. Have them tell the class what they would measure or count in their neighborhood.

PROMOTING CONCEPTS

1. Take the students on an estimation trip in the classroom just like Henry did with the jellybeans in a jar!

2. Set up 6–10 number stations around the room where the students can estimate quantity. Place a handful of counters (fewer than 100) on a paper plate. On a note card beside the paper plate, place 10 counters to represent a "benchmark." A benchmark or a reference group gives the students a visual image of "about how many make 10" and helps them make better estimates. Follow this procedure with beans, buttons, cubes, toothpicks, tiles, beads, jelly beans, etc.

3. Then, give the students an Estimation Recording Sheet I (Appendix A.15) and have them rotate through the estimation stations recording their estimates. Allow two or three minutes per station. Reminder: All of the estimation stations contain fewer than 100 items for initial estimation activities.

4. After recording estimates for each station, determine the actual number and establish a range of correct answers. For example, if there are 79 counters, then anything from 69 to 89 is an acceptable answer. Any response within this range is just as good as the exact amount.

5. Now, have the students make up an estimation station using objects in the room, such as how long is the chalkboard, how wide is a desk, how long are the windows, how wide is the classroom, etc. Plan an "about how many" or "about how long or how far" activity for each day.

Assessment

1. *Performance:* Have the students share aloud their estimates and the strategies they used. Share several of the estimation stations that students created and have them estimate and determine the actual quantity, length, or capacity.

2. *Writing:* Students can describe their thinking processes for estimating in their learning logs.

3. *Performance:* Check student responses on their Estimation Recording Sheet I. Determine the actual quantity and the range of acceptability at each estimation station. (See number 4 in "Promoting Concepts.")

Making Connections

OTHER CONCEPTS

Ratio and proportion, thinking logically, volume and capacity, estimating area.

OTHER BOOKS

The King's Commissioners, Aileen Friedman, Susan Guevara (Illus.) (1994)

A Remainder of One, Elinor J. Pinczes, Bonnie MacKain (Illus.) (1995)

Sir Cumference and the Dragon of Pi: A Math Adventure, Wayne Geehan (1999)

Spaghetti and Meatballs for All! A Mathematical Story, Marilyn Burns, Bebbie Tilley (Illus.) (1997)

WEBSITES

http://standards.nctm.org/document/eexamples/Chap4/4.6/index.htm

www.goenc.com

7.4

LESSON

Round Trip
Ann Jonas

Through the creativity of Ann Jonas, you are taken on a trip where you leave home in the early morning light and return in the dark. With the use of only two colors, you take a journey filled with the imagery of black and white; when you get to what you think is the last page, you turn the book upside down and find new images for the return trip. In daylight and in darkness, the shapes, the space, and your perceptions change as you alter your perspectives. A wonderful introduction to shapes, this book also provides an introduction to illusions.

GRADE LEVELS: 2–3

MATHEMATICS STANDARD ADDRESSED: geometry—analyze the characteristics of shapes, use visualization

LANGUAGE ARTS EXPERIENCE: visual representation

OBJECTIVES: to connect the names of geometric shapes to real-life objects in our environment; to construct a tessellation, a repeat tiling

KEY CONCEPTS: attributes of two-dimensional shapes such as squares, rectangles, triangles, and circles; art and illusion; tessellations

MATERIALS: tag board shapes of squares, rectangles, triangles, and circles in plastic bags for all students; black and white construction paper; scissors; glue; extra copies of this book (optional); examples of tessellations

Procedure

SHARING THE BOOK

1. Begin by identifying the two-dimensional shapes according to their geometric names (squares, rectangles, triangles, and circles). Have large examples of each on black paper and hold them up for all to see as you identify them.

2. Discuss the shapes of things around you. Have the students show you the shape that is like the top of your desk, the shape that is like the side of a house, the shape that is like the side of a drinking glass, and the shape that is like the top of a drinking glass. Encourage students to understand that how they look at something (side versus top) may change their perception of the object and its shape. Perspective changes perception.

3. Read the story and allow all students to see the scenes as the reader "travels" on the journey through the first part of the book.

4. Now, turn the book upside down for the journey home. Allow all students to see the illustrations from a different perspective as you "travel" home.

PROMOTING CONCEPTS

1. As you share pictures (railroad cars, rooftops, windows, trees, the moon, etc.), point to a specific item like a pine tree and have the students hold up an appropriately similar shape (triangle).

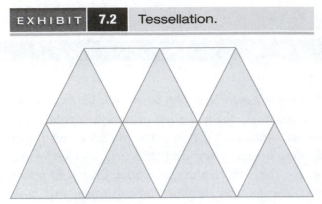

EXHIBIT **7.2** Tessellation.

2. Ask the students to identify objects in the classroom and classify them by shape. Discuss differences of opinion—for example, the top of a desk might be called a square or a rectangle—as they arise.

3. Have students classify or sort shapes by the number of sides they have. Discuss whether all three-sided objects are triangles and all four-sided objects are rectangles. Discuss the special properties of the rectangle called a square.

4. Discuss the special types of triangles and rectangles.

5. Explain what tessellation is—a repeating pattern of interlocking shapes that goes on forever with no overlapping and no gaps, such as a tile floor or patio (see the example in Exhibit 7.2). Select a triangle or square to create a tessellation, a repeat tiling. A tag board triangle or square can be used as a template.

6. Use black and white construction paper or two contrasting colors, similar to the book. Cut out enough squares or triangles to cover an 8½ x 11 sheet of construction paper. Lay the shapes out carefully, alternating colors, on a large sheet of construction paper, connecting the shapes at the vertices, then glue. Look closely for a visual pattern to emerge.

Assessment

1. *Observation:* Through the use of every-pupil-response techniques, have students hold up the shapes as you name them.

2. *Performance:* Have students create a bulletin board of shapes with appropriate names.

3. *Performance:* Construct a tessellation (a repeat tiling) using triangles or squares.

Making Connections

OTHER CONCEPTS

Measurement, optical illusions, quadrilaterals, regular two-dimensional shapes, three-dimensional shapes, relationships between and among the shapes, tessellations using a combination of shapes.

OTHER BOOKS

Color Dance (1989), *Quilt* (1984), *Reflections* (1987), and *The 13th Clue* (1992), Ann Jonas

It's Me, Marva: A Story about Optical Illusions, Marjorie Priceman (2001)

WEBSITES

http://library.thinkquest.org/16661/index2.html
www.cln.org/themes/tessellations.html
www.coolmath.com/tesspag1.htm
www.42explore.com/teslatn.htm
www.illusionworks.com/html/hidden_bird.html

7.5

Snowflake Bentley

Jacqueline Briggs Martin • **Mary Azarian, Illus.**

This Caldecott Medal picture book is a biography of Wilson "Snowflake" Bentley, a farmer from Jericho, Vermont, who was fascinated with snow crystals. His vision led him to collect images of what he considered masterpieces of design and miracles of beauty. Bentley's determination to capture the images of ice crystals led him to develop techniques of microphotography in the early 1900s. Unique to this book are the captions written in the side borders about Bentley's life, his experiments, and other interesting facts.

GRADE LEVELS: 2–3

MATHEMATICS STANDARDS ADDRESSED: geometry—characteristics and properties of two-dimensional shapes

SCIENCE STANDARDS ADDRESSED: science as inquiry—abilities necessary to conduct a scientific inquiry

LANGUAGE ARTS EXPERIENCES: writing (learning log), vocabulary study

LITERACY CONNECTION: monitoring

ARTS CONNECTION: photography

OBJECTIVES: to describe symmetry, to create lines of symmetry on snowflakes, to describe a snowflake

KEY CONCEPTS: lines of symmetry in two-dimensional shapes, crystal formation

MATERIALS: images of snow crystals, pencil, ruler, small mirror or Mira (a tool for reflectional symmetry), magnifying glasses

Procedure

SHARING THE BOOK

1. Show the students photographs of snow crystals. Beautiful examples are available on websites and in the informational books listed below under "Other Books." Walter Wick's *A Drop of Water: A Book of Science and Wonder* (1997) is a great source of snow crystal pictures. Other examples are available as posters from some websites.

2. Ask students to describe the snow crystals, guiding them to identify the branch-like formations in hexagonal shapes. Ask if they see other geometric shapes.

3. Inspect the photographs more closely with a magnifying glass. Techniques for growing crystals can be found at www.its.caltech.edu/~atomic/snowcrystals.

4. Explain that snowflakes are a collection of snow crystals.

5. Present *Snowflake Bentley* as a story about a man whose interest in snowflakes led him to a lifetime of observation, exploration, and documentation of snow crystals.

6. While reading, pause at various points to implement the Say Something activity (Harste, Short, & Burke, 1988). In this activity, students work in pairs to share their responses to a reading selection. Have the students take turns with their partners sharing one of the following types of responses to the reading (Beers, 2003); they can respond with:

   - A prediction
   - A comment
   - A clarification
   - A connection

   Post this list of possible responses for students to see and allow them to choose among them.

EXHIBIT 7.3 Symmetry.

7. Continue reading until the end of the book. Highlight for the students the interesting facts such as how Bentley had to wait season after season to perfect his imaging technique. Ask them how they might capture images of snow as it literally melts on contact.

PROMOTING CONCEPTS

1. Place a small mirror on an image of a snow crystal. Move the mirror around until half of the crystal is reflected in the mirror to present the concept of lines of symmetry. The line of symmetry identified can be marked with a pencil (see example in Exhibit 7.3). Define symmetry through this exploration.

2. Provide each student with a copy of the snow crystal.

3. Individually or in small groups, have the students speculate on the number of lines of symmetry on the crystal.

4. Discuss how they came up with their numbers (e.g., from one branch to the other branch on the opposite side).

5. Using mirrors, students can identify all of the lines of symmetry, confirming their speculations. Students can also mark the lines of symmetry as they identify them. If students are having difficulty identifying lines of symmetry, have them fold the snowflake.

6. Discuss which line of symmetry they may have missed in their speculations.

7. Predict what other polygons might be symmetrical. How many lines of symmetry would they have? As an extension of the lesson, test these predictions with paper shapes.

Assessment

1. *Observation:* Listen to students as they speculate about the number of lines of symmetry on the snowflake and their justifications.

2. *Performance:* Check the students' crystals and the marked lines of symmetry.

3. *Writing:* Create a learning log entry describing a snowflake using specific mathematical language. Emphasize the use of geometric vocabulary.

Making Connections

OTHER CONCEPTS

Lines of symmetry in three-dimensional shapes; symmetry in nature; translation (slides), reflections (flips), rotations (turns); patterns; fractals; tessellations.

OTHER BOOKS

A Drop of Water: A Book of Science and Wonder, Walter Wick (1997)

My Brother Loved Snowflakes: The Story of Wilson A. Bentley, the Snowflake Man, Mary Bahr Fritts, Mary Bahr, and Laura Jacobsen (2002)

Reflections, Ann Jonas (1987)

Round Trip, Ann Jonas (1983)

The Snowflake: Winter's Secret Beauty, Kenneth Libbrecht, Patricia Rasmussen (2003)

Snowflake Designs, Marty Noble, Eric Gottesman (2001)

The Snowflake Man: A Biography of Wilson A. Bentley, Duncan C. Blanchard (1998)

Snowflakes in Photographs, W. A. Bentley (2000)

WEBSITES

http://snowflakebentley.com
www.its.caltech.edu/~atomic/snowcrystals/

7.6

LESSON

The Keeping Quilt

Patricia Polacco

When Patricia's Great-Gramma Anna came to America, the only things she still had from her home in Russia were her dress and babushka. When she quickly outgrew them, her mother said, "We will make a quilt to help us always remember home. It will be like having the family in back home Russia dance around us at night." Throughout the next four generations, the quilt was used as a Sabbath tablecloth, a wedding canopy, a superhero cape, and a blanket to welcome each new child into the world. The Keeping Quilt became a symbol of love and faith for an immigrant Jewish family.

GRADE LEVELS: **2–3**

MATHEMATICS STANDARD ADDRESSED: geometry—spatial sense

SOCIAL STUDIES STANDARDS ADDRESSED: culture and cultural diversity; individual development and identity

LANGUAGE ARTS EXPERIENCES: small group discussions, visual representation

LITERACY CONNECTION: making connections

ARTS CONNECTIONS: colors, quilt making

OBJECTIVES: to explore triangles and squares, to investigate patterns, to construct a geometric quilt pattern; to discuss family traditions and beliefs; to make connections to personal history

MATERIALS: pattern blocks (or geometric shapes cut from poster board), geoboards, rubber bands, index cards, Classroom Quilt: Small Squares (Appendix A.16), Classroom Quilt: Large Squares (Appendix A.17)

Procedure

SHARING THE BOOK

1. After reading the story, ask the students the following questions:

   a. What was used to make the quilt? Can you describe the quilt in your own words? How was the quilt special to the family? How many different ways was the Keeping Quilt used in the story? Why do people use quilts?

   b. What is an immigrant? What country did Patricia's family leave? Where did they move to?

   c. What does the word "babushka" mean? What does the word "heirloom" mean? How many different generations used the Keeping Quilt?

   d. What are the colors of the Keeping Quilt? What are the colors of the other illustrations? Why were these colors used?

   e. Do you have quilts in your family? (If so, suggest that the students bring them to class to share.) Can you describe a quilt that your family owns? Does anyone in your family make quilts? If you were to make a patchwork quilt, where would you get the fabrics?

   f. What patterns do you notice in Patricia's quilt? What are the colors that repeat in the Keeping Quilt? Can you find a pattern in the clothing that you are wearing?

   g. What are some traditions that you have in your family?

2. Engage students in the activity Save the Last Word for Me (Short, Harste, & Burke, 1996) to promote text-to-self connections. On an index card, have each student write down a word that represents a connection they have made to the book. On the reverse side, have the student write down an explanation for his or her choice. In small groups of 3 or 4, have the students share their words. As each student shares the connection word, have all of the other students in the group respond to that word as they make their own connections. The student who "owns" the word will read or share the explanation last (hence the title, "Save the Last Word for Me"). Repeat until all group members have shared their words.

PROMOTING CONCEPTS

1. Have the students describe the pattern(s) in the Keeping Quilt. Explore quilt-like patterns using pattern blocks or geoboards. Review the definitions of triangles and squares. Have the students create a square on their geoboard and describe the number of sides and corners. Count the number of pegs that are inside, outside, and on. Repeat with a triangle. Create a shape that is *not* a square or triangle.

2. Name classroom or real-world objects that are squares (such as a stamp, a cracker, etc.) and triangles (such as a hanger, a tent, a pennant, etc.).

3. Create a repeating pattern with the pattern blocks and have the students show what comes next.

4. Look at the quilts that the students brought in and describe the patterns. Do you see any squares or triangles? Do you see any other patterns?

5. Let's make a class patchwork quilt! Using the Classroom Quilt: Small Squares (Appendix A.16), have the students draw diagonal lines from the corners of the square in each of the one-inch squares to create triangles. Encourage the students to create as many different patterns as they can by coloring only four triangles or selecting two colors and coloring four triangles with each color (see examples in Exhibit 7.4). Have the students describe their favorite pattern aloud.

EXHIBIT 7.4

6. Then, have students color their favorite pattern on the Classroom Quilt: Large Squares (Appendix A.17) to create their "quilt patch" for the classroom quilt. The "quilt patches" can be assembled on a bulletin board or glued to butcher block paper with a construction paper border.

Assessment

1. *Observation:* During the Save the Last Word for Me activity, students are observed by the teacher to assess their ability to communicate their connections to the text orally, express their ideas clearly, and listen when others are speaking.

2. *Performance:* Students' understanding of squares and triangles can be assessed by their ability to create and describe these shapes on a geoboard. A checklist and anecdotal recording sheet like the one shown in Exhibit 7.5 can be used with individual students, small groups, or the entire class. This particular tool was designed to gain insights into students' mathematical knowledge. Teachers observe the performance and write a description of what the student did. Students can also use the form to assess themselves. If students show unusual insights into creating geometric shapes and patterns they may want to keep a record to place into their best-work portfolio.

Assessing concept learning requires students to: (1) produce a correct definition of a concept, (2) produce a new or novel example of a concept, or (3) identify exemplars and nonexemplars of a concept (Jenkins & Deno, 1971). When assessing concept learning, a teacher should determine students' level of understanding. For example, the guidelines and charts shown in Exhibit 7.6 demonstrate how student learning of this lesson's concepts can be determined.

3. *Performance:* Students are evaluated by their completion of their "quilt patch" for the classroom quilt.

EXHIBIT 7.5 Checklist for assessing math knowledge.

Student name: **Date:**

	YES	NO	COMMENTS
Indicates that figures are triangles or squares			
Recognizes commonalities among the shapes			
Indicates classroom or real-world objects that are squares and triangles			
Completes a pattern using pattern blocks—triangles and squares			
Completes a pattern for a classroom quilt			

Adapted from: National Council of Teachers of Mathematics [NCTM] (2006). *PreK–2 Mathematics Assessment Sampler.* Reston, VA: Author.

EXHIBIT 7.6 Determining students' level of understanding.

Limited Understanding (Low): May state that a figure is a triangle but not be able to identify the attributes that make it so; may indicate that some of the figures are squares.

Developing Understanding (Moderate): Identifies characteristics of squares and triangles, may use inappropriate terminology.

Proficient Understanding (High): Recognizes triangles and squares, describes why each of the shapes is a square or triangle, and articulates a pattern using triangles and squares.

SAMPLE OF LIMITED UNDERSTANDING

Student name: Ray   **Date:** 10/14/XX

	YES	NO	COMMENTS
Indicates that figures are triangles or squares		X	"Some have three sides, some do not. They all have pointy corners."
Recognizes commonalities among the shapes		X	
Indicates classroom or real-world objects that are squares and triangles	X		
Completes a pattern using pattern blocks—triangles and squares		X	"Some look like triangles."
Completes a pattern for a classroom quilt	X		

Ray realized that triangles and squares had corners and that some of the shapes have three sides, but he was not sure if they were triangles.

(continued)

EXHIBIT 7.6 Continued.

SAMPLE OF DEVELOPING UNDERSTANDING

Student name: Gina **Date:** 10/14/XX

	YES	NO	COMMENTS
Indicates that figures are triangles or squares	X		"Triangles have 3 sides and 3 corners. Squares have 4 sides and 4 corners."
Recognizes commonalities among the shapes	X		
Indicates classroom or real-world objects that are squares and triangles	X		
Completes a pattern using pattern blocks—triangles and squares		X	"A coat hanger is the shape of a triangle and a cracker is the shape of a square."
Completes a pattern for a classroom quilt	X		

Gina seemed to focus on the number of sides that each shape has. She identified objects in the classroom that were the same shape as a triangle and a square. She was unable, however, to complete a pattern using the pattern blocks.

SAMPLE OF PROFICIENT UNDERSTANDING

Student name: Keith **Date:** 10/14/XX

	YES	NO	COMMENTS
Indicates that figures are triangles or squares	X		"Triangles have 3 sides and 3 corners. Squares have 4 sides and 4 corners."
Recognizes commonalities among the shapes	X		
Indicates classroom or real-world objects that are squares and triangles	X		
Completes a pattern using pattern blocks—triangles and squares	X		"Square, square, triangle is the pattern that is repeating."
Completes a pattern for a classroom quilt	X		

Keith successfully identified and created triangles and squares. He had no difficulty in completing linear patterns with pattern blocks using triangles and squares.

Making Connections

OTHER CONCEPTS

Classify the alphabet by the lines of symmetry, symmetry in geometric shapes, family trees, tessellations; create a story or memory quilt.

OTHER BOOKS

No Dragons on My Quilt, Jean Ray Laury, Ritva Laury (Contributor), Lizabeth Laury (Contributor) (2000)

The Patchwork Quilt, Valerie Flournoy, Jerry Pinkney (Illus.) (1985)

The Quilt Story, Tony Johnston and Tomie dePaola (1985)

The Seasons Sewn: A Year in Patchwork, Ann Whitford Paul, Michael McCurdy (Illus.) (1996)

Selina and the Bear Paw Quilt, Barbara Smucker, Janet Wilson (Illus.) (1999)

Sweet Clara and the Freedom Quilt, Deborah Hopkinson, James Ransome (Illus.) (1993)

WEBSITES

http://thecraftstudio.com/qwc/patterns.htm

www.pbs.org/americaquilts/America/

The Cloud Book

Tomie dePaola

"Multifaceted" is one way to describe this dePaola classic. The seemingly simple concept of clouds is presented in rich, complex, and multidimensional ways. After a brief science lesson on the formation of clouds, this book goes into detail about the different types of clouds in language that is accessible to young children. Other interesting facts are shared such as an ancient explanation of clouds and famous statements about clouds, particularly as they are believed to be predictors of weather. The Cloud Book is a good book to activate students' curiosity about clouds.

GRADE LEVELS: **2–3**

SCIENCE STANDARDS ADDRESSED: earth and space science—changes in Earth and the sky; science as inquiry—abilities necessary to do scientific inquiry

LANGUAGE ARTS EXPERIENCE: vocabulary study

LITERACY CONNECTION: summarizing/synthesizing

OBJECTIVES: to describe physical qualities of clouds, to identify different types of clouds, to observe and record different types of clouds and their possible connections to weather

KEY CONCEPTS: formation of clouds, types of clouds

MATERIALS: blue construction paper, white and gray chalk, chart paper, markers, informational books or references for clouds (or weather), Observation Log (Appendix A.18), Column Notes (Appendix A.19)

Procedure

SHARING THE BOOK

1. Look at the sky and observe the clouds. Have students describe the clouds in their texture, shape, height, color, etc. Ask students: What is a cloud?
2. Read the book and discuss the various elements that are shared such as the types of clouds, and cultural and sociological perspectives on clouds.

PROMOTING CONCEPTS

1. In small groups, have students make posters that describe each type of cloud using *The Cloud Book* and other resources. Some of the websites listed at the end of the lesson have great descriptions and pictures of clouds. Each poster should include the following information: type, physical appearance (as drawn on blue paper with white or gray chalk), nicknames, height, cloud color, sky color, and other descriptive terms. The types of clouds included in *The Cloud Book* are cirrus, stratus, cumulus, cirrocumulus, cirrostratus, altostratus, altocumulus, nimbostratus, stratocumulus, and cumulonimbus.
2. Using the Column Notes (Appendix A.19) format as shown in Exhibit 7.7, have students summarize the kinds of clouds presented in the book and their characteristics.
3. The students' posters can be discussed in class in order to identify the types of clouds. Place the posters at the students' eye level as resources for their observation log.

EXHIBIT 7.7   Using column notes to record cloud characteristics.

Type of Cloud	Characteristics
cumulus	Puffy. Looks like cotton balls
stratus	Horizontal, layered clouds stretch across the sky
cirrus	Thin and wispy, feathery
nimbus	Low, grayish, flat clouds

4. Collectively or individually, the students can observe and record clouds over a period of a week or a few weeks or even a month. Have students record the type, height, colors of clouds and sky, and other descriptions of clouds each day in their Observation Log (Appendix A.18). The students should refer to and consult their posters as these observations are made. In addition, measure the outside temperature and record the weather each day.

5. During this data collection, discuss with the students whether there is correlation between clouds and weather. Ask such questions as: Do the clouds predict weather conditions for the future? How correct is, "Evening red and morning gray, Set the traveler on his way. Evening gray and morning red, Bring down rain upon his head," as mentioned in *The Cloud Book?* Do the clouds predict precipitation? Do the clouds predict temperature?

6. As the days of data collection accumulate, discuss whether further evidence of a correlation between clouds and weather is presented.

7. At the end of the data collection, again discuss if their predictions were correct.

8. Ask the students whether observing clouds is an accurate way to forecast weather.

Assessment

1. *Performance:* Examine the students' posters to assess their understanding of the types of clouds.

2. *Observation:* Observe the students' discussion as data collection progresses.

Making Connections

OTHER CONCEPTS

Water cycle, weather, weather forecasting.

OTHER BOOKS

The Popcorn Book, Tomie dePaola (1989)
The Rains Are Coming, Sanna Stanley (1993)
Thunderstorm, Mary Szilagyi (1985)
Tornado Alert, Franklyn Branley (1998)
Weather, Seymour Simon (1993)

WEBSITES

http://vortex.plymouth.edu/clouds.html
www.aps.edu/aps/lavaland/weather.htm
www.inclouds.com/
www.met.tamu.edu/calss/Metr304/Exer10dir/clouds.html
www.pals.iastate.edu/carlson/

Hurricane

David Wiesner

The warm, moist end of summer brings threats of storms in much of the southeastern United States, especially along the Atlantic and Gulf coasts. David Wiesner tells us and shows us how one family prepares for, endures, and recovers from a hurricane. By looking at illustrations of taped windows, a wet cat, and a darkened home, we see the family's anxiety through the eyes of two boys, David and George. The hurricane swirls and twirls through the area, and David asks, "Do you think anything awful has happened outside?" "We'll see tomorrow," his brother replies. The destruction of a large elm tree provides a "new private place, big enough for secret dreams, small enough for a shared adventure," as the boys share fantasies about faraway places in the aftermath of the storm.

GRADE LEVELS: **2–3**

SCIENCE STANDARD ADDRESSED: Earth and space science—changes in Earth and sky

LANGUAGE ARTS EXPERIENCE: journaling

LITERACY CONNECTIONS: making connections, evaluating

OBJECTIVES: to explain the formation of hurricanes, to be familiar with the nature and power of hurricanes

KEY CONCEPTS: formation of hurricanes—effects of warm water and rotating Earth

MATERIALS: 4–5 large mixing bowls or small pails and 4–5 large spoons, K-W-L Chart (Appendix A.20)

Procedure

SHARING THE BOOK

1. Show your students the front cover of the book and discuss the title and the illustration by asking, "What are the boys thinking? Are they afraid? Why?"

2. Read the story aloud and share the pictures. After reading the story, ask questions. How did David and George's parents prepare for the storm? What damage was apparent? How did the boys use the fallen elm tree?

3. After the students have enjoyed the story for its narrative value, discuss the meaning of a hurricane. What do we know about hurricanes? Ask students if they have ever been in a bad storm. If so, how did it compare to the one in the book?

4. Begin the K-W-L chart (Appendix A.20) as shown in the example in Exhibit 7.8 and record student responses.

5. Share the sections of the book that deal with the hurricane (preparations, lack of power in the house, the strong wind and the intense rain, the uprooted tree).

6. Share information about when and where hurricanes occur. They occur in the late summer and fall when the waters of the Atlantic, the Caribbean, and the Gulf of Mexico are the warmest.

EXHIBIT 7.8 With students, fill in the K-W-L chart.

K what we know	W what we want to know	L what we have learned
Hurricanes produce strong winds. Hurricanes are made in the ocean. Hurricanes can result in devastating disasters.	How are hurricanes made? Why are hurricanes named after people? How do we protect ourselves from hurricanes?	

PROMOTING CONCEPTS

1. Review the information the students know and place comments in the "K" column (see Exhibit 7.8).

2. With the students, create some questions for the "W" column: Where do hurricanes start? Why do they start? What do they look like? Why are they accompanied by rain? What is the "eye" of the hurricane? What makes them spin? Where in the United States are they most likely to occur?

3. Provide informational books and reference materials about weather and hurricanes for students to use to answer some of the questions posed in the "W" column. The websites listed below are wonderful sources of information on hurricanes.

4. In four or five groups of four students each, have them conduct the following experiment to create their own small hurricane:
   - Fill the mixing bowls or pails about two-thirds full of water.
   - Mix by stirring the spoon in one direction, starting in the outside and moving slowly toward the center.
   - When the spoon reaches the center, take it out.
   - Notice the swirling water. This swirling water is what a hurricane looks like from high in the sky.
   - Can you identify the "eye" of the hurricane?

5. After all groups have completed the experiment, share the information gained and fill in the "L" column on the chart.

Assessment

1. *Observation:* Observe students' participation in the K-W-L chart and the information provided in the "L" column.

2. *Performance:* Students can write about how they can protect themselves in a hurricane or tornado (depending on their geographical location).

Making Connections

OTHER CONCEPTS

Investigations of destructive hurricanes (e.g., Andrew in 1992; Katrina in 2005; Gustav and Ike in 2008), tracking hurricanes through the Hurricane Tracking Center or the National Hurricane Center, other weather-related disasters such as tornadoes.

OTHER BOOKS

Hurricanes, Arlene Erlbach (1993)

1001 Questions Answered About Hurricanes, Tornadoes and Natural Disasters, Barbara Tuffy (1987)

On the Same Day in March: A Tour of the World's Weather, Marilyn Singer (2001)

Storms (1992) and *Weather* (2000), Seymour Simon

Twister Trouble, Ann Schreiber (2001)

Under the Whirlwind: Everything You Need to Know About Tornadoes but Didn't Know Who to Ask, Jerrine Verkaik and Arjen Verkaik (2001)

WEBSITES

http://kids.mtpe.hq.nasa.gov/archive/hurricane/index.html

http://tropical.atmos.colorado.edu

www.infoplease.com/spot/tornado1.html

www.nhc.noaa.gov/

7.9

LESSON

Sun Up, Sun Down

Gail Gibbons

This informational book chronicles a day, from sun up to sun down, in the life of a girl who observes and learns the properties and facts about the sun. Concepts included are seasons, location of the sun throughout the day, length of the shadows as they correspond to the location of the sun, distance from the planet Earth, gaseous state of the sun, properties of sunlight, and more. With a style distinct to Gibbons, the illustrations are bold, simple, and colorful; as usual, the book includes a "facts" page at the end.

GRADE LEVELS: 2–3

MATHEMATICS STANDARDS ADDRESSED: measurement—measurable attributes of objects and their units, systems, and processes of measurement

SCIENCE STANDARDS ADDRESSED: earth and space science—changes in Earth and sky; science as inquiry—abilities necessary to do scientific inquiry

LANGUAGE ARTS EXPERIENCE: visual representation

LITERACY CONNECTIONS: making connections, evaluating, summarizing/synthesizing

OBJECTIVES: to be aware of the location of the sun throughout the day by charting the length and location of shadows; to identify patterns as students chart the location of the sun, and plan and conduct a simple investigation using systematic observations; to relate the position of the sun with the length of the shadows

KEY CONCEPTS: patterns, Earth's rotation around the sun

MATERIALS: compass, yardsticks, chalk, data recording sheet displayed in the classroom, K-W-L Chart (Appendix A.20)

Procedure

SHARING THE BOOK

1. Using a K-W-L Chart (Appendix A.20), find out what students already know about the sun and what they may want to learn.

2. During the reading, highlight the cycles and patterns in the climate and weather that are generated by the sun.

3. Highlight the pages that discuss the length and position of shadows as they correspond to the position of the sun.

4. Ask the students questions similar to these examples. When the sun sets, where does it go? Does the sun really rise and set?

PROMOTING CONCEPTS

1. On the playground, have the students explore shadows and make observations. For example, as they move, do their shadows move? Do the shadows change directions? Where is the sun in relation to the shadows? Where are their own shadows in relation to other people's shadows? Discuss their observations.

2. Day two begins on the playground. With chalk, mark X on a spot. Hold a yardstick on the X. Note the location of the sun (by facing the sun and

EXHIBIT | 7.9 | Recording data about the sun.

TIME OF MEASUREMENT	LENGTH OF THE SHADOW	LOCATION OF THE SUN
8:30 a.m.	inches	
9:30 a.m.	inches	
10:30 a.m.	inches	
11:30 a.m.	12 inches	Southeast
12:30 p.m.	10 inches	South
1:30 p.m.	11 inches	Southwest
2:30 p.m.	14.5 inches	Southwest

checking the compass or facing a stationary object and noting the location of the sun). Trace the shadow of the yardstick and measure. Mark the time at the end of the shadow. Record the data on a chart as shown in Exhibit 7.9.

3. Ask students for their predictions of the length and position of the shadow. Discuss the reasons for their predictions.

4. At regular intervals, repeat step 2 using the X spot.

5. After the final collection of data, examine the traces of the shadow throughout the day. Ask the students if they see a pattern in the shadow traces. Ask them if the pattern would continue if the data collection continued until sundown.

6. Complete the K-W-L chart by recording what they have learned. Discuss the pattern they found.

7. Optional: This lesson can be repeated in different seasons to observe the different location of the sun.

Assessment

1. *Observation:* Observe the student's responses for the K-W-L chart, especially the "L" column.

2. *Observation:* Listen to students discuss their predictions and explanation of the pattern.

Making Connections

OTHER CONCEPTS

Phases of the moon; seasons; properties of the sun; telling time; measuring in inches, feet, and yards; passage of time.

OTHER BOOKS

The Moon Book, Gail Gibbons (1997)

Nine O'clock Lullaby, Marilyn Singer, Frane Lessac (1993)

Wake Up, World!: A Day in the Life of Children Around the World, Beatrice Holloyer (1999)

Weather (1993) and *The Sun* (1986), Seymour Simon

WEBSITES

www.hao.ucar.edu

www.nineplanets.org

www.windows.ucar.edu/tour/link=/sun/statistics.html

7.10

LESSON

So Say the Little Monkeys

Nancy Van Laan • **Yumi Heo, Illus.**

The monkeys featured in this cumulative tale are based on "blackmouth" monkeys that live near Rio Negro, the Black River, in Brazil. This Brazilian pourquoi folktale (a tale that explains why something is the way it is) attempts to explain the peculiar behaviors of the monkeys who live and sleep in the thorny palm trees. "Jibba, jibba, jabba," sing the monkeys all day long, doing everything but building permanent homes for themselves. Will tomorrow be the day?

GRADE LEVELS: 2–3

SCIENCE STANDARDS ADDRESSED: science as inquiry—abilities necessary to do scientific inquiry; life science—characteristics of organisms, organisms and environments

LANGUAGE ARTS EXPERIENCES: choral reading, expository writing, visual expression

LITERACY CONNECTION: evaluating

OBJECTIVES: to ask questions about animal behaviors that may seem peculiar and bizarre, to find answers to questions in multiple sources

KEY CONCEPTS: habits, animal behaviors, inquiry process

MATERIALS: Chart paper or a white board, K-W-H-L-H Chart (Appendix A.21), informational books and references about animals, access to the Internet if possible

Procedure

SHARING THE BOOK

1. Share the book as a shared reading experience. Through multiple readings, students should be able to participate in the chants that repeat throughout the book. This should be an enjoyable time for the students to play with the sounds in language.

2. Share the author's note in the beginning of the book because it presents the background of this tale, which comes originally from the native peoples who live along the Rio Negro and which attempts to explain the behavior of the monkeys.

3. Discuss what other tales or books students may know that attempt to explain the behaviors of animals. Books such as *Why Mosquitoes Buzz in People's Ears: A West African Tale* by Verna Aardema (2004) could be used as another example.

PROMOTING CONCEPTS

1. Generate a list of questions that students have about animals. Record these questions on chart paper or a white board.

2. Using one of the questions, model the inquiry process: How can the question be phrased for the inquiry? What is already known about the topic? Where can the answers be found? Demonstrate recording these thoughts

EXHIBIT 7.10	Using a K-W-H-L-H chart during the inquiry process.

K what is known	Frogs are amphibians. They live both in water and on land. Tadpoles turn into frogs.
W what we want to know	How long does it take a tadpole to turn into a frog?
H how we think we can find out	Informational books such as Frogs by Gail Gibbons. Internet websites
L what we learned	Tadpoles become frogs in about 12-16 weeks.
H how we learned about it	We learned that tadpoles at about three months still have their tails from Frogs book. www.allaboutfrogs.org had the answer under "Lifecycles of a frog."

From Soderman, Gregory, and O'Neill (2004).

and the inquiry process using a K-W-H-L-H chart (Appendix A.21) as shown in Exhibit 7.10.

3. Individually or in small groups, have the students investigate an authentic question they have about animals.

4. Sources of information can be provided, or the students themselves can research and locate sources appropriate for their inquiry.

5. Students' answers to their inquiry questions should be recorded on their K-W-H-L-H chart provided in Appendix A.21.

6. Students' findings can be presented to the class in various ways—poster session, presentation, expository writing, writing their own pourquoi tale, and so forth.

7. Revisit the students' K-W-H-L-H charts to discuss the process of their inquiry. Were the questions precise? Were the sources that they predicted to be helpful actually helpful? What sources were especially beneficial in answering their questions? If they were stuck, what strategies did they use to continue their inquiry? What did they learn about the inquiry process?

Assessment

1. *Observation:* Use students' reports on their animals to assess the successfulness of their inquiry.

2. *Writing:* Students' completed inquiry charts should document their process of inquiry.

3. *Observation:* Observe students' responses regarding their own inquiry process.

Making Connections

OTHER CONCEPTS

Inquiries in other content area topics; animals and their habitats; adaptation.

OTHER BOOKS

Big Cats (1994), *Snakes* (1994), *Crocodiles and Alligators* (2001), and numerous others, Seymour Simon

DK Science Encyclopedia (Rev. ed.), DK Publishing

Frogs (1994), *Pigs* (2000), and numerous others, Gail Gibbons

Touch and Feel: Jungle Animals, Geoff Dann, Inc. DK Publishing

WEBSITES

http://wcs.org/7617

http://wildwnc.org/af/

www.billybear4kids.com/animal/facts/animal.htm

www.kidsplanet.org/

www.phoenixzoo.org/

www.seaworld.org/

www.seaworld.org/animal-info/index.htm

www.zoo.org/

7.11

L E S S O N

Cactus Hotel

Brenda Z. Guiberson • **Megan Lloyd, Illus.**

In Cactus Hotel, the 200–year life cycle of a giant saguaro cactus, and how it provides nourishment and a home for many desert animals, is described. This simple story contains a large range of facts about the fragile habitat in the southwest desert that endures heat, cold, rain, wind, and sun. Jackrabbits, birds, bees, bats, Gila woodpeckers, and other desert creatures scurry around on a hot day looking for food. The saguaro provides food and shelter for many of these animals and is their hotel in the desert!

GRADE LEVELS: **2–3**

MATHEMATICS STANDARDS ADDRESSED: measurement—measurable attributes of objects and their units, systems, and processes of measurement

SCIENCE STANDARDS ADDRESSED: life science—organisms and environments and the life cycles of organisms; science as inquiry—abilities necessary to conduct scientific inquiry

LANGUAGE ARTS EXPERIENCE: writing (learning log)

LITERACY CONNECTIONS: evaluating, summarizing/synthesizing

OBJECTIVES: to describe the importance of the waxy covering on a cactus, to identify the characteristics of the saguaro cactus, to name the animals that live in saguaros, to investigate the life cycle of a saguaro cactus

KEY CONCEPTS: desert habitats, adaptation, adapting for survival, life cycle

MATERIALS: map of the United States or southwestern United States, two sponges (per group), petroleum jelly, measuring cups, a gallon container, water, paper towels, cacti, Observation Chart (Appendix A.22), learning logs, journals

Procedure

SHARING THE BOOK

1. Have the students locate the Sonoran Desert on the map (in southern Arizona and northern Mexico). Explain that the saguaro cacti live only in this region.

2. After reading the book, ask the students questions like the following:

   a. Does the saguaro cactus have wood? Does the saguaro cactus have fruit? Does the saguaro cactus have flowers? How long does a saguaro cactus live?

   b. Identify a deciduous tree that is familiar to students. Create a Venn diagram to compare the tree to the saguaro.

   c. How would you describe life in a desert environment? Describe the food and water supply in a desert environment.

   d. How has the saguaro cactus adapted to its environment? What does the saguaro cactus do when there is no rain? What have other plants and animals done to adapt to this environment? Can the saguaro cactus absorb too much water? Why or why not?

   e. Who makes their home in the saguaro cactus? Does it harm the cactus? Where are some other places for animals to live in the desert? About how much does a saguaro cactus weigh when it is full grown?

f. What do you think would happen in the Sonoran Desert without the saguaro cactus? What are "cactus hustlers"? Why are large saguaro cacti so valued today?

PROMOTING CONCEPTS

1. Distribute a cactus for each group of three or four students. Have them observe it closely. Ask the students, "Where are the leaves? What do you think the needles (or spines) do? Can there be a forest without leaves?"

2. Explain that the waxy substance on the cactus's outer covering helps it retain water during the long, dry periods in the desert. A broad-leaf tree can lose up to 100 gallons of water a day. Could that type of plant survive in the desert? Why or why not? A cactus has adapted so that it loses only one glass of water a day.

3. Conduct a scientific investigation to show how important the waxy covering is in retaining water. Give each group two sponges, one that is covered on all but one side with petroleum jelly and one that has nothing on it. Pour one-half cup of water onto each sponge (pour more water if using larger sponges).

4. Have each group record predictions of what will happen in an Observation Chart (Appendix A.22).

5. Allow the sponges to dry for several hours or overnight. Have the students predict what they will find when they return to their experiments.

6. Have them observe which of the sponges retained the most water and complete their Observation Chart by drawing and describing what is observed. Have the students discuss their observations with the class.

7. How many cups of water does it take to make a gallon of water? 100 gallons? Students can fill the one-gallon container to answer the question.

Assessment

1. *Writing:* Have the students record in their learning logs what they observed while doing the experiment and explain the results.

2. *Writing:* Have the students record in their journals what they learned about cactus in class today. Compare and contrast the cactus to plants in their environment.

Making Connections

OTHER CONCEPTS

Make a bar graph recording the high and low temperatures each day for a one-week period in the desert; explore deserts that are located in different parts of the world; compare two animals that live in the desert; have the students draw a desert scene; have the students draw a saguaro cactus during its five stages of life; other ecosystems and how organisms make adaptations to survive.

OTHER BOOKS

Cactus Desert, Donald M. Silver, Patricia J. Wynne (Illus.) (1997)

The Desert Alphabet Book, Jerry Palotta, Mark Astrella (Illus.) (1994)

Desert Giant: The World of the Saguaro Cactus (Tree Tales), Barbara Bash (1990)

Desert Voices, Byrd Baylor, Peter Parnall (Illus.) (1993)

Deserts, Gail Gibbons (1999)

Discovering Deserts, National Wildlife Federation (1998)

WEBSITES

www.desertmuseum.org/
www.geocities.com/Athens/Atrium/4649/index.html
www.oneworldjourneys.com/sonoran/index2.html
www.sonorandesert.org

The Dandelion Seed

Joseph Anthony   •   **Cris Arbo, Illus.**

"It is autumn in the garden," the story begins. The plants, the flowers, and the weeds have all dried up, but one dandelion seed remains connected to its dry, dead stem. Thus begins the journey of one tiny seed into the unknown, where it finally lands in the snowy faraway. But spring comes and the warm sunshine, the moisture, and the soil produce another dandelion plant from the one seed. The journey of the dandelion seed is a metaphor for all living things in this poignant story of life producing life. With beauty and clarity, the illustrations show the smallest detail of plants and animals in this wonderful story.

GRADE LEVELS: **2–3**

SCIENCE STANDARDS ADDRESSED: science as inquiry—abilities necessary to do scientific inquiry; life science—life cycles of organisms

---

LITERACY CONNECTION: evaluating

OBJECTIVES: to show that living things produce other living things in an endless cycle of life, to explain how plants make adaptations to survive, to observe structures of seeds, to inquire how seeds are dispersed in order to continue the cycle of life

---

KEY CONCEPTS: dispersion of seeds, adaptation, life cycle

MATERIALS: collection of seeds to represent a variety of ways that they travel (*Seeds: Pop, Stick, Glide* by Patricia Lauber [1981] is an excellent source for examples of seeds.), Column Notes (Appendix A.19), journals

---

Procedure   **SHARING THE BOOK**

1. Brainstorm with students what seeds are and what examples they know. Record their answers.

2. Each student or a small group of students can receive a pile of seeds to examine, explore, and observe. Which seeds have they seen before? What are some edible seeds? What are some seeds they may be able to see outside during an autumn day? As part of this exploration, students can classify the seeds. The various ways that students classify the seeds can be shared and discussed. What attributes did they use to classify seeds?

3. Read the book. Discuss, as presented in the book, how a plant completes a cycle of life. Seeds can be defined in the context of this discussion.

4. Take a nature walk. (Note: This lesson is most appropriate for late fall.) Collect seeds found during the walk. Note the physical appearance of the seeds as you find them: Is the seed prickly? Is it heavy? Is it fluffy? Does it look like something that students recognize? Think about where the seed came from. For example, if you find an acorn, see if there is an oak tree nearby.

PROMOTING CONCEPTS

1. Go back to the pile of seeds. The seeds collected during the nature walk can be added to the pile. After observing the seeds, have the students predict how different seeds may disperse themselves to replant. Patricia Lauber's

Seeds: Pop, Stick, Glide lists a number of different ways that seeds travel. As a whole-class or small group exploration, a Column Notes (Appendix A.19) such as the one shown in Exhibit 7.11 can be created as students make predictions about how different seeds travel.

2. As the chart is completed or when it is completed, discuss why plants and their seeds need ways of traveling. Why do they have to rely on other organisms or elements to travel?

3. Discuss concepts related to adaptation.

4. Ask the students to continue observing and identifying seeds and how they may travel to complete the cycle of life.

Assessment

1. *Observation:* Observe the discussion before, during, and after reading the book.

2. *Observation:* Are the students able to look at a seed and predict how it may travel? How does its structure help it to travel? Observe the responses on the chart.

3. *Observation:* Are the students reporting their observations of other examples after the lesson?

4. *Writing:* Have students hypothesize other ways seeds might travel. Ask them to write in their journals a story about "seed travelers."

EXHIBIT 7.11 Sample column notes.

METHODS OF TRAVELING	EXAMPLES OF SEEDS (YOU CAN TAPE OR DRAW THE SEEDS.)	WHY DO YOU THINK THE SEED TRAVELS THIS WAY?
Travelers with animals and people	Prickly seeds, burrs, or seeds with hooks travel with animals and people (sticklight, burdock, Queen Anne's lace). Other examples of seeds traveling with animals are edible seeds (apples, berries) eaten by animals and seeds that are buried in the ground by animals (acorns that are buried and forgotten by squirrels).	They stick to fur or clothes to be carried away and eventually dropped and planted. Seeds that must be eaten by animals in order to be replanted are attractive and bright.
Travelers with the wind	Small seeds that are light or dusty, seeds with silky hairs, winged seeds, and seeds with "parachutes" travel with the wind (Columbine, poppy, dandelion, maple).	They have mechanisms or qualities that allow them to "fly" and be carried away in the wind.
Travelers in water	(Most likely you will not have examples for this column.) Plants such as coconut and water lily can be mentioned. They live in or near the water.	Seeds that travel in water often have waterproof coatings.
Travelers that scatter themselves	Seeds in pods scatter themselves (violet, wood sorrel, touch-me-not).	They may be heavy enough to use gravity to drop and plant themselves.

Making Connections

OTHER CONCEPTS

Classifying living and nonliving things; plants as living organisms; resources needed for plants to grow; seed structures; plant classification.

OTHER BOOKS

The Gardener, Sarah Stewart, David Small (Illus.) (1997)

I Celebrate Nature, Diane Iverson (1995)

Lifetimes, David Rice (1997)

Seeds: Pop, Stick, Glide, Patricia Lauber, Jerome Wexler (Photographer) (1987)

WEBSITES

www.urbanext.illinois.edu/gpe/case3/case3.html

www.utm.edu/departments/cece/old_site/third/3F3.shtml

REFERENCES

Beers, K. (2003). *When kids can't read what teachers can do: A guide for teachers 6–12.* Portsmouth, NH: Heinemann.

Harste, J. C., Short, K. C., & Burke, C. (1988). *Creating classrooms for authors: The reading–writing connection.* Portsmouth, NH: Heinemann.

Jenkins, J. R., & Deno, S. J. (1971). Assessing knowledge of concepts and principles. *Journal of Educational Measurement, 8*(1), 95–101.

National Council of Teachers of Mathematics. (2000). *Principles and standards for school mathematics.* Reston, VA: Author.

National Council of Teachers of Mathematics. (2006). *PreK–2 Mathematics Assessment Sampler.* Reston, VA: Author.

National Research Council. (1996). *National science education standards.* Washington, DC: National Academy Press.

Nitko, A. J. (2004). *Educational assessment of students* (4th ed.). Englewood Cliffs, NJ: Merrill.

Ogle, D. (1986). K-W-L: A teaching model that develops active reading of expository text. *The Reading Teacher, 39,* 564–570.

Short, K. C., Harste, J. C., & Burke, C. (1996). *Creating classrooms for authors and inquirers.* Portsmouth, NH: Heinemann.

Soderman, A. K., Gregory, K. M., & O'Neill, L. T. (2004). *Scaffolding emergent literacy: A child-centered approach for preschool through grade 5* (2nd ed.). Boston: Allyn & Bacon.

Wood, C. (1997). *Yardsticks: Children in the classroom ages 4–14: A resource for parents and teachers.* Greenfield, MA: Northeast Foundation for Children.

CHILDREN'S LITERATURE

Aardema, V. (2004). *Why mosquitoes buzz in people's ears.* New York: Puffin/Dial.

Anthony, J. (1997). *The dandelion seed* (C. Arbo, Illus.). Nevada City, CA: Dawn.

Base, G. (2001). *The water hole.* New York: Abrams.

Clement, R. (1991). *Counting on Frank.* Milwaukee, WI: Gareth Stevens.

dePaola, T. (1975). *The cloud book.* New York: Holiday House.

Gibbons, G. (1983). *Sun up, sun down.* New York: Harcourt Brace.

Guiberson, B. Z. (1991). *Cactus hotel* (M. Lloyd, Illus.). New York: Holt.

Jonas, A. (1983). *Round trip.* New York: Morrow.

Lauber, P. (1987). *Seeds: Pop, stick, glide.* (J. Wexler, photog.). New York: Knopf.

Martin, J. B. (1998). *Snowflake Bentley* (M. Azarian, Illus.). New York: Houghton Mifflin.

Merriam, E. (1993). *12 ways to get to 11* (B. Karlin, Illus.). New York: Simon & Schuster.

Polacco, P. (1998). *The keeping quilt.* New York: Simon & Schuster.

Rice, D. (1997). *Lifetimes* (M. S. Maydak, Illus.). Nevada City, CA: Dawn.

Van Laan, N. (1998). *So say the little monkeys* (Y. Heo, Illus.). New York: Simon & Schuster.

Wick, W. (1997). *A drop of water: A book of science and wonder.* New York: Scholastic.

Wiesner, D. (1990). *Hurricane.* New York: Clarion.

8

*Experiencing
Mathematics, Science,
and Social Studies*

Grades 4–5

n this chapter, we capitalize on those experiences that students bring to the classroom. By using more excellent children's literature, we can make additional connections while teaching content area concepts. According to Wood (1997), students at this age have an intellectual curiosity and an awareness of the "bigger world." As well, they are beginning to develop an ability to handle abstract concepts. The lessons in this chapter link the concrete world to increasingly more abstract concepts. We often begin the lesson with both simple and complex understandings of their surroundings. We then move these ideas into more abstract concepts, challenging the boundaries of their knowledge about things they already know.

The two mathematics standards addressed are *Measurement* and *Geometry* (NCTM, 2000). The concept of geometry extends into connecting shapes of real-life objects and creating one's own three-dimensional structures. Collecting data, representing those data in a variety of meaningful ways such as graphs, and reading and interpreting maps based on the concept of coordinate grids are all part of how students experience geometry in this chapter.

Measurement is considered an opportunity for problem solving. For example, how are perimeters and areas similar and different? When you change the perimeter of a figure, does the area change? When you have the same area, can the perimeter be different? How do we know that? This is explored in Lesson 8.3 using *Spaghetti and Meatballs for All!* (Burns, 1997) with pentominoes. *Tuesday* (Wiesner, 1997) provides a surprising and engaging opportunity to experience measurement by making paper frogs jump. Students collect data by measuring the distances of frog leaps, then analyze the data set using mean, mode, and median.

Life Science and *Earth and Space Science* are the two science standards illustrated in this chapter (NRC, 1996). Discussions about environment and habitat begin with understanding the meaning of habitat, how each habitat sustains organisms within it, and how living and nonliving things interact with each other in their particular environments. These concepts are extended to include understanding the various threats to the environment (e.g., poisons, pollutions, and oil spills) that harm living things. There is a deliberate attempt to make students aware of the environment in which they live and how their actions may impact other living organisms. As well, the students are encouraged to take part in the social action related to sustaining a healthy environment for all.

Ann Garrett's *Keeper of the Swamp* (1999) describes the impact that humans have on an environment and its organisms. Breathtakingly beautiful illustrations provide a vivid look at the swamp as an ecosystem, and the poignant story reveals the fragile but important relationship between an old man and an alligator.

The notion of "environment" is broadened in our earth and space science lessons to include the hemispheres, planets, and the solar system. How does the tilting of the Earth's axis impact the climate and seasonal changes? How do we explore what seems unknown in our universe? What are the technological advancements that allow these human explorations? Several excellent books are included in this chapter for this science standard connection. Both the *Starry Messenger* (Sis, 1996) and *The Summer Solstice* (Jackson, 2001) challenge students to think and rethink about topics in space in ways that are systematic and scientific.

The study of social studies at this level offers a range of wonderful opportunities to learn history, power and authority, and physical landforms. Some books offer an alternate view to the stories that we already know. For example, *Flight: The Journey of Charles Lindbergh* (Burleigh, 1997) takes readers along on his famous flight across the ocean, and *Barn Savers* (High, 1999) illustrates that "recycling" can apply to saving a bit of the past. *Henry's Freedom Box* (Levine, 2007) shares a powerful story of a slave who mails himself to freedom; *Monday on the Mississippi* (Singer, 2005) offers new stories about the legendary Mississippi River; and *The First Marathon* (Reynolds, 2006) presents a story—of Pheidippides and the legend of the marathon—that students in grades 4–5 may not know. Many of these lessons also integrate wonderful and natural opportunities to develop mathematical concepts in measurement.

The lessons in this chapter allow students to glimpse at the larger world of which they are a part so they can better understand their place in that world. Students ought to be challenged to begin thinking about important issues and questions that involve not only their day-to-day lives, but also life for *all* organisms in remote and unfamiliar places.

8.1

LESSON

Betcha!

Stuart Murphy • **S. D. Schindler, Illus.**

Two friends, in an urban setting, set out to guess how many jelly beans are in a jar at the toy store in order to win two free tickets to the All-Star Game. Along the way, one of the friends estimates, while the other counts precisely, how many people are on the bus, the number of cars in the traffic jam, and the cost of items in a store window. Strategies are shared for determining an estimate. Through a fun trip to the toy store, the importance of estimation in everyday life is illustrated with a playful approach.

GRADE LEVELS:	**4–5**
MATHEMATICS STANDARD ADDRESSED:	measurement—select and use benchmarks to estimate measurements
LANGUAGE ARTS EXPERIENCE:	oral presentation
OBJECTIVES:	to estimate number through observation and analysis, to determine when it is appropriate to estimate, to explore the value of estimation as a practical life skill
KEY CONCEPTS:	estimating quantity, strategies for estimating, benchmarks or referents
MATERIALS:	jars and containers of various sizes and shapes (tall, short, round, square as shown in Exhibit 8.1); jelly beans, other types of beans, cereal, pretzels, popcorn, etc., Estimation Recording Sheet II (Appendix A.23)

Procedure

SHARING THE BOOK

1. Before reading the book, ask the students for examples of real-life situations that require estimations (e.g., food shopping, time to walk/drive to school, cookies for a class party).

2. Ask the students to explain what it means to estimate.

3. After reading the book, ask the students to describe what is happening in each picture. Encourage the students to share how they would estimate the number of people on a bus or the number of cars in a traffic jam, focusing on their thinking process. Encourage them to use different strategies to make their estimates.

4. Share an example of when you used estimation in your everyday life, similar to the friends in the story.

5. Discuss when it is appropriate to estimate and when you need an actual measurement. Give examples of both. List some tools that the students can use to measure.

PROMOTING CONCEPTS

1. Have the students estimate jelly beans in a jar, just like in *Betcha!*

2. Select a jar filled with jelly beans (or pinto beans, or some other similar

EXHIBIT 8.1 Jar and container varieties.

EXHIBIT 8.2 Sample estimation recording sheet.

STATION	ESTIMATE	ACTUAL	DESCRIBE STRATEGY
Jelly beans	580	492	I looked at the space that 10 beans took in the jar and estimated how many spaces the jar would contain.

item). Using the strategy in *Betcha!*, have students think about how many jelly beans are in one section. How many sections? About how many layers? What are some other ways of estimating the number of jelly beans?

3. Have the students check for the actual number of jelly beans. Establish an acceptable range for the number of jelly beans. Examine a referent group of 10 jelly beans to encourage better estimates.

4. Using various containers and jars (5 to 6; see Exhibit 8.1), have the students record an estimate and then determine the actual on the Estimation Recording Sheet II provided in Appendix A.23. Be sure to ask students to list the strategies they used when estimating on the form (see Exhibit 8.2). Establish an acceptable range for each estimate. Illustrate a referent or benchmark (place 10 of the item on an index card) to encourage better estimates.

Assessment

1. *Performance:* Have each student create an activity similar to *Betcha!* in their everyday life. Share these aloud with the rest of the class. Have each student explain why, in this instance, it is appropriate to estimate.

2. *Performance:* Have students in small groups create a daily bean guess for the entire class. Provide jars and beans. Count out the actual number in groups of 10s and 1s.

Making Connections

OTHER CONCEPTS

Estimating capacity, area, length, temperature, weight, time, angle measure, money, fractions, quotients, products; rounding; recognizing when an estimate is appropriate; a measurement scavenger hunt with no measuring instruments.

OTHER BOOKS

Counting Jennie, Helena Clare Pittman (1994)

Counting on Frank, Rod Clement (1995)

Coyotes All Around, Stuart J. Murphy, Steve Bjorkman (Illus.) (2003)

How Much Is a Million? David M. Schwartz, Steven Kellogg (Illus.) (1993)

Mapping Penny's World, Loreen Leedy (2000)

Measuring Penny, Loreen Leedy (2000)

Take a Guess (Spyglass Books), Janine Scott and Mary Beth Fletcher (2003)

Time to Estimate (Yellow Umbrella Book: Math), Betsy Franco, Claudine Jellison, and Johanna Kaufman (2002)

WEBSITES

http://mathforum.org/library/topics/

http://standards.nctm.org/document/

www.aaamath.com/B/est.htm

www.atozteacherstuff.com/

www.education-world.com/a_tsl/

8.2

LESSON

Tuesday

David Wiesner

Tuesday is an almost wordless picture book with illustrations that tell a strange tale about cavorting frogs that emerge from their pond for a wild and whimsical romp on a Tuesday night around eight o'clock. The book is a visual delight that invites readers to stretch their imagination. While the frogs rise from their lily pads, the inhabitants of the town are asleep. As dawn is breaking, the frogs return to their pond, waiting for another night of adventure. The only clues of their fantastic journey are the lily pads that mysteriously appear on the street. For those who doubt these events, remember, there is always another Tuesday.

GRADE LEVELS: **4–5**

MATHEMATICS STANDARDS ADDRESSED: measurement—centimeters; data analysis and probability—measures of central tendency

SCIENCE STANDARDS ADDRESSED: life science—organisms and environment

LANGUAGE ARTS EXPERIENCES: retelling, choral reading, narrative writing, learning log

LITERACY CONNECTION: summarizing/synthesizing

ARTS CONNECTION: origami

OBJECTIVES: to collect, analyze, and interpret data; to explore mean, mode, and median of a data set; to read and make a line graph

KEY CONCEPTS: data set, range, mean, mode, median

MATERIALS: Pass It On Activity Form (Appendix A.24), 3 x 5 index cards, centimeter rulers, graph paper, instructions for paper folding, calculators, Frog Leap Recording Sheet (Appendix A.25)

Procedure   SHARING THE BOOK

1. Before sharing the book, encourage the students to look closely for details about what is happening in the story because the author tells the story primarily through pictures and uses few words.

2. Tell the students to think about why the book is called *Tuesday* while you are reading.

3. Read the book aloud.

4. Engage the students in the Pass It On activity (Stephens & Brown, 2004). For this activity, have each student retell the story from *Tuesday* in writing, using the form in Appendix A.24. Allow approximately two minutes for the writing. After this round of writing, have the students pass their form to a peer to their right or left. Allow another two minutes for the second writer to continue the retelling in writing. Repeat the process until 3–4 students have added to the retelling of the original writer. Ask students to share their retellings aloud with the whole class.

5. Engage the students in a discussion about frogs by asking questions such as the following:

   a. Do any of you have a frog for a pet? What do they like to eat? How do they catch their food?

   b. To which animal class do frogs belong? What are the characteristics of an animal that is an amphibian? Can you describe their life cycle?

6. Provide each student with an index card. Engage the students in a paper-folding activity to create a frog (see www.frogsonice.com/froggy/origami/ for folding instructions). Encourage the students to color their frogs similar to a frog found in nature.

7. Have the students make their frogs leap.

PROMOTING CONCEPTS

1. In pairs, have the students collect data by measuring the length of each leap (using centimeter rulers) of one of their frogs in 15 attempts.

2. Using the Frog Leap Recording Sheet (Appendix A.25), have the student pairs record these 15 leaps. This is their *data set*.

3. Now rank the data. From the shortest leap to the longest leap, arrange the leaps in order. Have each student identify the shortest leap and the longest. Have them subtract the shortest from the longest—they now have the *range* of their data.

4. Have students determine the leap distance that appears most frequently. This is the *mode* of their data set.

5. Have the students identify which leap distance is in the middle. This is the *median* of their data set.

6. Explain to the students how to estimate the average leap of their frogs. The mathematical word for this is the *mean*. Add up all 15 leaps and divide by 15 to determine the mean of the data set. Provide calculators.

7. Now, using graph paper, have the pairs of students create a line graph to represent the 15 leaps made by each frog. Remind them to be sure to label all parts of the graph and create a title for the graph.

8. Determine a gold, silver, and bronze medallist for the frogs that have the greatest leaps in the classroom.

Assessment

1. *Performance:* The students should complete the line graph, as described above, that represents the 15 frog leaps.

2. *Writing:* Have the students write three questions in their learning logs that can be answered by getting information from the line graph they created or write a story to match the graph.

3. *Writing:* Have the students describe how to determine the mean, mode, and median of a data set.

Making Connections

OTHER CONCEPTS

Stem-and-leaf plots, box-and-whisker graphs (see Exhibit 9.4), circle graphs, scattergram, double bar graph, data predictions

OTHER BOOKS

Fantastic Frogs, Fay Robinson and Jean Cassels (2000)

Free Fall, David Wiesner (1991)

Frogs, Gail Gibbons (1994)

From Tadpole to Frog, Wendy Pfeffer (1994)

The Icky Sticky Frog, Dawn Bentley and Salina Yoon (1999)

If You Hopped Like a Frog, David M. Schwartz and James Warhola (1999)

Joseph Had a Little Overcoat, Simms Taback (1997)

Moon Frog: Animal Poems for Young Children, Richard Edwards, Sarah Fox-Davies (Illus.) (1992)

Officer Buckle and Gloria, Peggy Rathmann (1996)

Sector 7, David Wiesner (1999)

The Three Pigs, David Wiesner (2001)

WEBSITES

http://allaboutfrogs.org/

http://cgee.hamline.edu/frogs/

www.exploratorium.edu/frogs/

Spaghetti and Meatballs for All!

Marilyn Burns • **Debbie Tilley, Illus.**

Mr. and Mrs. Comfort decide to have a family reunion and begin planning a spaghetti and meatball dinner for 32 people. While Mr. Comfort cooks, his wife plans the seating arrangement. She orders 8 tables and 32 chairs to accommodate all of her guests. After the first few family members arrive, they begin rearranging the tables, much to Mrs. Comfort's distress. She is certain they will run out of room. Chaos soon develops as family members continue to arrive and seats must be found for them. Implementing a playful approach to area and perimeter, everyone at the reunion has a seat.

GRADE LEVELS: 4–5

MATHEMATICS STANDARDS ADDRESSED: measurement—area and perimeter; geometry—spatial sense; problem solving—formulate problems from everyday mathematical situations

LANGUAGE ARTS EXPERIENCES: retelling, listening, writing (learning log)

LITERACY CONNECTION: summarizing/synthesizing

OBJECTIVES: to define area and perimeter, to calculate area and perimeter, to describe the difference between area and perimeter, to discover and cut out pentominoes, to solve geometric puzzles using pentominoes

KEY CONCEPTS: area, perimeter, spatial relationships

MATERIALS: 5 one-inch square tiles per student, one-inch square graph paper (two sheets per student), scissors, learning log

Procedure

SHARING THE BOOK

1. After reading the book, do a Partner Retells (Hoyt, 2000). Pair up students and designate a storyteller and a listener in each pair. The storyteller retells the story, capturing as much detail as possible in the retell. The partner listens without looking at the book. When the retelling is finished, the listener turns to the book, marking the details that were included in the retelling with small sticky notes. The listener can encourage the storyteller to provide missing information by giving clues or prompts.

2. Ask the students such questions as: What is a family reunion? Have any of you ever been to a family reunion? How many people were at your family reunion? How many people were the Comforts expecting for their family reunion?

3. Together with students, use the tiles to illustrate the seating arrangement that Mrs. Comfort figured to seat all of the guests.

4. Each time guests arrived, they rearranged the tables into different rectangles so that more people could sit together. Using the tiles, illustrate a 2-by-4 rectangle. Ask the students what the perimeter of the rectangle is, how many people can be seated around it, and what the area of the rectangle is.

5. Later, after six more guests arrive, a 1-by-8 rectangle is created. Have the students show this using the tiles. Then, ask them what the perimeter of this

rectangle is, how many people can be seated around it, and what the area of the rectangle is.

6. Ask the students to think of a different arrangement that could seat all 32 guests. Have them use the tiles to illustrate the arrangement, and determine the perimeter and the area.

7. Have the students use their own words to describe the perimeter of a rectangle and the area of a rectangle.

PROMOTING CONCEPTS

1. Ask the students to complete the following:

    a. Using one tile, how many different ways can it be arranged if you flip, twist, and rotate it? *One* ▫

    b. Using two tiles that touch on a complete side, how many different ways can they be arranged? *One* ▭

    c. Using three tiles that touch on a complete side, how many different ways can they be arranged? *Two* ▭ ⌐

    d. Using four tiles that touch on a complete side, how many different ways can they be arranged? *Five* ▭ ⌐ ▦ ▤ ⌐

    e. Using five tiles that touch on a complete side, how many different ways can they be arranged? These arrangements are called *pentominoes*. Using the graph paper, find as many different arrangements of five tiles and cut each shape out. Remember, if you can flip, twist, or rotate the shape and fit it on top of another, it is the same shape. (Encourage the students, as part of the problem-solving process, to exhaust all the possibilities and to be confident that they have discovered *all* the pentominoes. There are 12 pentominoes, shown in Exhibit 8.3.)

    f. What is the area of each pentominoe piece? Explain how you know this.

    g. Do all the pentominoes have the same perimeter? Show an example of two pentominoes that have different perimeters.

    h. Using four pentominoes, create a 4-by-5 rectangle. What is the area and perimeter of this rectangle? Explain.

    i. Using five pentominoes, create a 5-by-5 square. What is the area and perimeter of this square? Explain.

| EXHIBIT | 8.3 | Twelve pentominoes. |

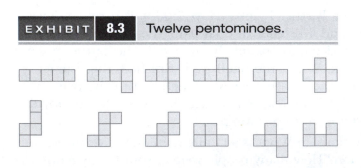

Assessment

1. *Observation:* Have students discover and cut out of the graph paper all 12 pentominoes.

2. *Writing:* Have students define area and perimeter and how to determine area and perimeter in their learning logs. Describe the difference between area and perimeter.

3. *Performance:* Have each student create a geometric puzzle using six pentominoes. Trace just the outline. Exchange with a classmate and solve each other's puzzle.

EXHIBIT **8.4** Scoring rubric for discovering pentominoes.

Name: _____ Date: _____

POINTS | **CRITERIA**

4
- ☐ You discovered and cut out all 12 pentominoes.
- ☐ You used reasoning and trial and error to discover all the pentominoes.
- ☐ Your display of the 12 pentominoes is organized, attractive, and complete.
- ☐ You discovered two pentominoes that have the same area and perimeter.
- ☐ You discovered two pentominoes that have the same area but a different perimeter.
- ☐ Your solutions for the 4-by-5 rectangle and the 5-by-5 square puzzles are accurate.
- ☐ The solutions for the area and perimeter of the rectangle and square puzzle are accurate.

3
- ☐ You discovered all 12 of the pentominoes.
- ☐ Your display of the 12 pentominoes is attractive and complete.
- ☐ Most of your solutions for area and perimeter of two pentominoes are correct.
- ☐ Most of your solutions for the area and perimeter of the rectangle and square puzzles are accurate.

2
- ☐ You did not discover all 12 of the pentominoes.
- ☐ You displayed the pentominoes you did discover in an organized manner.
- ☐ The rectangle and square puzzles are not complete.
- ☐ Determining the area and perimeter of the geometric puzzles is not complete.

1
- ☐ Please see the teacher for assistance in completing this project.

4. *Scoring:* Exhibit 8.4 offers a scoring rubric for discovering and cutting out pentominoes and solving geometric puzzles using pentominoes. This rubric can help guide a teacher's judgment in assessing the quality of a student's performance on this project.

Making Connections

OTHER CONCEPTS

Identify pentominoes that have a vertical or horizontal line of symmetry; identify pentominoes that will form a tessellation; hexominoes (six connected squares); double or triple a recipe for spaghetti sauce to use for a class luncheon.

OTHER BOOKS

Amanda Bean's Amazing Dream: A Mathematical Story, Marilyn Burns and Cindy Neuschwander, Lisa Woodruff (Illus.) (1998)

Anno's Mysterious Multiplying Jar, Masaichiro and Mitsumasa Anno (1983)

How Big Is a Foot? Rolf Myller and Susan McCrath (1991)

Math Appeal, Greg Tang (2003)

A Remainder of One, Elinor J. Pinczes, Bonnie MacKain (Illus.) (2002)

Sir Cumference and the First Round Table: A Math Adventure, Cindy Neuschwander, Wayne Geehan (Illus.) (1997)

Strega Nona, Tomie dePaola (1984)

WEBSITES

http://mathforum.org/paths/measurement/e.measlessons.html

www.math.clemson.edu/~rsimms/java/pentominoes/

8.4

LESSON

Barn Savers

Linda Oatman High • **Ted Lewin, Illus.**

The two main characters in Barn Savers, a father and son, dismantle a 100-year-old barn in order to save it from being crushed by the blade of a bulldozer. Wind and rain have taken their toll and left the boards weather-beaten and rugged; however, the barn savers can still see a beautiful place and can smell the hay and horses from years gone by. The barn savers save everything—from the joist and rafters to the floor and the roofing. In this way, the barn can be recycled and reused in new barns and houses so the old barn will never be gone. This is the hope of the barn savers. The text and the watercolors subtly deliver a message about the importance of preserving our past.

GRADE LEVELS: **4–5**

MATHEMATICS STANDARD ADDRESSED: geometry—exploring three-dimensional shapes

SOCIAL STUDIES STANDARDS ADDRESSED: production, distribution, and consumption—recycling

LANGUAGE ARTS EXPERIENCE: writing (learning log)

LITERACY CONNECTION: making connections

ARTS CONNECTION: architecture, geodesic dome

OBJECTIVES: to explore and investigate real-life representations of triangles, to construct a three-dimensional structure, to observe geometric shapes in architecture, to learn the importance of respecting historical buildings

KEY CONCEPTS: triangles, angles; three-dimensional construction; "reduce, reuse, recycle," preservation

MATERIALS: geoboards or square dot paper, rubber bands, centimeter rulers, gumdrops (11 per student), toothpicks (25 per student) [recommend one plastic bag per student containing the gumdrops and toothpicks], Connections Chart (Appendix A.10)

Procedure SHARING THE BOOK

1. Before reading the book, ask the students the following questions:
   a. Have you ever seen a barn? Where? Have you ever been in a barn? Can you share your experience?
   b. What do you think this book is going to be about from the title, *Barn Savers*? Who do you think the people are on the front cover? Why would you want to save barns?
2. After sharing the book, have students complete the Connections Chart (Appendix A.10) individually, then share them as a whole group (see the example in Exhibit 8.5). Observe how the students related to the characters and the events in the story, and the setting.
3. Engage the students in a discussion of the story by asking such questions as the following:
   a. What did the barn savers consider a treasure? Why?

EXHIBIT | 8.5 | Using a Connections chart to understand a story.

TEXT-TO-SELF	TEXT-TO-TEXT	TEXT-TO-WORLD
I have seen old barns that look like the ones shown in the book.	This book reminds me of remodeling shows on TV.	I know that some people try to reuse materials from old buildings.

b. What parts of the barn were saved? Name some of the parts.

c. What does it mean to recycle? Who would be interested in parts of the old barn?

d. What does the youngest barn saver save for his bedroom?

e. Should we save old barns? Why? What is the value of old barns? Other structures?

PROMOTING CONCEPTS

1. Copy the inside flap of the book. Have the students find as many triangles as they can in the old barns and point out any other geometric shapes.

2. Have students make a triangle on a geoboard or on square dot paper. Have the students create as many different triangles as they can. Then, challenge the students to create as many different triangles as they can with one constant side length.

3. In the field of architecture, the triangle is used in many creative and inventive ways. Ask students to name as many as they can.

4. In what other structures have they noticed triangles? Bridges, train trestles, skyscrapers, etc. Explain that this is because the triangle is considered the most stable, rigid polygon.

5. Explain that a geodesic dome is a type of structure shaped like a piece of a sphere or a ball. This structure is composed of a complex network of triangles that roughly form a spherical surface. The more complex the network of triangles, the more closely the dome approximates the shape of a true sphere.

6. Tell the students that Buckminister Fuller invented geodesic domes in the late 1940s.

7. Attempts to build triangulation and open networks of steel are evident in the geodesic dome. Ask students if they can name some existing examples of geodesic domes. (Epcot Center, play gyms, houses, greenhouses, etc.)

8. Have the students use the plastic bag of construction materials (11 gumdrops and 25 toothpicks) to build a geodesic dome.

9. Start with a gumdrop in the center and connect five toothpicks to create a star pattern (Exhibit 8.6a).

10. Place a gumdrop at the end of each of the toothpicks in the star pattern. Create a pentagon by placing toothpicks between the outer edge gumdrops (8.6b).

11. Along each edge of the pentagon, form an equilateral triangle using one more gumdrop and two more toothpicks. This makes five additional equilateral triangles (8.6c).

EXHIBIT 8.6 Building a geodesic dome using gumdrops and toothpicks.

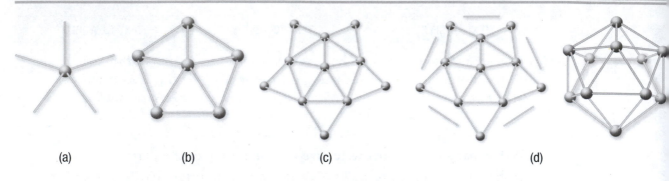

(a)   (b)   (c)   (d)

12. Now, connect the outer gumdrops with the five remaining toothpicks. The first center gumdrop becomes the apex of the geodesic dome (8.6d).

Assessment

1. *Writing:* Have the students describe the characteristics that all triangles have in common.

2. *Performance:* Complete the three-dimensional geodesic dome construction.

3. *Writing:* Have students explain the value of old barns and write about why we should save them.

Making Connections

OTHER CONCEPTS

Naming angles—acute, right, obtuse, and straight; classifying triangles—equilateral, isosceles, and right; using a protractor to measure angles; summing the angles of a triangle; other shapes in architecture; other space or three-dimensional shapes.

OTHER BOOKS

Architects Make Zigzag: Looking at Architecture from A to Z, Diane Maddex (1995)

Architecture, Shapes, Michael J. Crosbie and Steve Rosenthal (1995)

Beekeepers, Linda Oatman High, Doug Chayka (Illus.) (1998)

Dumpy LA Rue, Elizabeth Winthrop, Betsy Lewin (Illus.) (2001)

Fireflies! Julie Brinckloe (1985)

Frank Lloyd Wright for Kids, Kathleen Throne-Thomsen (1994)

How a House Is Built, Gail Gibbons (1996)

In November, Cynthia Rylant, Jill Kastner (Illus.) (2000)

Round Buildings, Square Buildings, and Buildings That Wiggle Like a Fish, Philip M. Isaacson (2001)

Under New York, Linda Oatman High, Robert Rayevsky (Illus.) (2001)

When I Was Young in the Mountains, Cynthia Rylant, Diane Goode (Illus.) (1982)

WEBSITES

http://worldtrans.org/whole/bucky.html
www.barnmaster.com/
www.bfi.org/
www.colonialbarn.com/
www.doorcountycompass.com
www.grunch.net/synergetics/domes/index.html

8.5

LESSON

Two Bad Ants

Chris Van Allsburg

In *Two Bad Ants, two greedy ants desert the safety of their colony to eat the delicious crystals (sugar) discovered in an unnatural place (a kitchen). The next morning at breakfast, the two ants enter the bizarre world of humans. Chris Van Allsburg creates dazzling illustrations—from an ant's perspective—of the exciting journey that begins with a giant silver spoon scooping into the crystals and dropping them into a brown lake (coffee). Their next hiding place was lifted, tilted, and heated to a warm red glow and then, suddenly, they were rocketed upward into the air (a toaster). Their journey continues with a fountain that plunges them into a dark chamber with wet food that spins (a garbage disposal) and a hiding place: two dark holes—but a force passes through them and blows them out of the holes like bullets (an electrical outlet). The battered ants step into line behind their fellow ants who have returned for more crystals, and each carries a single crystal home to their mother queen. The two ants are happy to hear the familiar sounds of their home and family, which is the real treasure after all.*

GRADE LEVELS: **4–5**

SCIENCE STANDARDS ADDRESSED: physical science—light, heat, electricity, and magnetism; life science—organisms and environments

LANGUAGE ARTS EXPERIENCES: visual expression, writing (learning log)

OBJECTIVES: to observe how objects become charged with static electricity and what some of its effects are, to create a scale drawing

KEY CONCEPTS: electric charges, static electricity, electric discharge, negative charge, positive charge, repel, attract; reduced, enlarged, scale

MATERIALS: balloons (latex, oblong shape is better than round), plastic wrap, wool cloth (100 percent wool), comb, puffed cereal grains, centimeter graph paper, centimeter rulers, Static Electricity Observation Chart (Appendix A.26)

Procedure

SHARING THE BOOK

1. While sharing the book, encourage the students to look closely and predict where the two ants are located throughout their journey. What are the clues the students use to help them figure out what is happening to the ants?

2. After reading the book, ask the students the following questions:

   a. What do we know about ants? To what animal class do ants belong? How many legs do they have? How many body parts do they have? Name them. *(head, thorax, abdomen)* Can you describe where ants live? *(colony)* Have you ever seen ants? Share your experiences with ants.

   b. What did the ants discover? What did the mother queen say about the discovery? As each ant is carrying a single crystal to the mother queen, two bad ants have a different idea. What did they decide to do? Why?

c. What are the crystals that the ants are carrying back to the mother queen? What do the crystals taste like?

d. Describe where the crystals were discovered. What makes you think that? Are the two bad ants in any danger? Are the crystals worth the risk?

e. Look closely at the size of the objects in the illustrations. Why are the illustrations drawn this way? Compare the size of sugar crystals in real life (as human beings see them) to the crystals the ants discovered. If you double the dimensions of an object, will its shape change? This is called an *enlarged scaled drawing*. A scaled drawing is like a photograph, it can be reduced or enlarged. Why would you use a scale drawing?

PROMOTING CONCEPTS

1. The two bad ants climbed into two dark holes similar to their underground home. Ask the students what these two dark holes are. A strange force passed through the wet ants. What do the students think that strange force was? Have they ever received an electric shock? Have those students describe what happened.

2. Ask the students if they have ever removed laundry from a clothes dryer and had their socks stick to their shirt. This is called *static cling*. This happens when there is a buildup of *electric charges*, and this is called *static electricity*.

3. Ask the students if they have ever walked across the carpet and then touched a friend's hand and received a mild shock. What causes the shock? Explain that when static electric charges jump off a charged object, an *electric discharge* takes place. A *charge* is too many electrons or too few electrons around an object's atoms, causing the object to have a negative (excess electrons) or a positive (too few electrons) charge. *Electrons* are tiny, negatively charged particles that, when separated from their atoms, form electricity. The freed electrons are the stuff of which electricity is made.

4. To demonstrate in class, blow up a balloon and rub it on a rug or sweater and bring the balloon close to a student's head. The student's hair rises to meet the balloon. By rubbing the balloon, it becomes electrically charged. The hair rises toward the balloon because of that charge.

5. The electrical charge is also strong enough to hold the balloon against a wall for a short time. Try it and see how long the balloon will stay.

6. Sometimes a balloon will stick to another balloon, and at other times it will not. Have the students try to figure out why.

7. Have each student blow up a balloon. In small groups, have the students rub their balloon with a wool cloth. Have students place two balloons about 10 cm apart, observe what happens, and record their observations on the Static Electricity Observation Chart (Appendix A.26).

8. Now, this time have each student rub the balloon with plastic wrap. Have students place two balloons about 10 cm apart, observe what happens, and record their observations on the chart.

9. Compare the observations and predictions after they have rubbed with the wool cloth and the plastic wrap. Rubbing a balloon with wool gives a *negative charge* to the balloon. Rubbing a balloon with plastic gives a *positive charge* to the balloon. Like charges repel each other; unlike charges attract.

10. From the behavior of the balloons, ask if the students can *infer* whether there is more than one kind of charge. Have them explain how they made their inference.

11. Repeat the earlier procedure but rub a comb with the wool cloth and then the plastic wrap. Have students record their observations on their chart.

12. Bring a charged balloon near a few puffed cereal grains (neutral charge) to see what happens. Then, bring a charged balloon near a wall (neutral charge) to see what happens. What conclusions can the students draw about the effect of a charged balloon on uncharged objects?

Assessment

1. *Writing:* Ask students to explain what happens when they rub a balloon with a wool cloth and it sticks to the wall or picks up puffed cereal grains.

2. *Writing:* If the students comb their hair in the dark, they may see sparks. Ask the students to explain, in their learning logs, why this happens.

3. *Performance:* Create a scale drawing. Enlarge the dimensions of a crayon or thumbtack to twice its size (measure and multiply by two). Draw it on centimeter graph paper.

Making Connections

OTHER CONCEPTS

Lightning, lightning rods, and lightning safety; current electricity; materials that are conductors and insulators of electricity; friction; things that need electricity; scaled drawings—reduced or enlarged.

OTHER BOOKS

Ben's Dream, Chris Van Allsburg (1982)

Electricity: Circuits, Conductors, Batteries, and Bulbs, Doug Sylvester (2000)

The Garden of Abdul Gasazi, Chris Van Allsburg (1979)

Lightning, Seymour Simon (1999)

The Mysteries of Harris Burdick, Chris Van Allsburg (1984)

What's the Big Idea, Ben Franklin? Jean Fritz, Margot Tomes (Illus.) (1996)

WEBSITES

www.ca.uky.edu/entomology/dept/bugfood1.asp

www.doyourownpestcontrol.com

www.hometrendscatalog.com

www.sciencemadesimple.com/static.html

www.terminix.com/information/default.aspx

Flight: The Journey of Charles Lindbergh

Robert Burleigh • **Mike Wimmer, Illus.**

No one had ever flown nonstop from New York to Paris, France, which is more than 3,600 miles away. In the early morning of May 20, 1927, Charles Lindbergh steps into the drizzle and goes to his small, single-engine airplane, The Spirit of St. Louis, *and takes off for Paris. He is alone with no radio or parachute. Using compasses and the stars as guides through 2,300 miles and six to seven hours of darkness, he is still over the ocean and 1,300 miles from Paris. After 29–30 hours, he sees the green coast of Ireland and knows that he can now land safely. His goal, however, is Paris. The use of dramatic paintings makes this story of courage inspirational.*

GRADE LEVELS: **4–5**

MATHEMATICS STANDARDS ADDRESSED: data analysis and probability—represent data; representation—model and interpret mathematical phenomena

---

SOCIAL STUDIES STANDARDS ADDRESSED: geography—draw maps as representations of places, physical features, and objects; determining location and direction

---

LANGUAGE ARTS EXPERIENCE: writing (learning log)

OBJECTIVES: to graph ordered pairs, to demonstrate that a pair of numbers describes the location of a point, to use number pairs to make coordinate graphs, to use directional words

---

KEY CONCEPTS: coordinates, graphing/naming ordered pairs for points on a grid; map reading, understanding grids, reviewing conventions of ordered pairs, using ordered pairs to draw figures

---

MATERIALS: centimeter grid paper, rulers, masking tape or sidewalk chalk, index cards, map of the world or globe, learning log

---

Procedure   SHARING THE BOOK

1. After reading the book, ask the students what Charles Lindbergh did that made history, and whether anyone else had done it before.

2. Locate Long Island, New York, and Paris, France, on the map. Engage the students in a book discussion by asking questions like the following:

   a. How many miles is it between New York and Paris?

   b. Charles Lindbergh flew across what ocean?

   c. How long did it take him?

   d. Who was going to fly with him?

   e. What tools did he have on board to help him during his flight? How did they help him?

   f. Do airplanes fly this same route today? How long does it take now?

   g. What was the name of Mr. Lindbergh's airplane? What nicknames did he have? How did he get this nickname?

   h. In his diary, how did he describe icebergs?

i. What were the difficulties that Charles Lindbergh faced to complete his solo flight? How did he overcome them?

j. What did Charles Lindbergh use to know whether he was on course?

k. What did the newspaper headlines say? How long did he go without sleep? Have you ever gone without sleep for a long time? If so, how did it make you feel?

PROMOTING CONCEPTS

1. Begin the lesson by having the students provide examples of people who use maps and grids (e.g., designers, truck drivers, air traffic controllers, and pilots).

2. Locate the Prime Meridian on the world map or globe. Did Charles Lindbergh cross the Prime Meridian? Have the students use directional words (*north, south, east, west*) to describe Charles Lindbergh's flight from New York to Paris.

3. Review the conventions of ordered pairs to help students recall that the first number tells how many lines to count across from zero and the second number tells how many lines to count up. You can use a pair of numbers to describe the location of a point. The numbers in the pair are called *coordinates.* Start at zero and go *right* as many units as the first number. Then, go *up* as many units as the second number and mark the point.

4. Create a life-size grid on the classroom floor using masking tape or go outside on the playground and use sidewalk chalk. Label the origin (0,0) and the x-axis and y-axis to approximately 6 or 7.

5. Give each student an index card with an ordered pair recorded on it, such as (2,5), (4,5), (4,1), (2,1), (1,3), (2,2), (5,2), (3,3), (4,3), etc.

6. Starting at (0,0) on the life-size grid, have each student, one at a time, walk the appropriate number of units to the right for the first number and then walk the appropriate number of units up for the second number. Remind students to always start at (0,0); it is the first point on the graph.

7. For students having difficulty, have them label their ordered pair with an arrow going right ⟶ for the first coordinate and an arrow going up ↑ for the second.

8. Ask a student to stand on a point in the grid; the rest of the class should record the ordered pair. Do this several times. Use (1,4), (2,1), (4,4), (3,2), etc.

9. Ask a student to restate the rules for using a number pair to identify points on a graph.

10. Have two students walk off the coordinates (2,4) and (4,2). Have the class observe closely and explain the importance of order.

Assessment

1. *Writing:* In their learning logs, have students explain why the order of the numbers in the ordered pair is so important. Show an example of what would happen if the numbers in an ordered pair are switched.

2. *Performance:* Using centimeter grid paper, have each student create a simple "Connect the Dots" picture for a classmate to complete (e.g., a pentagon using five number pairs for the points). Have the students exchange and complete each other's puzzles.

Making Connections

Explore similar figures on a grid; second, third, and fourth quadrants; using models to solve problems; create quadrilaterals using coordinates for each vertex.

OTHER BOOKS

Amelia and Eleanor Go for a Ride: Based on a True Story, Pam Munoz Ryan, Brian Selznick (Illus.) (1999)

The Fly on the Ceiling, Julie Glass, Richard Walz (Illus.) (1998).

Girls Think of Everything: Stories of Ingenious Inventions by Women, Catherine Thimmesh, Melissa Sweet (Illus.) (2000)

Mapping Penny's World, Loreen Leedy (2003)

Talking About Bessie: The Story of Aviator Elizabeth Coleman, Nikki Grimes (2002)

When Marian Sang: The True Recital of Marian Anderson, Pam Munoz Ryan, Brian Selznick (Illus.) (2002)

WEBSITES

www.acepilots.com

www.charleslindbergh.com

www.charleslindbergh.org

www.ibiscom.com/volindbergh.htm

www.lindberghfoundation.org

www.pbs.org (search for "Charles Lindbergh")

www.time.com (search for "Charles Lindbergh")

Starry Messenger

Peter Sis

In this Caldecott Honor book, Peter Sis shares extraordinary life stories of Galileo Galilei, the genius who changed the way we see the universe and who is now considered to be the first modern astronomer. Galileo's fascination with the stars, his persistence to study the object of his fascination, and his courage to stand for what he considered to be the truth all make him a great subject for this biography. The stories in the book reveal a passionate scientist, Galileo.

GRADE LEVELS: **4–5**

SCIENCE STANDARD ADDRESSED: earth and space science—Earth and other planets in the solar system

LANGUAGE ARTS EXPERIENCES: free writing, learning log

LITERACY CONNECTIONS: predicting, making connections

OBJECTIVES: to understand the vastness of the universe, to discover the distances between the objects in the universe, to create a scale model of the solar system

KEY CONCEPTS: universe, planets, space missions

MATERIALS: Pass It On Activity form (Appendix A.24), Internet, several pieces of paper, one roll of toilet paper, one ruler, one pair of scissors, one calculator, access to a long hallway or outdoor space, and one set of planet printouts and one table of distances of the planets, both downloaded from http://cse.ssl. berkeley.edu/AtHomeAstronomy/activity_10.html, Exploration sheet (Appendix A.27), learning logs

Procedure

SHARING THE BOOK

1. To activate prior knowledge, begin with the Pass It On strategy (Stephens & Brown, 2004) (see Exhibit 8.7 and Appendix 8.24). First, put students in small groups of 3 or 4. Using the word "universe" and whatever the students may know about the universe (e.g., facts, portrayals in books and media, their own observations), they should write quickly for about a minute. When done, they pass the papers to another group member who continues writing from where the first author left off. Pass the papers 3 or 4 times. When finished, the papers are passed back to the original authors. In the small group or with the whole class, share the papers generated about the universe.

2. Read the book. Have students discuss how Galileo transformed the way we think about Earth and the universe.

PROMOTING CONCEPTS

1. Among the many things that Galileo accomplished, the book talks about his discovery of "stars" (we now know them to be moons or satellites) of Jupiter. Collectively, they are called Galilean moons. More information about Jupiter can be found at www.kidscosmos.org/kid-stuff/Jupiter-facts.html or in Seymour Simon's *Jupiter* (1985). Discuss some of the interesting things learned about Jupiter and its moons. For example, did the students know that after Galileo discovered the four moons—Io, Europa, Ganymede, and Callisto—in 1610, it

EXHIBIT 8.7 Pass It On strategy using "Universe."

Pass It On Strategy Using "Universe"

Name _____ Date _____

Write as much as you can about "universe."
What do you know about it? How do you know about it?

The moon looks a little different every day. Its shape changes.	By looking at the sky.
The sun can only be seen during the daytime.	By looking at the sky.
The sun, moon, and stars move slowly across the sky.	By watching the sky.

Pass this on to a friend.

Respond to the writing above.

Sometimes the moon's shape is whole and filled-up with light.

Sometimes the moon can be seen during the day.

The sky looks different during the day, than it does at night.

Pass this on to a friend.   [Teacher: allow enough spaces for the number of responses you wish to get.]

was not until 1892 that the next satellite was discovered? Ask the students for their thoughts on why it took so long.

2. Not surprisingly, NASA named the spacecraft launched to study Jupiter and its moons *Galileo* and the entire mission The Galileo Project. The website www2.jpl.nasa.gov/Galileo and links on the site describe in detail this ambitious NASA project. One of the interesting facts from the project description is that the space shuttle *Atlantis*, carrying Galileo in its payload bay, left Earth on October 18, 1989, from Cape Canaveral, Florida. However, Galileo did not arrive at Jupiter until December 1995. What does this mean? Why did Galileo take more than six years to reach its destination?

3. The website http://cse.ssl.berkeley.edu/AtHome Astronomy/activity_10.html has an activity to explore the distances between planets in the solar system. A scale model of the solar system can be built using the table of distances of the planets provided on the website and sheets of toilet paper. First, have the students predict the distances and tape the planets along the hallway. Then, using the distance table, place the planets in scale. The students should complete the journal entry items in the Assessment section below either individually or in small groups after the model is complete and share their responses with the class.

4. Check out www.jpl.nasa.gov/solar_system/index.cfm for other NASA missions throughout the solar system.

Assessment

1. *Performance:* Have each student create a scale model of the solar system.
2. *Writing:* Have each student describe the distance from Earth to other planets (see Appendix A.27).
3. *Writing:* Have students write a paragraph in their learning logs reflecting on the vastness of the universe.

Making Connections

OTHER CONCEPTS

Light years, galaxies, gravity.

OTHER BOOKS

Jupiter, Seymour Simon (1985)

The Magic School Bus: Lost in the Solar System, Joanna Cole, Bruce Degen (Illus.) (1990)

The Universe, Seymour Simon (1998)

WEBSITES

http://cse.ssl.berkeley.edu/AtHomeAstronomy/activity_10.html

http://planetquest.jpl.nasa.gov/

www.exploratorium.edu/ronh/solar_system

www.jpl.nasa.gov/solar_system/index.cfm

www.kidscosmos.org/kid-stuff/jupiter-facts.html

www2.jpl.nasa.gov/galileo

www2.jpl.nasa.gov/galileo/jupiter/jupiter.html

The Summer Solstice

Ellen Jackson • Jan Davey Ellis, Illus.

The summer solstice symbolizes, both metaphorically and literally, the life source that the sun provides. Not surprisingly, the summer solstice continues to be celebrated around the world. The Summer Solstice documents the many ways people, past and present, acknowledge the sun and its power to sustain life for all living things. The stories of summer solstice celebrations, such as ancient Lithuanians rolling a blazing wheel down the hill into the river, are interesting and amusing. The book beautifully portrays the narrative and the scientific knowledge about the sun.

GRADE LEVELS: **4–5**

SCIENCE STANDARD ADDRESSED: earth and space science—changes in the Earth and sky

LANGUAGE ARTS EXPERIENCES: writing, vocabulary study

LITERACY CONNECTION: summarizing/synthesizing

OBJECTIVES: to demonstrate the Earth's movement that causes seasons, particularly how the tilting of the axis results in the summer solstice

KEY CONCEPTS: seasons, Earth's axis, Earth's rotation, equinox, solstice, hemisphere, equator

MATERIALS: skewers, oranges, flashlights, permanent markers, Equinox and Solstice Exploration sheet (Appendix A.28)

Procedure

SHARING THE BOOK

1. After reading the book, students in small groups of 3 or 4 should complete the Relay Summary (Saphier & Haley, 1993) by compiling a list of as many celebrations as they can. Each student in the small group contributes one response to the chart. Then, they return to the text to find examples (see Exhibit 8.8).

2. Ask students for their thoughts on why the summer solstice is celebrated around the world.

3. Engage the students in a discussion on how the sun sustains all living things on Earth.

EXHIBIT 8.8 Relay Summary chart for celebrations of the summer solstice.

CELEBRATIONS OF THE SUMMER SOLSTICE AROUND THE WORLD

WHO	HOW	ANCIENT OR MODERN
Carribean	Ships could sail off the world and into the sun	Ancient
Finland	Juhannus Day—dancing and singing outdoors	Modern
Great Britain	Bonfires—children allowed to stay up until dawn	Ancient

PROMOTING CONCEPTS

1. As illustrated in the book, demonstrate the change of seasons using an orange on a skewer and a flashlight. A variation is to mark the equator and the United States on the orange with a marker.

2. As the demonstration progresses, ask students to notice the amount of light the orange captures as it is both tilted on its axis and rotated. How does varying the two movements impact

how much sunlight a certain spot gets and how long the sunlight remains on the spot? Discuss the reversal of seasons in the two hemispheres, and that locations near the equator always receive the most sunlight.

3. Define *equinoxes* and *solstices* for the students. Or using sources provided, the students can compose their own definitions.

4. Students can speculate on the positions of the Earth in relation to the sun that result in solstices and equinoxes. In small groups, students can use their own oranges and flashlights to find their answers. Have them record their predictions and observations on the Equinox and Solstice Exploration sheet in Appendix A.28.

5. Ask the students to share their findings by discussing how they came up with their answers and demonstrating them with the oranges. Did the groups have similar responses?

Assessment

1. *Performance:* The students complete all the Equinox and Solstice Exploration sheet (Appendix A.28).

2. *Performance:* The students demonstrate, with oranges and flashlight, seasons, solstices, and equinoxes.

Making Connections

OTHER CONCEPTS

Latitudes, solar system, weather, climate.

OTHER BOOKS

The Autumn Equinox: Celebrating the Harvest, Ellen Jackson, Jan Davey Ellis (Illus.) (2000)

Celebrate the Solstice: Honoring the Earth's Seasonal Rhythms Through Festival and Ceremony, Richard W. Heinberg (1993)

The Return of the Light: Twelve Tales from Around the World for the Winter Solstice, Carolyn McVickar Edwards (2000)

A Solstice Tree for Jenny, Karen Shragg, Heidi Schwabacher (Illus.) (2001)

The Spring Equinox: Celebrating the Greening of the Earth, Ellen Jackson, Jan Davey Ellis (Illus.) (2001)

The Winter Solstice, Ellen Jackson, Jan Davey Ellis (Illus.) (1997)

WEBSITES

http://scienceworld.wolfram.com/astronomy/SummerSolstice.html

http://solar.physics.montana.edu/YPOP/Classroom/Lessons/Sundials/summer.html

www.religioustolerance.org/summer_solstice.htm

www.teachnet.com/lesson/seasonal/solstice061899.html

8.9

The Waterfall's Gift

Joanne Ryder • **Richard Jesse Watson, Illus.**

More than anything else, this Sierra Club book is about the reverence we feel—or should feel—for nature. With her mother and grandmother, a girl journeys northward to a small cabin built by her grandfather many years ago. As she walks through the woods to her "secret place," a waterfall she once shared with her grandfather, she remembers his words: "The old north woods hides treasure in its deepest places." Through lively, vivid illustrations, many treasures are revealed in this poignant story about a wonderfully wooded habitat and a girl's memory of her grandfather.

GRADE LEVELS: **4–5**

SCIENCE STANDARD ADDRESSED: life sciences—organisms and environment

---

LANGUAGE ARTS EXPERIENCE: expository/narrative writing

OBJECTIVE: to investigate the meaning of habitat by collecting and analyzing data

---

KEY CONCEPTS: habitats must have food, water, shelter, and air to sustain life

---

MATERIALS: drawing papers, crayons or markers, string (approximately 30 inches per student), magnifying glasses, poster charts

---

Procedure

SHARING THE BOOK

1. Before reading, review with students the necessities for sustaining life. Discuss our need for food, water, and shelter. What is meant by the word *shelter*? Is a home a shelter? What do we expect from a home (e.g., protection from cold, rain, harm)?

2. Share the two-page illustration (on pages 9–10) and have students explain what living things they see. Have them name at least 10 different living things.

3. Share the illustration, on the first two pages, of the girl who appears to be packing. Is this girl in her *habitat*, that place where a plant or an animal naturally lives or where a person is ordinarily found? How do you know? What can the students say about the girl from this illustration? Call attention to the flowers, pine cones, acorns, birch bark, and the picture of her grandfather. Ask the students whether they think this girl has an appreciation of things found in nature. Ask them how they know this.

4. Read the first paragraph of the story. Engage the students in a discussion of what Grandpa meant when he said "The old north woods hides treasure in its deepest places."

5. Read the story and ask students to remember the living things mentioned or pictured in the book.

PROMOTING CONCEPTS

1. Have students read and discuss the book in small groups, paying particular attention to the illustrations, and identifying the plants and animals in them.

2. This book shows that the girl has an understanding of the "north woods." Have the students explain what the girl means when she says, "We share the cabin with small ones who share the woods with us all."

3. Have students determine how many living things exist in this habitat called the "north woods." There are at least 30 (hawks, mice, squirrels, many kinds of birds, bear, caterpillars, deer, raccoons, pheasants, otters, lizards, butterflies, rabbits, worms, mushrooms, berries, crickets, spiders, fox, bushes, weeds, bees, frogs, several kinds of trees, several kinds of flowers, etc.). Then, have them discuss the reasons why the north woods provides a good habitat for all the animals and plants pictured in the illustrations.

4. Discuss the idea of multiple habitats (e.g., zoos, bird cages, fish tanks of various types) and why we have them. Are habitats necessary for all animals and plants—even for those that are nearing extinction?

5. Take students on a walking field trip on the school grounds or to a park nearby. Using string, have each student create a closed figure (e.g., circle, square, oval) on the ground in a grassy area. Then, each should generate a list of all things, both living and nonliving, within that space. They may use the magnifying glasses to examine things closely.

6. Create a class list of all things found during the walking field trip. Next, classify the items and create categories. Have the students decide on and define the categories. For example, they may begin with the broad categories of living and nonliving things. Have the students think about how these categories should be further divided. Examples of subcategories may be living vs. nonliving plants, broad leaf vs. needles, prickly vs. smooth, or colors and texture. Nonliving things can be classified by whether they are biodegradable, or human created vs. naturally occurring.

7. Based on the collection of data from their walking field trip, students should write a brief expository or narrative story and create illustrations about the habitat they just experienced.

Assessment

1. *Performance*: Students' illustrations of the "north woods."
2. *Performance*: Students' stories and illustrations of the habitat from the class walking field trip.

Making Connections

OTHER CONCEPTS

Habitats within the students' geographic region, matching habitats to geographic areas in the United States; habitats in other parts of the world; balance of living things within a habitat (food chain).

OTHER BOOKS	WEBSITES
One Day in the Woods, Jean Craighead George (1995)	http://birdwebsite.com/backyard.htm
Plantzilla, Geraldine Nolan (2002)	www.birdsforever.com/habitat.html
Pond, Gordon Morrison (2002)	www.fi.edu/fi/units/life/habitat/habitat.html
Prairie Dog, Dorothy Hinshaw Patent (1993)	www.nwf.org/backyardwildlifehabitat/
The Water Hole, Graeme Base (2001)	www.wildlifehc.org/
Who Lives in the Snow? Jennifer Barry Jones (2001)	

The Forest in the Clouds

Sneed B. Collard III • **Michael Rothman, Illus.**

In the forest in the clouds of Central America live thousands of different plants and trees, birds and animals, butterflies and insects. Because of the high mountains in the path of the trade winds blowing off the Caribbean Sea, clouds form when the moisture in the warm air becomes cooler as it blows high over the mountains. The clouds provide the moist air and rain necessary for all of the plant and animal life found in the mountains. This book describes the remarkable cloud forest ecology of Monteverde, Costa Rica. From Collard's vivid descriptions and the colorful illustrations, readers learn about varieties of hummingbirds, butterflies, frogs, and even birds that can swallow whole avocados. He discusses predators and animals of prey, and he takes you into a 100-foot fig tree to discover "air plants" or epiphytes, plants that live on other plants without harming the host. This is an excellent introduction to the special ecology of lush, high-mountain rain forests.

GRADE LEVELS:	**4–5**
SCIENCE STANDARD ADDRESSED:	life sciences—organisms and environments
LANGUAGE ARTS EXPERIENCES:	writing (learning log), concept mapping
OBJECTIVES:	to explain the relationship of one organism to another, to describe how organisms rely on the environment, to explore how organisms interact with each other to sustain life in a given environment
KEY CONCEPTS:	ecology to support life, food cycle, food web
MATERIALS:	large poster charts, markers, print and Internet resources about the rain forest

Procedure

SHARING THE BOOK

1. Discuss the relationship between living things and their environment. Have students provide some examples of how humans adapt to their environments. After some discussion, inform students that the relationship between living things and their environment is called *ecology.*

2. Ask students to name some of the things (e.g., food or nutrients, water, air) that are necessary to sustain life. Again, discuss the relationship of living things to their environment.

3. Tell students that you are going to share information about a special place in Central America that has a rather peculiar *ecosystem*. Ask them to note the different kinds of living things mentioned as you read the book.

PROMOTING CONCEPTS

1. After reading, discuss the relationships that exist among the following: birds, moths, grasshoppers, trees, clouds, soil, and the air. Ask if they can name other things that the creatures that inhabit the Monteverde Rain Forest use for food.

2. On a large poster chart, begin a concept map by listing living and nonliving examples mentioned in the book. Discuss how these living and nonliving things may be classified (e.g., animals and plants, birds, insects, flowering plants, epiphytes).

3. Once most living and nonliving things are classified and recorded, begin talking about the relationships among these organisms and nonliving things that exist for survival. For example, the relationship between the clouds and the plants, the relationship between plants and animals. Specifically, what is the relationship between a fig tree and an epiphyte? Between flowering plants and butterflies? What is eaten by what? Draw lines between the organisms with such relationships. You should end up with a messy web and many opportunities to engage the students in meaningful discussions about the key concepts.

4. Students can engage in individual or small group research to further investigate a particular relationship identified during the lesson.

Assessment

1. *Performance:* Create a concept map of living things, drawing lines between organisms that require each other for existence.

2. *Writing:* Write about one organism's relationship to another. For example, what does the rain forest provide for the hummingbird that sustains life? What would happen to the hummingbird in the Antarctic?

Making Connections

OTHER CONCEPTS

Organisms in other ecosystems, changes in the environment caused by organisms, impacts of humans on various environments around the world.

OTHER BOOKS

At Home in the Rainforest, Diane Willow, Laura Jacques (Illus.) (1992)

The Great Kapok Tree: A Tale of the Amazon Rain Forest, Lynne Cherry (1990)

The Most Beautiful Roof in the World: Exploring the Rainforest Canopy, Kathryn Lasky (1997)

Nature's Green Umbrella, Gail Gibbons (1997)

A Walk in the Rainforest, Kristin Joy Pratt-Serafini, Kristin Joy Pratt (Illus.) (1992)

WEBSITES

www.monteverdeinfo.com
www.ran.org/
www.wri.org/wri/

The Great Kapok Tree

A TALE OF THE AMAZON RAIN FOREST • **Lynne Cherry**

"Two men walked into the rain forest. Moments before, the forest had been alive with the sounds of squawking birds and howling monkeys. Now all was quiet as the creatures watched the two men and wondered why they had come." So begins this story of the animals in the Amazon rain forest. One by one, the animals whisper to the man with an ax, asleep while taking a break from chopping the great Kapok tree, about how they need the tree for their survival. A boa constrictor, a bee, monkeys, a set of exotic birds, tree frogs, and more plead to the man: "Señor, a ruined rain forest means ruined lives . . . many ruined lives. You will leave many of us homeless if you chop down this great Kapok tree." Cherry also provides a two-page informational spread with the many animals that make the rain forest their home, a map of the world with past and present rain forests, and the structure of a rain forest.

GRADE LEVELS: **4–5**

SCIENCE STANDARD ADDRESSED: life science—organisms and environments

LANGUAGE ARTS EXPERIENCES: narrative/expository writing, visual expression

LITERACY CONNECTIONS: evaluating, questioning

OBJECTIVES: to describe the rain forest as an ecosystem and name its components

KEY CONCEPTS: ecosystem, habitat, conservation, rain forest

MATERIALS: Inquiry Chart (Appendix A.14), reference and resource materials on rain forests, access to the Internet, drawing paper, bulletin board paper

Procedure

SHARING THE BOOK

1. Before reading, activate students' prior knowledge with such questions as: What do you know about the rain forest? What do you know about the Amazon rain forest? What animals do you know that make the rain forest their habitat? What animals do you see in the cover illustrations? What may be the consequences of deforestation of the rain forest?

2. During and after reading, ask, "What do the animals suggest as the possible consequences of deforestation in the story?"

PROMOTING CONCEPTS

1. The Inquiry Chart (Appendix A.14) is used as the post-reading activity. An Inquiry Chart allows the students' genuine questions about a specific topic to guide their learning. Using a chart of guiding questions and knowledge gathered from multiple sources of information gives students the opportunity to study a topic in depth and from potentially differing points of view. The Inquiry Chart can be completed individually, in small groups, or collectively as a whole class.

2. First, identify the topic from the book. Some suggested topics include rain forest or any other ecosystem around the world, a particular animal that uses the rain forest as its habitat, and deforestation.

3. After identifying the topic, have the students formulate some good guiding questions that they can use to gather information. For example, for deforestation, "What is the rate of deforestation in the rain forests around the world?" or "What are some reasons for deforestation?" may work as meaningful guiding questions.

4. Students can collect materials and resources such as informational books, textbooks, encyclopedias, and Internet sources that provide answers to their questions. If the whole class uses the same set of guiding questions, provide a set of resources for students to use.

5. Explore students' prior knowledge of the guiding questions and record students' responses in the "What We Know" row of the Inquiry Chart.

6. Read and record the information gathered from the research of the guiding questions.

7. Interesting facts and figures and new questions derived from students' research should be added to the chart.

8. Share the findings by summarizing each guiding question. The sharing can take other forms such as research papers, projects, multimedia presentations, fiction or nonfiction stories, and social action.

9. Continue the research to find answers to the new questions using additional rounds of Inquiry Charts.

Assessment

1. *Performance:* Complete an Inquiry Chart and other forms for final presentation and sharing.

2. *Performance:* Illustrate the rain forest and label all of its components using the Inquiry Chart.

3. *Performance:* Create a classroom mural of the rain forest using bulletin board paper. Have different groups of students responsible for illustrating specific components using the Inquiry Chart.

Making Connections

OTHER CONCEPTS

Life cycles, specific animal habits, ecosystems around the world.

OTHER BOOKS

Just a Dream, Chris Van Allsburg (1990)

Keeper of the Swamp, Ann Garrett, Karen Chandler (Illus.) (1999)

The Lorax, Dr. Seuss (1971)

The Water Hole, Graeme Base (2001)

WEBSITES

www.rainforest-alliance.org/

www.ran.org/

www.ran.org/rainforestheroes

8.12 LESSON

Keeper of the Swamp

Ann Garrett • **Karen Chandler, Illus.**

A boy has been waiting for this day, the day that his grandfather will finally let him feed Ole Boots. Grandfather has been the keeper of the swamp and Ole Boots, an alligator that he rescued and raised after its mother was killed by poachers. The special bond between a fragile, ailing man and a fierce creature of the swamp is deeply understood by the boy, who will eventually take on the responsibility of keeping the swamp. The nearly photographic illustrations of the freshwater swamp of the Louisiana Bayou are breathtakingly vivid and alive. Hidden among the pages are the wondrous creatures of the swamp. Keeper of the Swamp ultimately illustrates the beauty of the relationships among the environment, the creatures within, and the man.

GRADE LEVELS: **4–5**

SCIENCE STANDARD ADDRESSED: life science—organisms and environments

LANGUAGE ARTS EXPERIENCES: brainstorming, letter writing, learning log

LITERACY CONNECTION: predicting/inferring

ARTS CONNECTION: drawing

OBJECTIVES: to explore the impact humans have on the swamp and other environments and their organisms, to research organisms in a swamp and other environments using websites

KEY CONCEPTS: ecosystem, habitat, conservation

MATERIALS: Talking Drawings sheet (Appendix A.29), Internet, print resources about animals, learning logs

Procedure

SHARING THE BOOK

1. Before reading the book, use the Talking Drawings strategy (Appendix A.29) to activate students' prior knowledge about swamps. ("Talking Drawings" uses drawings to bridge prior knowledge to the target concept by asking students to visually represent what they know about a concept before it is taught and again after it is taught.) Have the students draw what they think a swamp might look like and include organisms/creatures that they think can be found in the swamp.

2. As the book is read, ask the students to notice and record the various organisms, both plants and animals, found in the book. What did they find?

3. Describe the swamp portrayed in the book. What are some characteristics of this environment?

4. Have students complete the Talking Drawings for post-reading. The "after" drawings serve not only as an opportunity for students to represent what they know after the lesson, but also as a useful assessment opportunity for the teacher.

1. Discuss the grandfather's very special role in this swamp by asking such questions as: What makes his role a special one? What may be some reasons why this man became the keeper of the swamp? What are poachers? What may be some reasons why they do what they do?

2. Humans seem to change environments in ways that can be either beneficial or detrimental to themselves and other organisms. As a whole class, brainstorm a list of examples that debate this issue. Check out www.saveour environment.org, the home page of A National Coalition for the Environment, for a list of environmental issues such as pollution, energy, clean water, and global warming.

3. Ask the students to identify some issues that they can help solve through active participation. Check out the various organizations that focus on environmental causes at www.saveourenvironment.org/about.html. Students can research a particular organization, find the ways the organization suggests for students to participate, and follow through on the action plan such as writing letters to legislators.

4. Based on the list of organisms from the Talking Drawings sheet, have small groups of students select one animal for an inquiry project that answers this question: What does the swamp provide the animal to sustain its life? Using the Internet and other resources about animals, have students conduct the research.

Assessment

1. *Learning log:* The students should describe in their learning logs the actions they can take to preserve the environment.

2. *Performance:* Use the Talking Drawings sheet to record prior knowledge and knowledge gained from research.

Making Connections

OTHER CONCEPTS

Life cycles, specific animal habits, ecosystems around the world.

OTHER BOOKS	WEBSITES
Marshes & Swamps, Gail Gibbons (1999)	www.epa.gov/owow/wetlands
Swamp, Donald M. Silver, Patricia J. Wynne (Illus.) (1997)	www.experienceneworleans.com/swamp.html
Wading into Wetlands, National Wildlife Federation (1997)	www.ran.org/rainforestheroes
Wild and Swampy, Jim Arnosky (2000)	www.saveourenvironment.org/

Prince William

Gloria Rand   •   **Ted Rand, Illus.**

This fictional account of a real-life oil spill provides excellent information about the harmful effects of human carelessness on our environment. An oil tanker crashes off the coast of Alaska, causing devastating effects. Through the eyes of a girl who rescues an oil-coated baby seal that she names Prince William, the reader learns about the threats of an oil spill to the wildlife on the coast of Alaska. Through tender, responsible human care, we see this seal nurtured to good health and returned to his natural habitat. We also learn about how oil spills are controlled and see the efforts of dedicated workers who clean and nourish other animals and birds back to good health.

GRADE LEVELS: **4–5**

SCIENCE STANDARD ADDRESSED: life science—organisms and environments

SOCIAL STUDIES STANDARD ADDRESSED: people, places, and environments—human effects on the environment

LANGUAGE ARTS EXPERIENCES: vocabulary study, learning log, expository writing

OBJECTIVES: to explore the effects of an oil spill on the environment, to explore the positive and negative effects that humans have on the environment

KEY CONCEPTS: oil spill, environment, habitat, pollution, poison, containment, disposal site, habitat destruction, renewable and nonrenewable resources

MATERIALS: clear bottle of water tinted with blue food coloring, cooking oil mixed with black tempura paint, cork or toy boat, cotton balls, paper towels and other clean-up materials, learning logs

Procedure

SHARING THE BOOK

1. Discuss the concepts *environment* and *habitat*. Talk about threats to the environment and the harm to living things that may be caused by *poison* and *pollution*.

2. Share a newspaper article or an Internet story about the 1989 *Exxon Valdez* oil spill in Alaska. Ask students what they know about the story (or other man-made disaster stories about damaging the environment).

3. Hold up a copy of the book and tell students that the story is about environmental pollution. Ask students to predict what they think the book is about.

4. Read the story and define unknown words like *skiff, volunteers, murres, kittiwakes, incubator,* and *wilderness* as appropriate.

5. Give students an opportunity to share ideas and raise questions about the book.

PROMOTING CONCEPTS

1. Have students work in teams of three or four on the Internet activity found at www.gma.org/surfing/human/savethebay.html—"Save Casco Bay from an Oil Spill."

2. Fill a clear glass bottle with water and add blue food coloring to make the "ocean." Then, pour one-half inch or more of cooking oil into the bottle to make the "oil spill." Have students observe where the oil congregates, what happens to an object (such as a cork) dropped into the bottle, and what happens to the oil. Ask what would happen to organisms that float on the surface. Explain that over time the water and oil mix somewhat, and some of the oil will sink to the bottom of the ocean.

3. Next, have students try to clean up the oil spill before the oil pollutes the water and harms the animals. Have groups of students use whatever materials they think will clean the oil from the top of the ocean. Students should try the materials and record their results.

4. Have students relate their findings to the story. Explain to them that an oil spill may release thousands of gallons of crude oil into the water, and the magnitude of the clean-up requires enormous human resources.

5. In groups of two or three, have students identify pollution or environmental threats in their community. Have them identify the cause and the likely harmful effect. Some expected answers might be automobile and truck exhaust that causes lung damage (and cancer), crop fertilizer that may wash into rivers and streams and find its way into drinking water, pollutants from garbage and waste that may also wash into streams and poison drinking water, smoking cigarettes and other tobacco products, and flushing used motor oil (cleaning fluids, nail polish remover, etc.) down the drain.

Assessment

1. *Writing:* The students should respond to the following questions in their learning logs: Why is it unwise to pour the unused portion of fingernail polish remover down the drain? Why should we be concerned about the exhaust fumes from automobiles, trucks, and diesel farm tractors?

2. *Writing:* Individually, the students should write a brief paragraph about how they will help maintain a clean and healthy environment based on their observations of how an oil spill impacts the environment.

3. *Writing:* Have the students write a story from the point of view of an animal that was affected by the oil spill. The story should detail how the animal was helped.

Making Connections

OTHER CONCEPTS

Exxon Valdez oil spill, other major oil spills, interdependence of living organisms in an ecosystem.

OTHER BOOKS

Chattanooga Sludge, Molly Garrett Bang (1996)

The Great Kapok Tree: A Tale of the Amazon Rain Forest, Lynne Cherry (1990)

J. Rooker, Manatee, Jan Haley (1996)

Maya and the Town That Loved a Tree, Kathryn Shaw, Kiki (Illus.) (1992)

The Shape of Betts Meadow, Meghan Nuttall Sayres, Joanne Friar (Illus.) (2002)

They Came from the Bronx: How the Buffalo Were Saved from Extinction, Neil Waldman (2001)

Wildfires, Seymour Simon (2000)

WEBSITES

http://projects.edtech.sandi.net/oceanpollution

www.gma.org/surfing/human/savethebay.html

8.14

LESSON

Henry's Freedom Box

A TRUE STORY FROM THE UNDERGROUND RAILROAD • **Ellen Levine** • **Kadir Nelson, Illus.**

Henry dreams of a life where he is allowed to celebrate his birthday. Henry's heart longs to be freed by his master; he is a slave. As a young child he is separated from his mother, and then later, as an adult, he is separated from his wife and children. In desperation for the free life that he longs for, Henry mails himself in a wooden crate to a place where there are no slaves. Henry traveled by horse-drawn cart, steamboat, and train. Then, after a harrowing journey of 350 miles and 27 hours, Henry arrives safely in Philadelphia, Pennsylvania. At last he has a birthday—March 30, 1849, his first day of freedom—and he also has a middle name, Henry "Box" Brown. Illustrations are muted soft colors that match the somber mood of this true story about one of the most famous runaway slaves who traveled on the Underground Railroad.

GRADE LEVELS: **4–5**

MATHEMATICS STANDARDS ADDRESSED: measurement, estimation

SOCIAL STUDIES STANDARDS: power, authority, and governance—time, continuity, and change; geography

LANGUAGE ARTS EXPERIENCES: expository writing, learning log

OBJECTIVES: to explore and estimate the length, width, height, and weight of boxes; to introduce the Underground Railroad

KEY CONCEPTS: Underground Railroad; slavery; estimating length, width, height, and weight; map reading

MATERIALS: map of the United States, an assortment of boxes (approximately 4–6; for example, shoe boxes, brown corrugated boxes for shipping), measuring tapes (standard or metric), scale, access to zip codes, Estimating the Measurement of Boxes Exploration (Appendix A.30), learning logs

Procedure

SHARING THE BOOK

1. Before reading the story, share the title of the book and guide the students in a discussion of the Underground Railroad. (*It was "underground" in the sense that it was a secretive anti-slavery movement or network of people. The railroad consisted of safe routes and meeting houses; it was not literally underground.*)

2. Define slavery. (*Certain people are deprived of their freedom, owned as property, and forced to work.*)

3. Have the students locate Richmond, Virginia (where Henry's journey began) and Philadelphia, Pennsylvania (where Henry's journey ended) on the map of the United States.

4. After reading the book, ask the students if they would mail themselves in a box, like Henry, in order to be free?

5. Describe Henry's life. Ask them how that makes them feel.

6. Describe Henry's journey. Where did it begin? Where was his destination? What did he take with him on his journey?

PROMOTING CONCEPTS

1. After reading the book, set up boxes (approximately 4 to 6) around the classroom in stations. Select one of the boxes and guide the students through an estimation of its length, width, height, and weight. As a class, use measuring tape to determine the actual length, width, height, and a scale to determine weight for the selected box. This can be recorded in Box Number 1 on Appendix A.30—Estimating the Measurement of Boxes Exploration.

2. After estimating and determining the actual measurements of the selected box as a class, have the students go to the stations to estimate the length, width, height, and weight of the remaining boxes. Then have them determine the actual length, width, height, and weight for each of the boxes. They can use Appendix A.30 to record the information.

3. Encourage the students to create a benchmark or referent for themselves. For example, if the class is using the metric system, the width of a student's pinky finger is about 1 centimeter and the width of a palm is about 1 decimeter. If using the standard system, the width of a student's three middle fingers is about 1 inch and the span from thumb to pinky finger is about 6 inches. Have the students share their estimates and their strategies for determining their estimates with the class. Benchmarks/referents that the students find useful can be recorded on a class chart.

4. Next, in cooperative groups, choose one box from the stations and ask the students to decide its origin including the zip code (or select the town where they live or the school address as the origin of the box). In their group, then decide the destination of the box including the zip code (go to www.zip-code-database.org to look up zip codes). Locate the destination of the box on the U.S. map.

5. In conclusion, ask the students, "If you could mail yourself in a box, where would your destination be? Why?" Discuss the different destinations. Locate the destinations on the U.S. map. Estimate the size of the box needed.

Assessment

1. *Performance*: Complete the form "Estimating the Measurement of Boxes Exploration" (Appendix A.30). Encourage the students to share their benchmarks for estimating length, width, height, and weight.

2. *Writing*: If you could mail yourself in a box, where would your destination be? Have students write a paragraph to explain why they selected this destination. Illustrate on a map the origin and the destination. Estimate how much it would cost to mail oneself in a box.

3. *Learning log*: Have students describe in their learning logs the actions they would take to help the slaves if they had lived during that time.

4. *Questioning*: Questioning is a way of teaching that actively invites students to convey what they are thinking. As discussed in Chapter 5, **probing questions** are a teaching/assessment strategy that provides insight into the mental processes students use by engaging them in conversation about the subject. Following are sample probing questions for measurement to use with this lesson:
   - How did you estimate the length (or height or width)?
   - What strategy did you use?
   - Have you used this estimation strategy before?

- Can you show us how you did that?
- What benchmarks or referents are you using for the length (or height or width)?
- How are you estimating the weight?
- What is your benchmark or referent for the weight?
- Could you do it another way?

Making Connections

OTHER CONCEPTS

Plantation, fugitive slave, American Civil War, Thirteenth Amendment, abolitionism, emancipation, volume, capacity.

OTHER BOOKS

An Apple for Harriet Tubman, Glennette Tilley Turner, Susan Keeter (Illus.) (2006)

Barefoot: Escape from the Underground Railroad, Pamela Duncan Edwards, Henry Cole (Illus.) (1999)

Elijah Buxton, Christopher Paul Curtis (2007)

The Escape of Oney Judge, Emily Arnold McCully (2007)

Feathers, Jacqueline Woodson (2007)

A Freedom River, Doreen Rappaport, Bryan Collier (Illus.) (2000)

Freedom Ship, Doreen Rappaport, Curtis James (Illus.) (2006)

Mailing May, Michael O. Tunnell, Ted Rand (Illus.) (1997)

The Secret to Freedom, Marcia Vaughan, Larry Johnson (Illus.) (2005)

Sweet Clara and the Freedom Quilt, Deborah Hopkinson, James Ransome (Illus.) (2003)

Under the Quilt of Night, Deborah Hopkinson, James E. Ransome (Illus.) (2005)

WEBSITES

http://images.library.uiuc.edu/projects/tdc/LessonPlans/UndergroundRailroad.html

www.atozteacherstuff.com/pages/450.shtml

www.greece.k12.ny.us/ath/library/webquests/underground/default.htm

www.nationalgeographic.com/railroad/index.html

www.nku.edu/~undergroundrr/lessonplans

www.songsforteaching.com/newlin/undergroundrailroadlesson.htm

www.the-ugrr.org

www.undergroundrailroadinc.org

www2.lhric.org/pocantico/tubman/tubman.html

Monday on the Mississippi

Marilyn Singer • **Frané Lessac, Illus.**

The legendary Mississippi River has many stories as it winds its way from its source at Lake Itasca, Minnesota, to its mouth into the Gulf of Mexico at its Louisiana delta. As the meandering and majestic river glides its way through cities and villages, farmlands and lakes, tales are told that are old and new. This journey down the river takes place all in a week's time. As the book describes the mighty Mississippi River flowing through ten states from beginning to end, historical information and maps are included. Lyrically written and illustrated with folk-art pictures, this book describes an exciting river journey and celebrates one of America's most renowned rivers.

GRADE LEVELS:	**4–5**
MATHEMATICS STANDARDS ADDRESSED:	measurement—ranking data shortest to longest
SOCIAL STUDIES STANDARDS ADDRESSED:	people, places, and environment—locate and distinguish landforms
LANGUAGE ARTS EXPERIENCES:	reading and writing legends, research skills
OBJECTIVES:	to order lengths from longest to shortest, to collect data for a spreadsheet, to interpret data, to describe parts of a river
KEY CONCEPTS:	how rivers are formed, factors that affect the formation of rivers, length of rivers, rivers' origin and mouth
MATERIALS:	one large as well as individual maps of the United States, map of the world or globe, Internet, encyclopedias, atlas (or other resources) for research, Exploration: Longest Rivers in the World (Appendix A.31), Ranking the Longest Rivers in the World (Appendix A.32)

Procedure   SHARING THE BOOK

1. Discuss the concept of *river*—a body of fresh water flowing from an upland source to a large lake or to the sea. Define *origin* (the source of the river) and *mouth* (the lowest point to which it can flow) of a river.
2. Other words to define: *tributary, drainage basin,* and *confluence* as appropriate.
3. Discuss the differences among lakes (a large body of water surrounded by land), streams (flowing body of water smaller than a river), and rivers.
4. Ask the students to identify what rivers are nearest geographically to where they live. Using a map, have the students locate the rivers.
5. Ask the students if they have ever gone for a walk or hike beside a river? Taken a boat ride on a river? Ridden over a river on a bridge? Share these experiences.
6. Ask the students to name other rivers in the United States. Locate the rivers on a map.
7. Locate the Mississippi River on the U.S. map. Read the story and then ask the students if they have visited any of the locations mentioned in the story.
8. Define the term *legend*. (*A legend is a narrative of human actions that are perceived both by teller and listeners to take place within human history and to possess certain qualities that give the tale the appearance of being real.*) Ask if

they have heard any "river legends" such as the adventures of Tom Sawyer or Huckleberry Finn.

PROMOTING CONCEPTS

1. After reading the story, use the U.S. map to follow the path of the Mississippi River, from its source in Minnesota to the Louisiana delta. Point out each of the ten different states and the major cities that the Mississippi River travels through.
2. Notice how towns and cities tend to be located next to rivers. Why? (*Rivers provide essential water for both small towns and large cities.*)
3. What are some nicknames for the Mississippi River? (*Big Muddy, Old Man River, The Father of Waters.*)
4. What is the longest river in the United States? (*Missouri*) How many miles long is it? The second longest river in the United States? (*Mississippi*) How many miles long is it? Locate the rivers on the map.
5. How do you measure the length of a river? (*Measuring a river is like taking a snapshot because rivers are in constant state of change.*)
6. Using the Exploration: Longest Rivers in the World (Appendix A.31), have the students work in pairs to research the longest and the second longest river on each continent.
7. Next, using the data collected during the previous exploration, have the students answer the questions on the Ranking the Longest Rivers in the World exploration (Appendix A.32). Encourage them to use the Internet, encyclopedias, an atlas, and other resources to help their research. One helpful website is http://ga.water.usgs.gov/edu/riversofworld.html.

Assessment

1. *Performance:* Using Appendix A.31, have each student rank the world's longest rivers in descending order from longest to shortest.
2. *Writing:* Have the students write their own river legend. Select any river and write a legend/tale that might have happened alongside the route of the river. Use the scoring rubric (Exhibit 8.9).

| EXHIBIT | 8.9 | Rubric for writing a legend. |

Name:				Date:	
SCORE	Outstanding	Excellent	Proficient	Developing	Emerging
CRITERIA					
Clear communication of the main idea, well developed	5	4	3	2	1
Organization	5	4	3	2	1
Sentence fluency	5	4	3	2	1
Descriptive vocabulary (when and where)	5	4	3	2	1
Clear statement of the problem facing the main character	5	4	3	2	1
Creativity	5	4	3	2	1
Mechanics/grammar/spelling	5	4	3	2	1

Making Connections

OTHER CONCEPTS

Conservation and preservation; measuring rivers; pollution (factories on rivers); flooding; levees, dikes, and dams; whitewater rafting; wildlife along rivers; water cycle; surface runoff; confluence; steam boats; Mark Twain.

OTHER BOOKS

The Amazon River (Rookie Read-About Geography), Mary Schulte (2006)

Letting Swift River Go, Jane Yolen (1995)

Liquid Locomotive: Legendary Whitewater River Stories, John Long (1999)

The Mississippi River (Rookie Read-About Geography), Allan Fowler (2000)

The Nile River (Rookie Read-About Geography), Allan Fowler (2000)

A River Ran Wild: An Environmental Story, Lynne Cherry (2002)

WEBSITES

http://en.wikipedia.org/wiki/River

http://42explore.com/rivers.htm

http://ga.water.usgs.gov/edu/earthrivers.html

http://ga.water.usgs.gov/edu/riversofworld.html

www.americanrivers.org/site/PageServer

www.answers.com/topic/river?cat=technology

www.experiencemississippiriver.com/home.cfm

www.firstpeople.us/FP-Html-Legends/HowtheFlySavedtheRiver

www.nationalgeographic.com/geographyaction/rivers/

www.socialstudiesforkids.com/articles/geography/longestriverstable.htm

8.16

LESSON

The First Marathon: The Legend of Pheidippides

Susan Reynolds • **Daniel Minter, Illus.**

Twenty-five-hundred years ago a boy named Pheidippides (Fi-DIP-uh-deez) lived in Athens, the largest city in Greece (then and now). All Greek boys were encouraged to be athletes, so Pheidippides ran for miles and miles and won many races. All Greek boys were also expected to join the army, so as a soldier Pheidippides served as a herald and ran to deliver messages for the generals. When a powerful army from Persia invaded Greece on the plain of Marathon, the generals sent Pheidippides to run from Athens to Sparta to get help. The journey from Athens to Sparta, up and down mountains, is 140 miles (driving on a modern highway would take two to three hours). Pheidippides ran for almost 36 hours without stopping. By law the Spartans could not send their army until there was a full moon, so Pheidippides ran back to share the sad news with the generals and then he marched with the army for 25 miles to the plain of Marathon for battle. After winning the battle against the Persians, once again Pheidippides ran 25 miles to Athens to share the news: "Rejoice! We have won!" Those final miles were more than his brave heart could take, and he died. Today Pheidippides is remembered as a Greek hero and to runners everywhere who run marathon races.

GRADE LEVELS:	**4–5**
MATHEMATICS STANDARD ADDRESSED:	measurement—the units, systems, and process of measurement
SOCIAL STUDIES STANDARDS ADDRESSED:	time, continuity, and change—stories about past events and people
LANGUAGE ARTS EXPERIENCES:	using metric vocabulary in place of well-known vocabulary in familiar expressions and everyday language, journaling
OBJECTIVES:	to measure everyday objects with metric tools; to use metric vocabulary; to establish referents for metric measurements; to develop meaning and feeling for the units through estimation; to identify people, places, and situations of the past
KEY CONCEPTS:	the metric system of measurement; linear metric units—centimeters, decimeters, meters, kilometers; marathon; herald; Greek history
MATERIALS:	classroom map of the world or globe, centimeter rulers, meter sticks, metric trundle wheel, yarn, an assortment of objects in the classroom, Metric Scavenger Hunt (Appendix A.33), Metric Vocabulary (Appendix A.34)

Procedure

SHARING THE BOOK

1. After reading the book, ask if any students like to run like Pheidippides. What is the greatest distance they have run? Where? Have any students or their parents run in races or in marathons? Where?

2. Are marathons still run today? Do you know the names of any marathons run today? (*New York City Marathon, Boston Marathon, San Francisco Marathon, etc.*)

3. Could the Athenian generals have contacted Sparta for help in any other way? Telephone? Telegraph? Cars? Computers? Other ideas? (*These technologies did not exist then.*)

4. Do you think Pheidippides is a hero? Why? What makes someone a hero?

5. Locate Greece on the map/globe. Then trace Pheidippides's route from Athens to Sparta. Describe for the students what life was like for Greek boys at this time in history.

6. What is the official distance of a modern-day marathon? (*26.2 miles*) Why? (*Because, during the 1908 Olympics in London, King Edward VII wanted the finish line to be in front of his royal box; the marathon was thus declared to be 26.2 miles. At the 1924 Paris Olympics, the marathon was officially declared to be 26.2 miles.*)

PROMOTING CONCEPTS

1. In Greece, do they measure a marathon in miles? (*No*) Why not? (*They use the metric system*) What percentage of the world uses the metric system? (*90%*)

2. How long is a marathon using the metric system? (*40 km*)

3. Show the students a centimeter ruler. Explain that a millimeter is a small unit for measuring length. Ask the students to find items in the classroom that are one millimeter (mm) in length, such as the width of a standard paper clip or the width of a pencil point. Then ask the students to find items in the classroom that are one centimeter (cm) in length, such as the width of a pencil, a fingernail, the light switch, and so on. Follow the same procedure with the decimeter (dm), finding items such as a note pad, the length of a crayon, palm/hand, and so on.

4. Next, give the students meter sticks and have them walk around the classroom and find items that are one meter (m) in length, such as the distance from a doorknob to the floor, height of the teacher's desk, the width of a table, etc. (If you do not have enough meter sticks, use a piece of yarn that is one meter in length.)

5. Use a trundle wheel or meter stick to map out 10 meters in the hallway or classroom (depending on space). How many times would you have to repeat this path to equal 100 meters? (*10 times*) To equal a kilometer (km)? (*100 times*) How many meters equal one kilometer? (*1,000 meters*) Kilometers are used for measuring greater distances, and students will use this unit of measurement in the future when reading maps.

6. Point out the important relationships between units within the metric system. (*1 km = 1,000 meters; 1 meter = 10 dm = 100 cm = 1,000 mm; 10 mm = 1 cm*)

7. Guide the students in establishing meaning and feeling for the units by focusing on estimating and creating a benchmark or referent. Encourage a personal benchmark; for example, a fingernail is about 1 cm. (Exact conversions between the metric and the customary U.S. system are not recommended. Focus on friendly and useful conversions.) Some suggestions include the following:
   - mm—width of a paperclip
   - cm—fingernail
   - dm—palm/hand/a slice of bread
   - m—length of a baseball bat
   - km—about 1/2 mile (select a local site)

8. Then, using the Metric Scavenger Hunt (Appendix A.33), have the students estimate and determine the actual measurement of the listed objects.

Assessment   1. *Performance:* Complete the Metric Scavenger Hunt (Appendix A.33).

2. *Performance:* Complete Metric Vocabulary (Appendix A.34).

3. *Writing:* Have students write a journal entry in which they compare and contrast the differences between finishing and winning a marathon. Which is more important to them? Why?

Making Connections

OTHER CONCEPTS

Greek history; Spartans; ancient Olympic Games; modern Olympic Games; running/exercise for good health; Olympic marathon; first women's Olympic marathon; half marathon; Ironman competition; the Boston Marathon; the New York City Marathon; other famous marathon runners; other types of marathons—dance, skating, etc.; marathon world record holders.

OTHER BOOKS

Athens Is Saved!: The First Marathon, Stewart Ross, Sue Shields (Illus.) (1997)

The Mystery on the Freedom Trail: The Boston Marathon Mystery, Carol Marsh (2003)

Pellie Runs a Marathon, Michelle Bredice Craemer, Elizabeth Lavin (Illus.) (2003)

Run, Dad, Run, Dulcibella Blackett, Andy Yelenak (Illus.) (2004)

See Mom Run, Carol Douglass Thom, Lilly Golden (Illus.) (2003)

WEBSITES

http://ctc.coin.org/marathon.html

http://en.wikipedia.org/wiki/Marathon

http://en.wikipedia.org/wiki/Pheidippides

www.helleniccomserve.com/olympicmarathon.html

www.helleniccomserve.com/pheidippides.html

www.marathonguide.com/

www.marathonguide.com/features/firstmarathons.cfm

www.olympic.org/uk/athletes/profiles/bio_uk.asp?PAR_I_ID=18263

8.17

Zachary Zormer Shape Transformer

A MATH ADVENTURE • **Joane Reisberg** • **David Hohn (Illus.)**

Friday is Zachary's favorite day at school because all the students bring to class something interesting to measure. Hmm ... but on this particular Friday Zachary forgot. What can he do with the scrap of paper in his pocket? Can you double the length of a strip of paper without cutting it? In this book Zachary creates three transformations out of scraps of paper. Zachary uses his imagination to create his projects and explains each of them while using mathematical terms and concepts. Zachary's projects are entertaining and explained at the end of the book for students to try on their own.

GRADE LEVELS: 4–5

MATHEMATICS STANDARD ADDRESSED: geometry—to apply transformations to analyze mathematical situations and spatial sense

SCIENCE STANDARD ADDRESSED: science as inquiry—ability to conduct a scientific inquiry

SOCIAL STUDIES STANDARD ADDRESSED: global connections—symbols used worldwide

LANGUAGE ARTS EXPERIENCES: shared and independent writing, retelling a story

OBJECTIVES: to create a Möbius strip; to make predications and test for the results; to think critically in situations that do not always follow traditional reasoning; to observe that symbols have meaning and are recognized globally

KEY CONCEPTS: transformations, spatial sense, the scientific method—observing, predicting, collecting, and recording data

MATERIALS: adding machine tape—2 1/2–3 inches wide and 20–24 inches long (or any paper that can be cut into strips); each student will need 10 strips, scissors, transparent tape, crayons or markers, geometric shapes, Möbius Strip: The Mystery Twist (Appendix A.35)

Procedure   SHARING THE BOOK

1. Have the students define the word *transformer* in the title of the book. Some will be familiar with the movie, cartoons, and toys with the same name.
2. Continue the discussion about an untwisted strip of paper. Ask how many surfaces does it have. (*two*) Ask for suggestions on how you could prove it. (*Put a mark on the front and the back of the paper*) Describe a Möbius strip. (*an unending loop; a continuous loop having only one side and one edge*)
3. Share other geometric shapes (basic shapes they are familiar with), and ask the students to describe the number of surfaces.
4. After reading the book, ask the students to describe in their own words what Zachary did in his classroom.

PROMOTING CONCEPTS

1. As a class, create a Möbius strip like Zachary. First, model for the students by taping the ends of a strip of paper together (tape all the way across) *without* any twists. Ask the students how many surfaces there are? (*two*) Ask the stu-

dents what will happen if you cut down the middle. Record their predictions. Cut down the middle and record the results.

2. Next, have the students create a strip (each student will need a strip of paper and transparent tape) with a half twist and tape all the way across. Ask the students how many surfaces there are. Have them draw a line down the middle without picking up the point. Ask again about the number of surfaces. (one) What would happen if we cut along this line? Make a prediction. Carefully pinch the band and cut down the middle. Have the students record the results by describing and drawing.

3. Continue the exploration using Möbius Strip: The Mystery Twist (Appendix A.35). Have the students collect and record observations by varying the distance from the edge of the paper and the number of twists. Ask them to record a prediction each time before cutting the paper. Then record how many sides they get after the cut, the length of each side, and the total length of all the sides. Have the students record the results by describing and drawing.

EXHIBIT 8.10

4. Then have the students write a formal report in groups about what happened in their exploration. Present this to the class. Encourage the students to experiment and to enjoy the amazement of math using a Möbius strip.

5. What real-life symbol is the same shape as a Möbius strip or unending loop? (*the universal symbol for recycling, as shown in Exhibit 8.10*)

6. For the fun of it:

   Q: Why did the chicken cross the Möbius strip?

   A: To get to the same side. (see www.pballew.net/arithm12.html)

Assessment

1. *Performance:* Complete the exploration, collection, and recording of data on the Möbius Strip: The Mystery Twist data sheet (Appendix A.35).

2. *Writing:* Write a formal report about what happened during the exploration.

3. *Performance:* Retell the story using one of Zachary's transformations as a visual aid.

4. *Writing:* Explain why the Möbius loop shape is an appropriate symbol for recycling.

Making Connections

OTHER CONCEPTS

Topology; surfaces; belts in machinery; August Möbius; M. C. Escher; distorting surfaces; curves; Klein bottle; other symbols for recycling.

OTHER BOOKS

The Journey of Möbius and Sidh, Mark Kashino (2002).

Mummy Math: An Adventure in Geometry, Cindy Neuschwander, Bryan Langdo (Illus.) (2005)

Sir Circumference and the Sword in the Cone: A Math Adventure, Cindy Neuschwander, Wayne Geehan (Illus.) (2003)

What's Your Angle, Pythagoras? A Math Adventure, Julie Ellis, Phyllis Hornung (Illus.) (2004)

WEBSITES

http://findarticles.com/p/articles/mi_qa3666/is_200308/ai_n9292464

http://gk12.uark.edu/lessonplan/Mobius%20Bands.ppt#25 (PowerPoint)

http://mobius.us

http://pbskids.org/zoom/activities/phenom/mobiusstrip.html

www.abc.net.au/science/news/stories/2007/1979384.htm

www.abc.net.au/spark/experiments/s1476371.htm

www.boingboing.net/2004/07/28/moebius-double-twist.html

www.cut-the-knot.org/do_you_know/moebius.shtml

www.gnarlymath.com/gnarart3.html

www.sciencenews.org/articles/20070728/mathtrek.asp

REFERENCES

Hoyt, L. (2000). *Snapshots: Literacy minilessons up close.* Portsmouth, NH: Heinemann.

National Council of Teachers of Mathematics. (2000). *Principles and standards for school mathematics.* Reston, VA: Author.

National Research Council. (1996). *National science education standards.* Washington, DC: National Academy Press.

Saphier, J., & Haley, M. A. (1993). *Summarizers: Activity structures to support integration and retention of new learning.* Acton, MA: Research for Better Teaching.

Stephens, E. C., & Brown J. E. (2004). *A handbook of content literacy strategies: 125 practical reading and writing ideas* (2nd ed.). Norwood, MA: Christopher-Gordon.

Wood, C. (1997). *Yardsticks: Children in the classroom ages 4–14: A resource for parents and teachers.* Greenfield, MA: Northeast Foundation for Children.

CHILDREN'S LITERATURE

Burleigh, R. (1991). *Flight: The journey of Charles Lindbergh* (M. Wimmer, Illus.). New York: Puffin.

Burns, M. (1997). *Spaghetti and meatballs for all!* (D. Tilley, Illus.). New York: Scholastic.

Cherry, L. (1990). *The great kapok tree: A tale of the Amazon rain forest.* New York: Harcourt Brace.

Collard III, S. B. (2000). *The forest in the clouds* (M. Rothman, Illus.). Watertown, MA: Charlesbridge.

Garrett, A. (1999). *Keeper of the swamp* (K. Chandler, Illus.). New York: Turtle Books.

High, L. O. (1999). *Barn savers* (T. Lewin, Illus.). Honesdale, PA: Boyds Mills Press.

Jackson, E. (2001). *The summer solstice* (J. D. Ellis, Illus.). Brookfield, CT: The Millbrook Press.

Levine, E. (2007). *Henry's freedom box: A true story from the Underground Railroad* (K. Nelson, Illus.). New York: Scholastic.

Murphy, S. J. (1997). *Betcha!* (S. D. Schindler, Illus.). New York: HarperCollins.

Rand, G. (1992). *Prince William* (T. Rand, Illus.). New York: Holt.

Reisberg, J. (2006). *Zachary Zormer shape transformer: A math adventure* (D. Hohn, Illus.). Watertown, MA: Charlesbridge.

Reynolds, S. (2006). *The first marathon: The legend of Pheidippides* (D. Minter, Illus.). Morton Grove, IL: Albert Whitman.

Ryder, J. (2001). *The waterfall's gift* (R. J. Watson, Illus.). San Francisco: Sierra Club Books for Children.

Singer, M. (2005). *Monday on the Mississippi* (F. Lessac, Illus.). New York: Henry Holt.

Sis, P. (1996). *Starry messenger.* New York: Farrar, Straus & Giroux.

Van Allsburg, C. (1988). *Two bad ants.* Boston: Houghton Mifflin.

Wiesner, D. (1997). *Tuesday.* New York: Houghton Mifflin.

CHAPTER

9

Investigating Mathematics, Science, and Social Studies

Grades 6-8

n this period of early adolescence, we see enormous physical, emotional, social, and cognitive changes. It is essential during these years that we help students maintain a positive view of themselves as they continue to mature and as they, themselves, deal with the mysteries of biological change. Teacher (and parents) must be reminded that even though 12- and 13-year-olds often act with remarkable maturity, they are still 6 to 8 years away from the maturity of adulthood.

In order to use students' tendency to investigate for themselves the kinds of evidence that confirm or challenge their current beliefs and concepts at this age (NRC, 1996), we focus on standards that allow students to understand mathematics, science, and social studies in concrete, but perhaps new ways. Adding to the *experiencing* we did in Chapter 8, the lessons in this chapter challenge students to make larger connections to self and the world, often using objects or topics already familiar to them.

In mathematics, the chapter focuses on the *Data Analysis and Probability* and *Algebra* standards (NCTM, 2000); both connect with the experimental and investigative nature of the science lessons. How are big and small numbers represented? How do we organize these numbers to illustrate particular features? How do scientists use numbers in their scientific endeavors? How do we represent data in various forms? How do we make sense of data as they relate to our lives? We believe that *Anno's Mysterious Multiplying Jar* (Anno & Anno, 1983), *The Eleventh Hour: A Curious Mystery* (Base, 1996), and *Sir Cumference and the Great Knight of Angleland: A Math Adventure* (Neuschwander, 2001) provide excellent opportunities to answer these questions and others in the selected areas of mathematics.

The two primary science standards used are *Physical Science* and *History and Nature of Science* (NRC, 1996). Students explore the characteristic properties of matter and how these properties intersect and interact with energy and motion using the lessons in physical science. Students are asked to experiment, observe, record, make hypotheses, explain, plan, and further speculate using a number of different situations and contexts found in books such as *The Great Serum Race* (Miller, 2002). At the same time, they read about and learn from those who have gone through such scientific processes to envision and to actualize new possibilities in human experiences through our lessons in history and the nature of science; for example, they can read *The Top of the World: Climbing Mount Everest* (Jenkins, 1999). The science lessons explore such topics as water, life-saving serums, the impact of weather on human conditions, the invention of common objects, and more. In the process, we ask students to look and look again at the familiar objects in their lives in new and different scientific and mathematical ways. Simultaneously, we challenge students to think about the role of science and mathematics in their own lives.

The standards in the social studies are more broadly represented. *Sweet Music in Harlem* (Taylor, 2004) focuses on how arts contribute to the development and transmission of culture through a tale of the artists portrayed in Art Kane's famous photograph taken in Harlem in 1958. The book serves as a beautiful springboard to learn about contributions made by some famous and many unknown African American artists, filling the gap that may exist in dominant curriculum. Other books with social studies concepts take an integrated approach with other content areas. *Weslandia* (Fleischman, 1999) begins with the concept of a staple food crop to address production, distribution, and consumption. The nutritional information of mega crops are then used to calculate daily calorie requirements and analyze the nutritional value of common cereal brands. *Flotsam* (Wiesner, 2006) explores the impact of people on environments using a conservation theme. Students will learn about the difference between flotsam and jetsam, biodegradable and nonbiodegradable materials, and recyclable and nonrecyclable trash as they begin thinking about small actions they can take to help save the Earth.

As we think about creating engaging learning opportunities in mathematics, science, and social studies, we are reminded of the value of picture books for older readers. Even though the format in which the stories are presented is seemingly simple, the content and the concepts are complex and challenging. These books offer many opportunities to focus on concepts appropriate for grades 6–8. With the proper introduction and guidance, the picture books used in this chapter will engage the students' thinking about challenging concepts and the wonders that surround all of us.

9.1

L E S S O N

Anno's Mysterious Multiplying Jar

Masaichiro and Mitsumasa Anno

Inside Anno's Mysterious Multiplying Jar amazing things happen. The text and pictures combine to present a lesson on the concept of factorials, from the concrete to the abstract. This astonishing mathematical relationship, which occurs in many things and events, is illustrated using simple images. Inside the mysterious jar, objects are arranged in an ordered mathematical fashion to develop this numerical pattern. Anno shows us using dots and mathematics how the jars are multiplied.

GRADE LEVELS: 6–8

MATHEMATICS STANDARD ADDRESSED: algebra

LANGUAGE ARTS EXPERIENCES: brainstorming, writing (learning log)

OBJECTIVES: to express factorials in standard notation, to create arrangements (permutations) of sets

KEY CONCEPTS: investigate patterns, permutations, factorials

MATERIALS: calculators, color tiles, Permutations Exploration sheet (Appendix A.36)

Procedure   SHARING THE BOOK

1. Before reading the book, ask the students how many different ways red, yellow, and green can be arranged on a flagpole. Use color tiles to model the arrangements.

     RYG RGY YRG YGR GRY GYR

2. Explain that a *permutation* is an arrangement of a given number of letters, people, or objects.

3. Act out the many ways (permutations) four people can ride on a roller coaster using the following: A = Angelo, B = Barbara, C = Carlos, and D = Debby. How many different ways can the students arrange A, B, C, and D? ABCD, ACDB, ADCB, ADBC, ABDC, ADCB; then put B in the first place; then put C in the first place, and so on.

_____	_____	_____	_____
1st Place	2nd Place	3rd Place	4th Place

   An important component of problem solving is to eliminate all possibilities.

4. Calculating permutations involves finding the product of a sequence of counting numbers (e.g., 4 x 3 x 2 x 1 = 24). This calculation is called a *factorial*. There are 24 ways, or permutations, to arrange four people on a roller coaster. In these arrangements *order matters*, each arrangement of a permutation is unique.

5. *Anno's Mysterious Multiplying Jar* teaches the students a special mathematical notation for permutations.

6. While reading the book, have the students note any patterns that emerge.

7. Retell the beginning of the story, and ask the students to explain what begins to happen on arrival at the island and what they notice about the pictures. Record the student responses about the growth of the numbers, and ask if they notice a pattern.

8. Each box in the story contains 10 jars. But how many jars are in all of the boxes altogether (3,628,800)? How did there come to be so many jars? What can you say about writing large numbers?

9. If there are five students A, B, C, D, and E, in a classroom, how many different ways could we arrange their desks? Act this out and record the arrangements or permutations. This is a special kind of numerical relationship.

PROMOTING CONCEPTS

1. Record the pattern growth—from 1 (island) to 2 (countries) to 6 (mountains) to 24 (walled kingdoms)—in the story until an amazing number is revealed.

2. Mathematicians like to find short ways to say long numbers. So, for 3,628,800 jars, a mathematician would say there are 10! or "10 factorial" jars. This calculation is written as follows: 10! = 10 x 9 x 8 x 7 x 6 x 5 x 4 x 3 x 2 x 1 = 3,628,800. Explain that "factorial" is a word used to describe a special kind of numerical relationship.

3. The mathematical symbol for a factorial is an exclamation mark (!). That signals that the number it follows stands for the product of that number multiplied by the next smaller number, multiplied by the next smaller number, and so on all the way down to one. This is based on the *fundamental counting principle* for calculating the total number of possible outcomes for probability experiments that involve the combination of two or more independent events.

4. When computing probabilities, it's often necessary to compute the number of ways that things can be ordered within a group (permutations) or selected from a group (combinations).

5. As stated above, 10! factorial is equal to 10 x 9 x 8 x 7 x 6 x 5 x 4 x 3 x 2 x 1 = 3,628,800.

6. Ask students to write "5 factorial." Then, using their calculators, have them determine what 5! equals.

7. Have the students complete the Permutations Exploration sheet (Appendix A.36).

Assessment

1. *Writing:* Have students write about amazing mathematical patterns they have observed.

2. *Performance:* Have students participate in brainstorming really large numbers, such as the population of the United States, the distance to the sun, atoms in the human body, and so forth.

3. *Performance:* Complete the Permutations Exploration sheet (Appendix A.36). Check for participation.

Making Connections

OTHER CONCEPTS

Prime numbers, combinations, probability experiments, Choice Principle, independent and dependent events.

OTHER BOOKS

The Grapes of Math: Mind Stretching Math Riddles, Greg Tang, Harry Briggs (Illus.) (2001)

How Much Is a Million? David M. Schwartz, Steven Kellogg (Illus.) (1993)

Math Curse, Jon Scieszka, Lane Smith (Illus.) (1999)

WEBSITES

http://mathforum.org/dr.math/
www.cs.uml.edu/~ytran/factorial.html
www.mathpages.com/home/icombina.htm
www.mathpages.com/home/kmath165.htm

9.2

One Grain of Rice: A Mathematical Folktale

Long ago in India, a greedy raja keeps nearly all of the people's rice. When famine comes, he refuses to share the rice with his hungry people. A clever village girl, Rani, devises a resourceful plan. After doing a good deed for the raja, she is allowed to select her reward. Rani asks for just one grain of rice, doubled every day for 30 days. What a surprise when one grain of rice doubles into one billion grains of rice! Rani teaches the selfish raja an important lesson about being fair. The illustrations in One Grain of Rice are inspired by traditional Indian miniature paintings and create a sense of culture in this instructive mathematical folktale, especially when 256 elephants march across a four-page spread to deliver one billion grains of rice.

GRADE LEVELS: **6–8**

MATHEMATICS STANDARD ADDRESSED: algebra

SOCIAL STUDIES STANDARDS ADDRESSED: culture and production; distribution and consumption; characteristics of government

---

LANGUAGE ARTS EXPERIENCES: vocabulary study, character study, learning log

---

LITERACY CONNECTIONS: predicting/inferring

OBJECTIVES: to express numbers using exponential notation, to identify powers and exponents, to record numbers in a standard form of notation, to describe the qualities of a good leader

---

KEY CONCEPTS: investigate patterns, doubling, powers of two, exponential notation, powers, base, factor

---

MATERIALS: Story Impressions sheet (Appendix A.37), world map or globe, a jar filled with rice, Exponential Notations Exploration sheet (Appendix A.38), calculators, learning logs

---

Procedure   SHARING THE BOOK

1. Before reading the book, ask the students what today's leaders are called in the United States and other countries.

2. Use the Story Impressions activity (McGinley & Denner, 1987) to engage the students in vocabulary study. Using the clues from the book's cover and illustrations, have students write their predictions on the Story Impressions sheet in Appendix A.37. Define and discuss words that students may not know before they make any predictions.

3. After reading the book, ask the following questions to expose the students to geography, the Indian culture, vocabulary, and mathematics:

   a. Where does this story take place? (locate India on the map)

   b. What is a raja?

   c. What did the villagers do for food? Why was rice so important to the villagers? Where did most of the rice go each year? What is a famine? What would you do with the rice in the royal storehouses?

d. The raja believes he is wise and fair. Do you agree? Why or why not?

e. Rani does a good deed for the raja. Can you describe what she did? How would you describe Rani? Would you have returned the rice to the raja?

f. What happened when the raja heard about Rani's good deed? What did he offer her? What did Rani ask for from the raja? Isn't one grain of rice a modest request? Two grains on day two, four grains on day three— but when the rice doubles for 30 days, what begins to happen?

g. How was the rice delivered to Rani?

h. Does the raja understand the process of doubling? Do you think Rani is a good mathematician? How did she use mathematics to trick the raja?

i. How is rice bought today? Ask the students to estimate how many grains of rice are in the jar.

4. Have students return to their Story Impressions to see how many words they were right about.

PROMOTING CONCEPTS

1. Describe how our democracy is *similar* to the royal government in the story. Describe how our democracy is *different* from the royal government in the story. As a class, brainstorm a list of governments that are democratic and governments that have a monarchy (are ruled by royalty). Discuss the advantages and disadvantages of these forms of government.

2. What are the qualities of a good leader in either type of government, monarchy or democratic?

3. Have students describe the pattern that starts to develop on day two, day three, day four, and so on. What can they tell you about the power of doubling?

4. Ask the students to predict how many grains of rice Rani will have after four days, eight days, fifteen days. What do they think is the total number of grains of rice for 30 days? Record the students' predictions.

5. Encourage students to verbalize the patterns they see.

6. Have students complete the Exponential Notations Exploration sheet in Appendix A.38 for number of grains of rice for each day and add up all the grains of rice for the 30 days. Use calculators for the computation.

7. Explain that mathematicians like to find short ways to say long numbers. Introduce exponential notation. If the same addend is repeated, we can use multiplication. If the same factor is repeated, we can use exponents (e.g., $2 \times 2 \times 2 \times 2 \times 2 = 2^5$). The repeated factor is the *base* and the number of times the factor is repeated is the *exponent*. The number represented by the base with its exponent is called a *power of the base*. Thus, 2^5 is the fifth power of two, or two to the fifth power.

8. Using exponential notation, have the students record the number of grains of rice on the 11th day, 15th day, 19th day. Then, write the number of grains of rice for each of the 30 days using exponential notation.

9. Using a calculator's constant feature, the students key in $2 \times 2 = = = =$ (that is, have them press the equals sign again and again). What is happening? Record the numbers that are in the viewing rectangle. Then, have them write the same numbers in exponential notation and using the multiplication symbol.

Assessment

1. *Performance:* Students will complete the chart (Appendix A.38) for the number of grains of rice for each day using whole numbers and exponential notation.

2. *Writing:* Have students write in their learning logs about the power of doubling, how knowing mathematics helped Rani trick the raja, or whether they think Rani was a good mathematician.

3. *Writing:* Have students compare the raja's government with the U.S. democracy.

Making Connections

OTHER CONCEPTS

Estimating quantities of rice in different size containers; determine the number of grains of rice in one cup; the weight of one cup of rice; the weight and the number of cups of rice on a specific day in the book; squares; square roots.

OTHER BOOKS

Anno's Mysterious Multiplying Jar, Masaichiro and Mitsumasa Anno (1982)

How Big Is a Foot? Rolf Myller and Susan McCrath (1991)

The King's Chessboard, David Birch, Devis Grebu (Illus.) (1988)

Math Curse, Jon Scieszka, Lane Smith (Illus.) (1995)

Sir Cumference and the First Round Table: A Math Adventure, Cindy Neuschwander, Wayne Geehan (Illus.) (1997)

WEBSITES

http://en.wikipedia.org/wiki/Raja

www.frmco.com/history.html

www.riceweb.org/

The Eleventh Hour: A Curious Mystery

Graeme Base

Horace is celebrating his 11th birthday by inviting his friends to a party. The sumptuous feast he prepared mysteriously disappears while the guests are playing games and awaiting the 11th hour. Throughout the detailed, intricate, and fun illustrations are clues as to who devoured the birthday banquet. With close observation and simple deduction, a clever detective will discover which of the 11 animals stole the feast. (The top secret "The Inside Story," located at the end of the book, is where the author reveals a detailed explanation of all the clues and puzzles in the illustrations.)

GRADE LEVELS: 6–8

MATHEMATICS STANDARDS ADDRESSED: measurement, problem solving

---

LITERACY CONNECTIONS: summarizing/synthesizing, predicting

OBJECTIVES: to compute with intervals of time, to solve for elapsed time, to add and subtract hours and minutes, to regroup minutes to hours and minutes, to regroup hours and minutes to minutes, to apply time computations in real life

---

KEY CONCEPTS: units of measure for time, elapsed time, regrouping hours and minutes to minutes and vice versa, A.M., P.M.

MATERIALS: digital and analog clocks, other devices that measure time, several copies of the book, Column Notes (Appendix A.19), Time Computation Exploration sheet (Appendix A.39), Microsoft Calendar Wizard

---

Procedure

SHARING THE BOOK

1. Before reading, ask questions like the following to prepare the students for what is to come in the book:

   a. Who has a birthday on the 11th day of the month? Who has a birthday in the 11th month of the year? Who is 11 years old?

   b. Does the number 11 appear anywhere in your life, such as in your telephone number or in your street address?

   c. How about on a clock face? What devices tell time? Before we had clocks, as we know them today, what was used to tell time (e.g., sundial, hourglass)?

2. Ask the students if they are skillful detectives. Tell them to look and listen closely for details as the book is read to see if they can unravel the mystery. There are visual clues, as well as clues in the text. Look closely for the clocks and the time. Look for the representations for the number 11. Graeme Base, the author, says, "Use your eyes and head."

3. As the book is read by the teacher, individually by the student, or in small groups, have students complete a Column Notes (Appendix A.19) using PAGE and CLUE(S) to document the clues from both the text and the illustrations.

4. Then, part way through the story, have them write (in the left-hand column) who they think stole the banquet, how it was done, and how do they know.

After the reading, they can record the answers to those questions from the story to verify their predictions.

5. After reading the book, ask who ate the birthday banquet. More important, how was it done? Check each response with the code provided by the author to decode the hidden message on the last page of the book. The thief is one of the 11 animals, not some other unknown or obscure animal. Did the students break the code?

6. Discuss observation and deduction as another method to figure out which animal is the thief. Can they deduce which of the 11 is the thief?

7. Then, explain the method of detecting the numerous messages hidden throughout the book. Did they notice any clues in the text of the book?

8. As a class, go over the clues and puzzles in "The Inside Story."

PROMOTING CONCEPTS

1. To begin the discussion on time computation, ask questions such as:
   a. What time is it when Horace is in the study?
   b. What time is it when Horace is in the kitchen?
   c. How much time has passed?

2. Review that 10:45 means 10 hours and 45 minutes. Point out that 6 hours and 75 minutes is the same as 7 hours and 15 minutes.

3. Review the relationship between seconds, minutes, hours, and days. Be sure students understand the use of A.M. and P.M. Point out that when it is exactly 12:00 noon or 12:00 midnight, it is neither A.M. nor P.M.

4. Then, focus on the relationship between days, weeks, months, years, and centuries. Create a list of equivalent measurements:

60 sec = 1 min	52 wk = 1 yr
60 min = 1 hr	12 mo = 1 yr
24 hr = 1 day	10 yr = 1 decade
7 days = 1 wk	100 yr = 1 century

   a. Using this list, have the students figure out what the difference is between the number of hours in seven days and the number of hours in five days.
   b. How many minutes is 7,200 seconds?
   c. How many hours is 7,200 seconds?
   d. What is 2 hr 20 min later than 3:45?
   e. What is 3 hr 30 min earlier than 12:45 P.M.?

5. Continue the review with questions such as the following: 5 h = ___ min; 3 yr = ___ days; 240 sec = ___ min; 65 mo = ___ yr ___ mo.

6. Ask students: What time did the guests arrive at Horace's gate? Hint: Look closely on the Zebra's scooter. How long was it until time to eat the banquet?

7. Say to students: Looking at our class schedule (use your own), it is now (say the time), how long until we are dismissed from school? Express precisely in hours and minutes. How much time has passed since your arrival at school? How much time has passed since you began mathematics class? Students can also create elapsed time problems of their own.

8. Using the Time Computations Exploration sheet (Appendix A.39), have the students compute the number of hours Keith and Gina worked. They earn different hourly pay rates. What is their pay for the week?

Assessment

1. *Performance:* Students create a schedule of daily activities and create a problem that can be solved using the schedule.

2. *Performance:* Students create a monthly or yearly calendar using Microsoft Calendar Wizard and create problems that can be solved using the calendar.

3. *Performance:* Students complete the hourly rate charts and create one of their own.

Making Connections

OTHER CONCEPTS

Twenty-four-hour clock; units to measure time; time zones; how to read and use a schedule; travel arrangements; plan a five-day trip; other timekeeping systems; history of timekeeping devices; telling time without a clock; A.M., P.M.; time travel.

OTHER BOOKS

The Backwards Watch, Eric Houghton (1992)

The House with a Clock in Its Walls, John Bellairs (1989)

Pastime: Telling Time from 1879 to 1969, Philip Collins, Garry Brod (Photographer) (1993)

Telling the Time (Everyday History), Rupert Matthews, Kevin W. Maddison (Illus.), Joanna Williams (Illus.), Stefan Chabluk (Illus.) (2000)

Tom's Midnight Garden, Philippa Pearce (1959)

Tuesday, David Wiesner (1991)

WEBSITES

http://hea-www.harvard.edu/ECT/Daymarks/

http://sln.fi.edu/qa00/attic3/index.html

www.timeanddate.com/worldclock/

Math Curse

Jon Scieszka • **Lane Smith, Illus.**

On the jacket cover, inside panels, and the dedication page, and from the first page to the last page, this book contains exciting and fun mathematics problems that encourage students to think about mathematics in a different way. Beautifully illustrated, each page can be used as an introduction to the wonderful world of problem solving in mathematics. The girl's teacher, Mrs. Fibonacci, says that you can think of almost everything as a math problem. The next day, the girl wakes up and experiences many mathematics problems in real-life situations throughout her day. She calculates the time required to get dressed, combinations of outfits in her wardrobe, quarts in a gallon, pints in a quart, inches in a foot, and feet in a yard, and this is just the beginning. When she realizes that two halves make a whole, she escapes the math curse through a hole!

GRADE LEVELS: **6–8**

MATHEMATICS STANDARDS ADDRESSED: algebra, problem solving

LANGUAGE ARTS EXPERIENCE: writing (learning log)

OBJECTIVES: to write factors of numbers, to identify prime and composite numbers

---

KEY CONCEPTS: primes, composites, factors

MATERIALS: connecting cubes or tiles (approximately 24 for each group), numeral cards 2 to 50, Hundreds Chart (Appendix A.6), learning logs

---

Procedure

SHARING THE BOOK

1. Before reading, show the students the cover and ask what they notice. Do they know what some of the mathematical symbols mean, and what a "math curse" is?
2. Looking at the dedication page, what do they notice? Can they figure out how many dedications are for the author and the illustrator?
3. Read the book.
4. Ask whether they have had any mathematics problems like this girl. Then, have the students answer some of her questions from the book. How many quarts in a gallon? How many pints in a quart? How many inches in a foot? How many feet in a yard? How many yards in a neighborhood? How many ounces in a pint? How many feet in a pair of shoes?

PROMOTING CONCEPTS

1. How many students are in Mrs. Fibonacci's class? Count out cubes/tiles to represent the class. Use tiles to make different class arrangements. If the class sits in four rows, how many desks are in each row? What if Mrs. Fibonacci rearranges the desks to make six rows, eight rows, three rows, two rows, one row?
2. How many different rectangles can the students make with their 24 cubes/tiles? Have them display their rectangles/arrays (e.g., 6 by 4, 4 by 6, 3 by 8, 8 by 3, 2 by 12, 12 by 2, 1 by 24, 24 by 1). The multiplication sentence for each rectangle is: 6 x 4, 4 x 6, 3 x 8, 8 x 3, 2 x 12, 12 x 2, 1 x 24, 24 x 1.

3. Explain that these are the factors for 24. *Factors* are numbers that are multiplied to find a product. How many different whole numbers are factors for 24? (8)

4. Look at the number 5. How many rectangles can the students make? (*1 by 5 and 5 by 1*) The numbers 1 and 5 are factors of 5. Because 5 has only two factors, it is a prime number. A *prime number* has exactly two factors, itself and 1.

5. Explain that a whole number such as 24 is called a *composite* because it has more than two factors. (Special note: The numbers 0 and 1 are neither prime nor composite.)

6. Conduct the following activities:
   a. How many different rectangles can students make from 10 tiles? What are the multiplication facts for the rectangles? What are the factors for 10? Is it prime or composite?
   b. Make a list of prime numbers between 1 and 10. (2, 3, 5, 7) Make a list of the composite numbers between 1 and 10. (4, 6, 8, 9)
   c. Draw tiles from a bag containing the numbers 2 to 50. The object is to make as many rectangles as possible using that number of cubes/tiles. (*Determining the factors.*) Students get a point for each rectangle that they make.

7. Prime numbers are used in cryptography and encryption. Large numbers from the products of primes are used to encode messages, and the factors are needed to decode the message.

8. Using the Hundreds Chart (Appendix A.6), follow the Rules of Eratosthenes, a Greek mathematician who devised a system for finding primes:
   a. Cross out 1.
   b. Cross out all the multiples of 2 that are greater than 2.
   c. Cross out all the multiples of 3 that are greater than 3.
   d. Do the same for the multiples of 5 and 7.
   e. The remaining numbers are prime.

Assessment

1. *Writing:* Have students describe the meaning of prime numbers and composite numbers in their learning logs. Have the students select 10 even numbers and write them as the sum of two primes.

2. *Performance:* Find all of the prime numbers between 1 and 100 following the system that Eratosthenes, a Greek mathematician, devised using the Hundreds Chart (Appendix A.6).

Making Connections

OTHER CONCEPTS

Measurement; twin primes; abundant, deficient, and perfect numbers; Eratosthenes; prime factorization, multiples.

OTHER BOOKS

Anno's Mysterious Multiplying Jar, Masaichiro and Mitsumasa Anno (1983)

The Grapes of Math: Mind Stretching Math Riddles, Greg Tang, Harry Briggs (Illus.) (2001)

How Big Is a Foot? Rolf Myller and Susan McCrath (1991)

Sir Cumference and the First Round Table: A Math Adventure, Cindy Neuschwander, Wayne Geehan (Illus.) (1997)

Sir Cumference and the Great Knight of Angleland: A Math Adventure, Cindy Neuschwander, Wayne Geehan (Illus.) (2001)

WEBSITES

http://mathforum.com/library/view/13358.html
http://primes.utm.edu/glossary/home.php

9.5

LESSON

People
Peter Spier

People is a delightful book that exposes students to the human diversity on Earth. In this tale of heterogeneity, there is a deeper message: differences between people produce great riches for us all. Each page is a celebration of the excitement of the differences, similarities, and the value of being unique among six and a half billion people. Peter Spier communicates visually that we can live together harmoniously by accepting one another.

GRADE LEVELS: **6–8**

MATHEMATICS STANDARD ADDRESSED: algebra

SOCIAL STUDIES STANDARDS ADDRESSED: people, places, and environments; global connections and interdependence; world population distribution; geographic perspectives of the world

LANGUAGE ARTS EXPERIENCE: expository writing

OBJECTIVES: to write whole numbers in scientific notation, to write standard numerals for numbers expressed in scientific notation, to describe how we are different from and similar to other people on this Earth

KEY CONCEPTS: scientific notation, standard form, nonscientific notation, powers of 10, living harmoniously together by understanding and accepting one another

MATERIALS: list of real-life large-number values, globe/map of the world, reference resources such as the Internet, atlas, almanac, Standard/Scientific Notation Exploration sheet (Appendix A.40)

Procedure

SHARING THE BOOK

1. Before reading the book, ask how many people are there in the world (*approximately 6.7 billion, January 2009*). If we all joined hands, how long would the line stretch? How many times could this line wrap around the equator?

2. After reading the book, ask what are some similarities we share with every other human being on this planet (*we were all babies; we all have noses, eyes, lips, hair, etc.; we all love to play; we all have homes, pets, language, etc.; we all breathe the same air and in the end we all must die*).

3. Ask students: How are we different from and similar to other people on this Earth? Continue this question by selecting specific countries on the map or globe, such as Bolivia, South America; Thailand, Asia; Nigeria, Africa; and so on.

4. How are you like the person sitting beside you? How are you unique from the person beside you and all the other people in the world?

5. Imagine what the world would be like if everybody looked, thought, ate, dressed, and acted the same! What would that world look like to you? How would you feel about that kind of world? Let's celebrate the differences!

PROMOTING CONCEPTS

1. Looking at the globe or map of the world, how many continents are there? Have the students list them.

2. What is the population of these continents (or the world's largest countries)? What is the total number of people on this planet? Students can research the answers to these questions using a website such as http://geography.about.com/od/obtainpopulationdata/Population_Data.htm.

3. Write "4.75" billion on the chalkboard. This was the world's population in 1983. Lead a discussion that focuses on the numerical value (in standard form) of that number in the abbreviated form. Ask the class to think of another way to write the number in an abbreviated form. Assure them that there may be many ways to express the value of a number and that each can be considered correct (e.g., 4,750,000,000 or 47,500,000,00.0 x 10).

4. Explain that in the scientific community, it is universally accepted to use scientific notation to express numbers because notations require less space and time and are useful when making comparisons. Performing calculations when many digits are involved is difficult, and even calculators allow only for a limited number of digits.

5. In *scientific notation*, the first factor must be equal to or greater than 1 and less than 10 (in this case, 4), and the second factor is a power of 10 (in this case 10^9). For example, 4.75×10^9. Place a decimal between the first two digits, and the exponent is the number of places the decimal was moved.

6. *Scientific notation* does not make the number larger or smaller; it is just a way of rewriting it. It allows us to write large numbers (or small numbers) in a compact and efficient manner. *Scientific notation* has applications in many fields of science.

7. Many ways exist to express the value of a number, and each is considered correct. Show students the chart in Exhibit 9.1.

8. Then, explain that there are many ways to write a number in nonscientific notation, but only one way to write a number in both standard form and scientific notation. What advantages and disadvantages might there be for each notation method if you are writing reports? Making calculations?

9. Ask students: When is it appropriate to use scientific notation? Responses may include: when the numbers are very large and when the precision needed is only two to four digits.

10. Have the students compose a list of large numbers and write them in scientific notation, as shown in Exhibit 9.2.

    List the distance from the sun to each planet in our solar system. Write in standard form and scientific notation.
    www.nasa.gov/

11. Have the students complete a place values chart of the population of the world's largest countries (or by continents) and write it in standard notation

EXHIBIT **9.1**   Ways to express the value of a number.

STANDARD FORM	ABBREVIATED FORM	SCIENTIFIC NOTATION	NONSCIENTIFIC NOTATION
4,750,000,000	4.75 billion	4.75×10^9	475×10^7
3,642,000	3.642 million	3.642×10^6	36.42×10^5
812.5	8.125 hundred	8.125×10^2	1.3×5^4

	STANDARD NOTATION	SCIENTIFIC NOTATION
Minutes in 1,000 years	500,000,000	5×10^8
Centimeters in a 100 meter dash	10,000	10×10^4
Total number of seats/chairs in the school		
Total number of pages in the mathematics textbooks in the class		

and in scientific notation, looking for patterns. (As the populations get larger, the exponents get larger.) Students can use research resources available to them such as the atlas, the almanac, the website www.ibiblio.org/lunarbin/worldpop, and the Standard/Scientific Notation Exploration sheet in Appendix A.40.

Assessment

1. *Performance:* Students write an individual or group explanation of how to express a standard number in scientific notation.
2. *Performance:* Students write an explanation (individually or as a group) of how to compare two numbers written in scientific notation.
3. *Performance:* Students complete the Standard/Scientific Notation Exploration sheet (Appendix A.40) for the population of the world's largest countries using standard notation and scientific notation.
4. *Performance:* Students locate the world's largest countries (or the continents) on a map/globe and record their populations using scientific notation.
5. *Writing:* Describe ways in which communities reflect the cultural backgrounds of their inhabitants through such items as languages, food, clothing, homes, and so forth.

Making Connections

OTHER CONCEPTS

Decimals, multiplying decimals, multiplying powers of 10, estimation using the rounding strategy, geography, population, diversity, surface area, land area, water area, smallest countries, richest countries, largest cities, largest deserts, tallest mountains.

OTHER BOOKS

How Much Is a Million? David M. Schwartz, Steven Kellogg (Illus.) (1993)

If the World Were a Village: A Book About the World's People, David J. Smith and Shelagh Armstrong (2002)

If You Made a Million, David M. Schwartz, Steven Kellogg (Illus.) (1994)

Imagining the Universe: A Visual Journey, Edward Packard (1994)

Material World: A Global Family Portrait, Peter Menzel, Charles C. Mann, and Paul Kennedy (1995)

One Million, Hendrik Hertzberg (1993)

WEBSITES

http://geography.about.com/cs/worldmaps/

http://geography.about.com/od/obtainpopulationdata/Population_data.html

http://janus.astro.umd.edu/AW/awtools.html#classroom

http://worldatlas.com

www.census.gov/

www.ibiblio.org/lunarbin/worldpop

www.nasa.gov/

www.nyu.edu/pages/mathmol/textbook/scinot.html

9.6

LESSON

Sir Cumference and the Great Knight of Angleland

A MATH ADVENTURE • **Cindy Neuschwander** • **Wayne Geehan, Illus.**

Radius, son of Sir Cumference and Lady Di of Ameter, sets out on a mathematics adventure to earn his knighthood. Equipped with only a family medallion (a protractor) for luck, Radius encounters many dangers including a dragon. The ultimate challenge lies in a mysterious castle with a maze of angles. Students can join the mathematics adventure by measuring angles in the castle maze using the medallion (protractor) found at the back of the book.

GRADE LEVELS: **6–8**

MATHEMATICS STANDARDS ADDRESSED: geometry, measurement

LANGUAGE ARTS EXPERIENCES: vocabulary study, visual representation

OBJECTIVES: to measure angles using a protractor, to classify angles according to their measure

KEY CONCEPTS: right, acute, obtuse, and straight angles; measuring with a protractor

MATERIALS: chalkboard protractor, student protractors, Measuring Angles Exploration sheet (Appendix A.41)

Procedure   SHARING THE BOOK

1. Before reading the book, ask the students if they know what a circumference, an angle, a right angle, and a straight angle are. What tools are used to measure angles? What experiences have they had measuring angles?

2. After reading the book, state that Sir Cumference and Lady Di gave Radius a medallion for his journey. Then ask students the following:

   a. Can you describe the medallion? What is the unit of measure for an angle? (*degree [°]*) What is written on the medallion? (*0°, 90°, 180°*)

   b. Radius entered a circular chamber, and a parchment told him, "You must make a Knightly Right." What does that mean? Describe how to create a "Knightly Right" using the medallion (*protractor*).

   c. The parchment said, "Finding next Big, Straight, and Slight." What does that mean? In the book, how many degrees was a Big angle, a Straight angle, and Slight angle? What did Radius call angles that were less than 90°? What did Radius call angles that were more than 90°?

   d. According to Radius, a circle is divided into how many parts? (360) These parts are named in honor of Radius's teacher, Sir D'Grees. What are they called?

   e. When the two dragons, "Pair of Lells," stretched across the moat, what did they form? What does parallel mean today?

   f. Who became the Knight of Angleland? Why? What country is Angleland known as today?

PROMOTING CONCEPTS

1. Draw several angles on the chalkboard or use an overhead projector. Have selected students use the protractor to measure the angles. Caution: Align

the vertex of the angle with the center point of the protractor. Align the side of the angle with the protractor. Make sure the appropriate scale is used on the protractor.

2. Have the students follow these steps to draw ∠ABC with measure 35°.

   a. Draw ray $\overrightarrow{AB}$.

   b. Place the protractor arrow on A and mark point C at 35°.

   c. Remove the protractor and draw ray $\overrightarrow{AC}$. The measure of ∠ABC is 35°.

3. Have students construct angles (e.g., 60°, 25°, 145°, 170°, 25°, 80°) without using a protractor. Then, measure each angle to check their estimate. Classify each angle, acute, right, obtuse, or straight by their measure.

4. Ask students to find some realistic situations in which angles are used in the classroom (e.g., bulletin board, desk, door). Estimate the number of degrees and measure with a protractor, when possible.

5. Using the Measuring Angles Exploration sheet in Appendix A.41, ask the students to find as many angles as they can. Next, have them estimate the number of degrees in these angles and then measure the angles to check.

6. Conclude the lesson by walking to the cafeteria, gym, library, or playground and looking for angles in the school. Have the students try to find an example of each classification: acute, right, obtuse, and straight.

Assessment

1. *Performance:* Students complete the Measuring Angles Exploration sheet (Appendix A.41) or locate and measure each type of angle in the classroom.

2. *Observation:* Students successfully locate angles of each type in real-life situations.

3. *Observation:* Students draw, estimate, and measure angles using a protractor.

Making Connections

OTHER CONCEPTS

Angles and locating aircraft; complementary and supplementary angles; notation for angles; perpendicular lines; parallel lines; triangles.

OTHER BOOKS

The Adventures of Penrose the Mathematical Cat, Theoni Pappas (1997)

Fractals, Googols and Other Mathematical Tales, Theoni Pappas (1993)

The Grapes of Math: Mind Stretching Math Riddles, Greg Tang, Harry Briggs (Illus.) (2001)

The Greedy Triangle (Brainy Day Books), Marilyn Burns, Gordon Silveria (Illus.) (1994)

Sir Cumference and the First Round Table: A Math Adventure, Cindy Neuschwander, Wayne Geehan (Illus.) (1997)

WEBSITES

www.kidport.com/Grade6/Math/MeasureGeo/
   MeasuringAngles.htm

www.mathforum.org/geometry/k12.geometry.html

www.mathleague.com/help/geometry/angles.htm

www.teachervision.fen.com/geometry/printable/6173.html

Tiger Math: Learning to Graph from a Baby Tiger

Ann Whitehead Nagda and Cindy Bickel

Tiger Math is a heartwarming story about TJ, a Siberian tiger born in captivity in the Denver Zoo. TJ's mother dies when he is 10 weeks old, and the staff of the zoo's animal hospital raises him. After five days, however, the tiny orphan cub has not eaten anything. Through forced feeding and the care of several hospital assistants, TJ begins to grow, and at 14 weeks he weighs 19 pounds. TJ later becomes so familiar with the hospital that he learns to open the refrigerator door and to play hide-and-seek with the hospital workers. The text is paired with different graphs (picture, line, bar, and circle) that show information about tigers and TJ's growth and that encourage students to interpret data. Rich and beautiful photos of TJ throughout the book are captivating, a terrific enhancement to any graphing lesson.

GRADE LEVELS: **6–8**

MATHEMATICS STANDARD ADDRESSED: data analysis and probability

LANGUAGE ARTS EXPERIENCES: expository writing, learning log

OBJECTIVES: to interpret and construct box-and-whisker plots; to determine quartiles and extremes; to interpret data from picture, bar, line, and circle graphs

KEY CONCEPTS: box-and-whisker graph, median, upper extreme, lower extreme, data set, quartiles

MATERIALS: graph paper, rulers, globe or map of the world, learning logs

Procedure

SHARING THE BOOK

1. Before reading the book, ask the students if they have seen tigers at the zoo. What did they look like? What were they doing? How big were they? Can students estimate their weight?

2. Ask if they know where tigers are found in the wild. Locate India, Burma (Myanmar), and Sumatra on the globe or map. What are the different kinds of tigers found in the wild (see the graph on page 8 of the book)? Where are Siberian tigers found in the wild? Locate Russia (specifically Siberia), Korea, and China on the map.

3. After reading the book, look back at each graph and ask the students to interpret the representation of the data in each type of graph—picture, line, bar, and circle. Specific questions may include the following:
   a. How many tigers are still in the wild today? (see the graph on page 10)
   b. Describe TJ's weight the first few weeks of his life. (see the graph on page 12)
   c. How much did TJ weigh at 10 weeks old? (see the graph on page 14)
   d. Compare TJ's weight to his father's weight. (see the graph on page 16)
   e. What does the graph on page 18 tell us?
   f. At 12 weeks old, what can we say about TJ's weight? (see the graph on page 20)
   g. Describe the graph on page 22.

h. What did the staff at the hospital zoo do in order to keep TJ alive? What did the staff feed TJ?
i. At what age did TJ start gaining weight?
j. What is the trend in the graph on page 24?
k. How do mother tigers teach their cubs to hunt? What kind of games did the nursery staff play with TJ?
l. At 18 weeks, compare TJ's weight to his father's weight. (see the graph on page 26)
m. When TJ was two years old, where did he go? How much did he weigh when he was two years old?
n. At four years old, how much did TJ weigh? (see the graph on page 28)

4. What will tigers in captivity do if they are especially fond of a person? Several years later, did TJ recognize Cindy, the veterinary assistant? How did he respond?

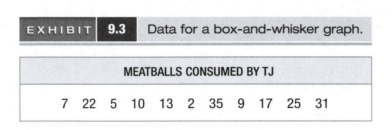

EXHIBIT	9.3	Data for a box-and-whisker graph.

MEATBALLS CONSUMED BY TJ
7 22 5 10 13 2 35 9 17 25 31

PROMOTING CONCEPTS

1. Box-and-whisker graphs are used to organize and group data. Also, they show the distribution of the numbers in a set. Ask the students to hypothesize how many meatballs TJ ate and make a box-and-whisker graph of the data shown in Exhibit 9.3.

2. Walk the students through the steps for creating a box-and-whiskers graph, as shown in Exhibit 9.4:
   a. First, rank the data from the least to the greatest.
   b. Then, create a number line from 1 to 40 because that is the appropriate range for our data set. In our data set, 2 is the *lower extreme* and 35 is the *upper extreme*.
   c. Next, identify the median (middle piece of data). Put a triangle around the median. Mark a line segment for the *median* underneath the number line. The median divides the set of data into two parts.

EXHIBIT	9.4	Box-and-whisker graph.

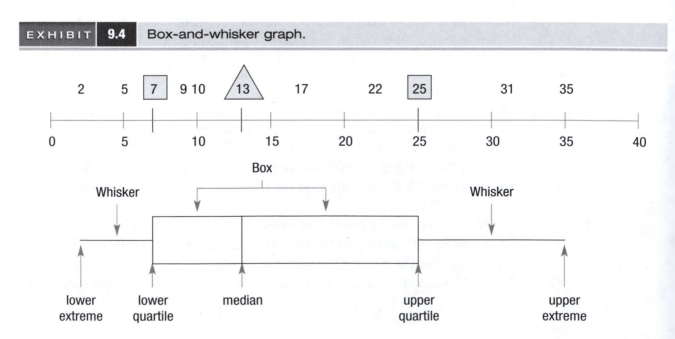

d. Now, identify the middle piece of data in each half of the data set. The middle number in the lower half of the data set is 7, which is the *lower quartile*. The middle number in the upper half of the data is 25, which is the *upper quartile*. Put a square around the quartiles and mark a line segment for each underneath the number line. Quartiles divide the set of data into four parts.

e. Connect the three segments to form two rectangles (the box).

f. Plot the value for the least and greatest data (the extremes). Extend lines (the whiskers) from the extremes to the box.

g. Guide students to conclude that the box contains two central quartiles, separated by the median. The whiskers represent upper and lower quartiles.

3. Make a box-and-whisker graph (using the data in Exhibit 9.5) to represent the number of basketballs (fictitious) that TJ destroyed while in the nursery.

EXHIBIT 9.5	Data for a box-and-whisker graph.

TJ'S BASKETBALLS										
8	12	5	7	10	9	11	3	4	2	13

4. Complete a number line appropriate for the range of the data. Order the data from least to greatest. Determine the median. What is the lower extreme and the upper extreme? What is the lower quartile and the upper quartile?

Assessment

1. *Performance*: Complete a box-and-whisker graph for the set of data for TJ's basketballs.

2. *Writing*: Write three questions that can be answered using your box-and-whisker graph for TJ's basketballs in your learning log.

3. *Writing*: Select a graph (picture, bar, line, or circle) from the book and write a paragraph explaining the data represented.

4. *Writing*: Explain how the box-and-whisker graph divides the data into four parts. What fraction of the data in a set is included in the whisker of a box-and-whisker graph?

Making Connections

OTHER CONCEPTS

Extrapolation, interpolation, scattergram, correlation, mean, mode, stem-and-leaf plots, circle graphs; coordinate grids x and y axis.

OTHER BOOKS

The Adventures of Penrose the Mathematical Cat, Theoni Pappas (1997)

Chimp Math: Learning About Time from a Baby Chimpanzee, Anne Whitehead Nagdo and Cindy Bickel (2002)

The Grapes of Math, Greg Tang, Harry Briggs (Illus.) (2001)

Sir Cumference and the First Round Table: A Math Adventure, Cindy Neuschwander, Wayne Geehan (Illus.) (1997)

Spaghetti and Meatballs for All: A Mathematical Story, Marilyn Burns, Debbie Tilley (Illus.) (1997)

Why Do Tigers Have Stripes? (Usbornes Starting Point Science), M. Unwin (1994)

WEBSITES

http://nm.essortment.com/aboutbengalwhi_pnz.htm

http://tiger.to/

www.abc-kid.com/tiger/

www.allsands.com/Science/Animals/siberiantiger_zqf_gn.htm

www.siberian-tigers.com/links.htm

Sir Cumference and the Dragon of Pi

A MATH ADVENTURE • **Cindy Neuschwander** • **Wayne Geehan, Illus.**

Sir Cumference, Lady Di of Ameter, and their son Radius take us on a mathematics adventure to discover the magic number that is the same for all circles. When Sir Cumference drinks a potion that turns him into a dragon, his son Radius searches for the magic number known as pi that will restore him to his former shape. As Radius travels on his quest, he encounters Geo and Sym, the Metry brothers, and his cousin, Lady Fingers, who is making pies. They help Radius unravel the riddle of pi. This book develops the concept of pi in an understandable and fun approach that is developmentally appropriate for young readers. Radius measures around the outside edge of a wheel and divides by the measurement across the middle of the wheel. His result is 22/7. Whether he measures an onion slice, a basket, a bowl, or a round of cheese, he gets the same result. This is the fascinating number pi, which can be expressed as 22/7, 3.14, or the Greek symbol, π.

GRADE LEVELS:	**6–8**
MATHEMATICS STANDARDS ADDRESSED:	geometry, measurement
LANGUAGE ARTS EXPERIENCE:	writing (learning log)
OBJECTIVES:	to measure diameter, to measure circumference, to determine the ratio between the circumference and the diameter (circumference divided by the diameter), to calculate the approximate value of pi
KEY CONCEPTS:	diameter, circumference, pi, radius, ratio
MATERIALS:	a chalkboard compass; string; measuring tapes; calculator; Pi Exploration sheet (Appendix A.42); a collection of circular tops, jars, cans, and containers

Procedure

SHARING THE BOOK

1. Before reading the book, ask the students if they know the name of the line segment that passes through the center of the circle and has endpoints on the circle. (*diameter*) What is the name of the segment from the center of a circle to a point on a circle? (*radius*) What is the name for the distance around the outside of a circle. (*circumference*) Do you recall the formula for the circumference of a circle?

    $C = \pi d$ or $C = 2\pi r$

2. Mathematicians have been finding approximations for pi since ancient times. Read the book to see how Radius discovers the magic number. After reading, ask the following questions to stimulate a book discussion:

    a. When Sir Cumference drank the potion for his belly, what happened? What did the knights plan to do the next day to the dragon?

    b. Radius spotted a curious-looking container with a poem "The Circle's Measure." What do you think it means?

    c. What did Radius discover in the Carpenters' workshop? What did the brothers Geo and Sym point out to Radius?

d. In the kitchen, Lady Fingers was making a pie and asked Radius to help her. What did Radius notice about the pie that was similar to the wheel in the Carpenters' workshop?

e. When Radius measured big wheels and small wheels, what were the measurements?

f. Radius measured an onion, a basket, a bowl, and a round of cheese. What were his measurements? Did Radius successfully figure out the magic in circles? Explain. Did he successfully rescue his father? Explain how.

g. Geo and Sym gave Radius a special present. What was it? What does it do?

PROMOTING CONCEPTS

1. Draw four different circles on the chalkboard using a chalkboard compass. Using string or a measuring tape, measure the diameter and circumference of each circle. Record these measurements. Divide each circumference by the diameter of each circle for an approximation of pi. Use calculators to compute the answers. There may be some variations in answers; it is approximately 3.14.

2. Working in pairs, have the students complete the Pi Exploration sheet (Appendix A.42). Answers will vary. Dividing the circumference by the diameter will always be close to 3.14, no matter what size circle is used. Archimedes (287–212 B.C.) calculated the value of pi to be 3.14. Computers have calculated the value of pi to more than 500,000 decimal places.

3. Set up centers around the room with various containers, lids, and cans for the students to use to measure the circumference and diameter. Place a measuring tape at each center.

4. At each center, the students should measure the diameter and circumference of the lids and containers, making a record of each measurement. Then, have them compute the approximation for pi by dividing the circumference by the diameter.

Assessment

1. *Performance:* Complete the Pi Exploration sheet (Appendix A.42).
2. *Observation:* Participate in the measurements and calculations at each center.
3. *Writing:* In learning logs, explain the magic that is in all circles.

Making Connections

OTHER CONCEPTS

Fraction to a decimal, decimal to a fraction, repeating decimals, rounding to the nearest hundredth, perimeters, area of a circle.

OTHER BOOKS	WEBSITES
The Adventures of Penrose the Mathematical Cat, Theoni Pappas (1997)	www.teachervision.fen.com/math/lesson-plan/3430.html?detoured=1
Fractals, Googols and Other Mathematical Tales, Theoni Pappas (1993)	www.kidport.com/Grade6/Math/MeasureGeo/MeasuringAngles.htm
The Grapes of Math: Mind Stretching Math Riddles, Greg Tang, Harry Briggs (Illus.) (2001)	www.mathleague.com/help/geometry/angles.htm
The Greedy Triangle, Marilyn Burns, Gordon Silveria (Illus.) (1994)	
Sir Cumference and the First Round Table: A Math Adventure, Cindy Neuschwander, Wayne Geehan (Illus.) (1997)	

A Drop of Water

A BOOK OF SCIENCE AND WONDER • **Walter Wick**

Using exquisite photographs, Walter Wick presents water in both familiar and mysterious ways. Incredible close-up pictures of tiny water drops on the head of a pin and revealing sequence shots of a drop of water falling from a spout are just two examples of Wick's magic that draw us to the hidden beauty and science of water. Although we experience water in its plentiful and mundane ways in our daily lives, the photographs make us pause to look closer, to wonder, to read, and to learn. The words that accompany the pictures are minimal; however, the simplicity of the text complements the beauty of the photographs. A Drop of Water is still an informational book filled with explanations of how a steel pin is able to float on water, how water flows upward, how water molecules travel, and much more.

GRADE LEVELS: **6–8**

SCIENCE STANDARD ADDRESSED: physical science—properties and changes of properties in matter

LANGUAGE ARTS EXPERIENCES: vocabulary study, expository writing

LITERACY CONNECTION: evaluating

OBJECTIVE: to describe the effect of energy on water molecules

KEY CONCEPTS: water molecules, state of matter, adhesion, cohesion

MATERIALS: wax paper, eyedroppers, multiple copies of the book, clear jars, hot water, ice cubes, thermometer, timers, measuring cups, blue (or any other color) food coloring, colored pencils, Molecules in Motion Exploration sheet (Appendix A.43), Inquiry Chart (Appendix A.14)

Procedure

SHARING THE BOOK

1. Generate a list of how students used water before they arrived at school (e.g., drinking, showering, flushing the toilet, brushing teeth, cooking, etc.).

2. Provide a piece of wax paper to small groups of students. Using an eyedropper, put a few drops of water on the wax paper. (The beads of water represent the *cohesive* nature of water molecules: water molecules attract other water molecules.) Have the students look at the water drops. What do they see? Move the wax paper delicately. How do the water drops move? Move the wax paper again, this time a bit more aggressively. When the water drops touch each other, what happens? Do the water drops on the wax paper resemble the water the students have used and consumed? Have they ever observed and thought about water in such a precise and careful manner?

3. In small groups, students can read the book together. Although multiple copies of the book will be needed, the collective way in which the book is experienced will generate reader responses and student dialogues as they read.

4. After the small group reading, ask and discuss what the students have learned. What new terms have they learned? Which photographs captured

their interest? What did they know before? What else would they like to know? (Concepts to make explicit from this discussion include: even one tiny droplet of water is made up of more than three hundred trillion water molecules, and the molecules are in constant motion.)

PROMOTING CONCEPTS

1. Fill a jar with water and put a single drop of food coloring in it as shown on page 18 of *A Drop of Water*. Have students observe as the blue drop of food coloring travels through the water and ultimately turns the entire jar of water blue. What does this illustrate? (*The water molecules are in motion in the* liquid *state.*)

2. Fill two jars with equal amounts of water—one with hot water and the other with cold water. (The greater the difference in water temperature, the easier it is to observe the effect.) Have students record the water temperatures on #1 of the Molecules in Motion Exploration sheet (Appendix A.43). Have students hypothesize and record what will happen to the blue drop in each of the jars (#2). Record and then discuss the reasons why they would make the hypothesis (#3). After group discussion, allow students to record other responses that they liked (#4).

3. Simultaneously, drop equal amounts of food coloring in each of the jars. (The stronger the concentration of food coloring and greater the amount, the easier it is to observe the effect.) Time *how fast* the drop of food coloring travels through each jar and eventually colors the whole jar (#5). Observe and describe *how* each drop travels in the jar of water (#6). Students can also draw what they see (#7). Note that the food coloring in the cold water may not completely dissolve into the water. Repeat the process if necessary or desired.

4. What does this experiment illustrate? From step #1, above, as well as from reading the book, the students established that water molecules are constantly in motion. What do they know about the effect of heat (energy) on molecules? Students' explanations can be recorded in boxes #8 and 9. (*Molecules move faster with more energy.*) After a group discussion of responses, students can summarize the experiment in box #10.

5. From reading the book, what other questions do students have about water? As a class, complete an Inquiry Chart (Exhibit 9.6 and Appendix A.14) using another concept from the book.

Assessment

1. *Performance:* Complete the Molecules in Motion Exploration sheet (Appendix A.43).

2. *Performance:* Students read their responses to #11 aloud.

3. *Writing:* Hypothesize about the effect of other forms of energy on water molecules in a paragraph.

Making Connections

OTHER CONCEPTS

Adhesion and cohesion properties of water—capillary attraction; states of water—melting, boiling, and freezing points, evaporation, condensation, frost formation, sublimation; surface tension; water cycle; water as an essential human resource.

EXHIBIT 9.6 Inquiry chart.

GUIDING QUESTIONS

TOPIC Drinking water	1. Where does drinking water come from?	2. How do I know if tap water is clean?	3.	4.	INTERESTING FACTS AND FIGURES	NEW QUESTIONS
WHAT WE KNOW	We know from the book that we rely on the water cycle for drinking water.	Many people purchase drinking water.				
1. http://ga.water.usga.gov	Only 3% of Earth's water is usable by humans.	Different treatment is used to clean the water depending on the water source.				
2. http:www.epa.gov	Most water systems use a ground water source, but most people are served by a water system that uses surface water such as river, lakes, and streams.	The Safe Water Drinking Act sets standards for tap water quality.				
3.						
4.						
SUMMARY						

(SOURCES — vertical label along left side)

OTHER BOOKS

Letting Swift River Go, Jane Yolen, Barbara Cooney (Illus.) (1992)

A River Ran Wild, Lynne Cherry (1992)

Snowflake Bentley, Jacqueline Briggs Martin, Mary Azarian (Illus.) (1998)

Water Dance, Thomas Locker (1997)

WEBSITES

www.biologylessons.sdsu.edu/classes/lab1/lab1.html

www.oceansonline.com/resources/index.html

www.uni.edu/~iowawet/H2Oproperties.html

The Great Serum Race

BLAZING THE IDITAROD TRAIL • **Debbie S. Miller** • **J. V. Zyle, Illus.**

This is a true story about the hardships of brutally cold weather and the bravery of men and dogs as they race to deliver life-saving serum to the Alaskan town of Nome. In January 1925, an outbreak of diphtheria infects many of Nome's 1,400 residents. With the nearest supply of antitoxin serum in Anchorage 1,000 miles away, the delivery of the serum becomes a race for life. The closest railroad link to Nome is 700 miles east. Battling ice, snow, darkness, and temperatures as low as 64 degrees below zero, 20 dog teams— working in intervals—deliver the serum in just over five days, saving hundreds of lives.

GRADE LEVELS: **6–8**

SCIENCE STANDARDS ADDRESSED: physical science, life science, history and nature of science

SOCIAL STUDIES STANDARDS ADDRESSED: people, places, and environments; geography

LANGUAGE ARTS EXPERIENCES: retelling, brainstorming

LITERACY CONNECTION: summarizing/synthesizing

OBJECTIVES: to investigate the forces of weather and rugged terrain in the far north (north of the 60th parallel); to determine the effect of temperature on solids, liquids, and gasses; to examine the characteristics of chemical change

KEY CONCEPTS: physical and chemical change, states of matter

MATERIALS: map of Alaska showing Nome and Anchorage, sequence flowchart (Exhibit 9.7), bowl or small pail full of ice cubes, thermometer, pan, hot plate, candle, match, drawing paper

Procedure

SHARING THE BOOK

1. With students, discuss hardships and, in particular, life in cold, winter weather.
2. Discuss the nature of freezing and the temperature at which water freezes. Ask students, why is freezing weather a hardship for humans?
3. Review the concepts of *solids*, *liquids*, and *gas* and provide examples of each.
4. On a map or a board, indicate the towns in Alaska where the story takes place. A simple outline map copied from the inside cover of the book will suffice.
5. Read the story aloud, share illustrations, and refer to the map as necessary.
6. Using a sequence flowchart as shown in Exhibit 9.7, retell the story.
7. What are the indications that the people of Nome were in desperate trouble? What are the indications that the men who guided the dog sleds, the *mushers,* were brave men? What are the indications that this effort required enormous cooperation? Ask students about times when they cooperated with others to accomplish something. Were they able to achieve their goal? Why or why not?
8. Discuss the hardships of travel in rugged terrain without highways or roads. Discuss the lack of modern conveniences like indoor plumbing, electricity, and telephones. Ask students how inventions of the twentieth and twenty-first centuries make our lives easier and safer.

EXHIBIT 9.7 Sequence flowchart.

TITLE

Dr. Welch recognizes diphtheria in three of his patients.

⬇

Dr. Welch sends a desperate plea for help.

⬇

Serum was packed in Anchorage for a long journey.

⬇

⬇

PROMOTING CONCEPTS

Part I

1. Place the thermometer in the bowl of ice and note the temperature (it should be between 25 and 30 degrees Fahrenheit). Have a few students place their fingers in the water to note the stinging coldness.

2. Place a few ice cubes from the bowl into a pan on a hot plate and heat the pan. Note what happens after a few minutes. What will happen if the water (a liquid that was formerly a solid) continues to heat?

Part 2

1. Return to the text and find instances of protecting the bottles of serum from freezing. How were the bottles of serum protected? Discuss students' speculation of why the delivery teams needed to protect the serum from freezing.

2. Present the concepts of *physical change* and *chemical change*. The difference between the two is that during chemical change, the nature of the substance changes. Use water as an example of a substance that goes through physical change with varying temperatures—freezing point, boiling point, melting point. Another example of physical change is the melting wax of a candle as it solidifies again.

3. Sometimes, we can use our senses to observe chemical changes. The presence of smoke, light, and heat; bubbling or fizzing; and changes in color are a few signs of chemical change. Demonstrate this by lighting the candle. Have students observe the lit candle. Ask students to notice any signs of chemical change. Responses should include changes in the color, production of heat, and presence of smoke.

4. Why was the serum protected from freezing? (*To prevent a chemical change that would substantively change the serum and make it ineffective.*)

Assessment

1. *Performance:* Students illustrate the rugged terrain in the far north, emphasizing how the forces of weather created this appearance.

2. *Performance:* Students demonstrate the effect of temperature on solids, liquids, and gases.

3. *Performance:* Students generate other examples of the importance of physical and chemical change in their own lives.

Making Connections

OTHER CONCEPTS

Toxin, antitoxin, and serum; immunization; measuring distances and estimating time; ocean currents and their impact on climate.

OTHER BOOKS

Buried in Ice: The Mystery of a Lost Arctic Expedition, Owen Beattie and John Geiger (1992)

Dog Heroes: True Stories About Extraordinary Animals Around the World, Tim Jones (1995)

Gold Rush Dogs, Claire Rudolph Murphy and Jane Haigh (2001)

Polar Animals: Over 100 Questions and Answers to Things You Want to Know, Jen Green, Michael Posen (Illus.) (2000)

WEBSITES

http://teacher.scholastic.com/activities/iditarod/index.htm
www.iditarod.com
www.lessonplanspage.com/ScienceDistinguishSolidLiquidAndGas24.htm
www.school-for-champions.com/science/matter_states.htm
www.sciencegems.com/physical.html

The Top of the World: Climbing Mount Everest
Steve Jenkins

In descriptive detail, this book takes readers on a step-by-step trip to the top of Mount Everest. Filled with historical, mathematical, and scientific information, Jenkins discusses the attraction this enormous mountain holds for mountain climbers and provides specific information on the careful planning necessary for a successful ascent. He also vividly shows the hardships and hazards that challenge even the most experienced climbers. Avalanches, freezing cold, high winds, limited oxygen, and moving glaciers all mitigate against those who try to reach the top of this 29,000-foot peak.

GRADE LEVELS: 6–8

MATHEMATICS STANDARD ADDRESSED: data analysis and probability

SCIENCE STANDARD ADDRESSED: physical science

SOCIAL STUDIES STANDARDS ADDRESSED: people, places, and environment; geography

LANGUAGE ARTS EXPERIENCES: graphic organizers, vocabulary study, expository writing

LITERACY CONNECTION: evaluating

OBJECTIVES: to analyze how man is able to overcome the almost insurmountable forces of nature

KEY CONCEPTS: altitude and its impact on weather and human conditions

MATERIALS: map of the world or globe, rulers, paper and pencils, cookie tray with sand or soil, K-F-N chart (Exhibit 9.8)

Procedure

SHARING THE BOOK

1. Begin with a semantic mapping exercise with "high mountain" as the key concept around which the students will create categories. Raise this question: What might be some of your concerns about climbing a high mountain that extends four or five miles into the sky? (Answers will vary. Clothing, food, weather, snow, ice, oxygen, avalanches, and ropes are all topics that may be mentioned. If the software Inspiration is available, this activity may be done on a computer so that the semantic map may be easily converted into categories.)

2. Individually or in small groups, direct students to identify the kind of planning they must do to safely climb a mountain five-and-a-half miles high. Have them record their planning and share with the class.

3. Ask students to locate Mount Everest on the map or globe. In what country is Mount Everest? (*Nepal*) What is the nearest city? (*Kathmandu*)

4. Discuss Mount Everest briefly, its height, its location, and its challenges to mountain climbers.

5. Generate a list of key words that are important to the story. Have students categorize the words using the Know-Familiar-New Chart (see Exhibit 9.8). Look at the words in the Familiar and the New columns. Define and discuss

EXHIBIT 9.8   Know-Familiar-New chart.

KNOW	FAMILIAR	NEW
mountain climbing	calories	Nepal
weather	oxygen	Sherpas
temperature	altitude	snowblume
	avalanche	

some of the words that are easily definable. If the context of the story is helpful to understand the words, point them out so that students can look for them.

6. Read the book aloud (omitting most of the insets that provide specific historical, mathematical, or scientific information). Discuss the book and introduce specific information from the insets as appropriate.

7. After reading, have students compare their plans to those in the book. What important ideas did they miss and how would they affect the mountain-climbing experience?

PROMOTING CONCEPTS

1. Discuss again the importance of planning for any dangerous event. Listed below are several mathematical problems that require the analysis of data and the planning necessary for climbing a treacherous mountain:

   a. If you are to climb Mount Everest, you must hike 100 miles from Kathmandu, the capital city of Nepal, to the base of the mountain. This trek takes about three weeks. If you consume between 1,800 and 2,000 calories of food each day, how many calories will you consume for this part of the trip? (*21 days x 1,800 calories = 37,800 calories; 21 days x 2,000 calories = 42,000 calories.*)

   b. If the food for one day weighs about 1.5 pounds, how many pounds of food must you carry for this portion of the trip? (*21 days x 1.5 = 31.5 pounds.*)

   c. Assuming you must consume close to 3,000 calories of food per day from the time you reach the base camp until you reach the top, how many pounds must you carry with you? (*2,000 calories = 1.5 pounds, so 3,000 calories = 2.25 pounds; 2.25 pounds for at least five days = 11.25 pounds of food.*) In very extremely cold temperatures of 20 to 40 degrees below zero, most climbers will need about 6,000 to 7,000 calories of food to sustain them. Why would a wise climber carry more than 11.25 pounds of food on this part of the climb?

   d. If the temperature is about 33 degrees Fahrenheit at the base camp and the temperature decreases about 3.5 degrees for every 1,000 feet (in elevation) climbed, what is the temperature at the peak? (*29,028 − 17,600 = 11,428 or 11.4 "thousands," and 11.4 x 3.5 degrees = 39.9 or 40 degrees lower than 33 degrees is about 7 degrees below zero Fahrenheit*). With a wind of 10 miles per hour and a temperature of 40 degrees below zero, what would the wind chill be?

   e. Challenge items: Assuming a consumption of about two quarts of water per day, how many pounds of water must each climber consume on the trek to the peak (one gallon of water is about seven pounds)? Why isn't it necessary to carry all this water? (*Climbers melt snow for drinking.*) With all of the equipment necessary to climb Mount Everest, how many total pounds of weight must each climber carry? (Have students visit equipment sites to determine the weight of various items like tents, boots, oxygen tanks, etc. For most climbers, the total weight will be from 60 to 80 pounds.)

2. In addition to food and warm clothing, what other provisions must be taken to the base camp and then up the slope to the top of Mount Everest? (See the pictured items in the book on pages 10 and 11 for a complete listing.)

3. Why is oxygen necessary for most climbers of Mount Everest?

4. Most commercial airplanes fly at about 30,000–33,000 feet or slightly higher than the peak of Mount Everest. The temperatures at these altitudes are sub-zero. Discuss the safeguards provided for people at high altitudes (including those in airplanes).

5. India is moving northward at about 2.5 inches per year. What effect does this have on the Himalayan Mountains (of which Mount Everest is a part)? Use the soil on the cookie sheet to demonstrate what happens when part of the soil is pushed against other soil.

6. The effects of elevation on vegetation are seen on page 12 of the book. Ask students, what happens to trees, bushes, and other plants as you move up the side of Mount Everest?

Assessment

1. *Performance:* Divide the students into groups and have them write two or three "test" items that require mathematical analysis and computation or describe the physical science of the Himalayan mountains and Mount Everest.

2. *Writing:* Students write a paragraph describing other events in which humans have overcome insurmountable weather conditions.

3. *Writing:* Students create a plan for climbing Mt. Everest, making a list of the materials that are essential for a successful trip. They should rank the list from 1 to 10 and provide a rationale for the most important items for survival.

Making Connections

OTHER CONCEPTS

Measurement of peaks, survival skills.

OTHER BOOKS

Blizzard! Jim Murphy (2000)

Everest: History of the Himalayan Giant, Roberto Montovani (1997)

The Great Serum Race: Blazing the Iditarod Trail, Debbie Miller (2002)

Mountains, Neil Morris (1986)

WEBSITES

www.everestnews.com

www.mountainzone.com/

www.nationalgeographic.com

9.12

So You Want to Be an Inventor?

Judith St. George • **David Small, Illus.**

From air bags and bifocal glasses to Velcro and windshield wipers, this book provides information on 41 creative men and women and their many inventions. From devices we use often like dishwashers, computers, rubber tires, and telephones to some gadgets that didn't catch on like eyeglasses for chickens and a haircutting helmet that burned hair shorter, this book provides information on individuals who have generally made our lives easier. The characteristics of inventors are shared in humorous detail. For example, the authors discuss inventors who were stubborn, those who worked alone, and those who were dreamers. In most cases, these creative individuals found a need and invented something to fill it.

GRADE LEVELS: 6–8

SCIENCE STANDARD ADDRESSED: the history and nature of science

SOCIAL STUDIES STANDARDS ADDRESSED: time, continuity, and change; science, technology, and society

LANGUAGE ARTS EXPERIENCES: researching, expository writing

LITERACY CONNECTION: evaluating

OBJECTIVES: to analyze how inventions require new applications of science; to explain how curiosity about how scientific principles is applied to create new things, to identify major scientific discoveries and technological innovations

KEY CONCEPTS: scientific knowledge is fundamental to the invention of new things

MATERIALS: a small container of fine sand, K-W-H-L-H chart (Appendix A.21)

Procedure

SHARING THE BOOK

1. Identify with students three or four inventions such as automobiles, airplanes, dishwashers, and zippers, and discuss how life would be different if we did not have these conveniences today. Ask students to identify other examples.

2. Discuss the nature of inventors and inventions. What talents and expertise must inventors have?

3. Place a small amount of sand in the students' hands and have them allow it to fall into a container. Be sure that all students understand that this is common sand. Discuss inventions that have been created from common sand (all glassware and most ceramics, microchips, etc.).

4. Read the story aloud and have students note any special inventors they would like to learn more about.

PROMOTING CONCEPTS

1. Take one single invention, the helicopter, that is based on a scientific principle (Bernoulli's Principle) that some—including many adults—have difficulty understanding. Discuss how Igor Sikorsky developed blades that had a camber

or a shape similar to an airplane wing that would whirl *above* the aircraft and lift it *straight up into the air.* Some discussion about the application of Bernoulli's Principle to make airplanes fly may need to precede the discussion about helicopters.

2. Josephine Cochran, tired of washing dishes by hand, invented the dishwasher and filled a critical need. Are there critical needs today? Encourage students to think broadly.

3. Discuss other women inventors such as Melitta Bentz (drip coffee maker), Letitia Geer (medical syringes), Mary Anderson (windshield wipers), Ida Forbes (electric hot water heater), Stephanie Kwolek (Kevlar, super strength cloth), and Jeanie Low, who, when she was 10 years old, invented a stool that folds into a cabinet.

4. Many organizations help young people with their creative talents. Encourage students to check out the following resources: Camp Invention, operated by the National Invention Center in Akron, Ohio; Inventors Clubs of America in Atlanta, Georgia; the National Science Teachers Association scholarship competition for students; and the Young Inventors and Creators Program in Richardson, Texas.

5. Provide students with a K-W-H-L-H Chart (Appendix A.21). Each student or small groups of students can identify one object they would like to research to find out how it works. Through the various books listed below in the "Other Books" section of this lesson, other print resources, and Internet resources, students can conduct their own research about the object and its inventor. The final project can be anything—diagrams, models, written reports, or experiments.

Assessment

1. *Performance:* Students complete the K-W-H-L-H Chart (Appendix A.21).

2. *Writing:* Students write about an invention they would like to create to make life easier.

3. *Questioning:* Students select one of the women inventors listed in #3 under *Promoting Concepts* and do additional research about the woman and her invention.

Making Connections

OTHER CONCEPTS

Ethical debates surrounding new scientific discoveries such as dynamite, the guillotine, and cloning; patents.

OTHER BOOKS

The Genius of Leonardo, Guido Visconti (2000)

Girls Think of Everything: Stories of Ingenious Inventions by Women, Catherine Thimmesh (2000)

How Things Work, David Macaulay (2002)

The Inventors: Nobel Prizes in Chemistry, Physics, and Medicine, Nathan Aaseng (1988)

Toilets, Toasters, & Telephones: The How and Why of Everyday Objects, Susan Goldman Rubin, Elsa Warnick (Illus.) (1998)

Women Inventors and Their Discoveries, Ethlie Ann Vare and Greg Ptacek (1993)

WEBSITES

www.enchantedlearning.com/inventors/indexa.shtml

www.invent.org

www.inventors.about.com

www.NSTA.org

www.totallyabsurd.com

Sweet Music in Harlem

Debbie A. Taylor • Frank Morrison, Illus.

In 1958, a young photographer named Art Kane takes a legendary photograph of 57 famous jazz musicians on the steps of a brownstone in Harlem, New York, as his first professional assignment for Esquire *magazine. Among those photographed are jazz giants such as Charles Mingus, Thelonius Monk, Count Basie, Dizzy Gillespie, and Lester Young. Known to be the single most significant jazz portrait taken in the twentieth century, the photo serves as an inspiration for* Sweet Music in Harlem. *Taylor imagines a colorful and rhythmic life in Harlem for a boy, CJ, who is sitting among the dozen children also captured in the photograph just before history is made with a single POP! of the flash.*

GRADE LEVELS:	**6–8**
MATHEMATICS STANDARDS ADDRESSED:	problem solving—making combinations (permutations), identifying patterns
SOCIAL STUDIES STANDARDS ADDRESSED:	culture—the arts contribute to the development and transmission of culture; time, continuity, and change—be able to identify and describe selected historical periods and patterns of change within and across cultures
LANGUAGE ARTS EXPERIENCES:	visual representation, research
ARTS CONNECTIONS:	jazz, musical notation, photography, Harlem Renaissance, African American art
OBJECTIVES:	to gain an appreciation for the significance of the Harlem Renaissance in the world of music and art and in other events of American history such as the Civil Rights Movement; to gain knowledge about notable figures of the Harlem Renaissance; to observe mathematical patterns in music
KEY CONCEPTS:	Harlem Renaissance, jazz, black urban migration
MATERIALS:	Inquiry chart (Appendix A.14), note cards

Procedure

SHARING THE BOOK

1. Play selected jazz pieces from such artists as Charles Mingus or Count Basie for students before reading the book. Internet sites such as www.pbs.org/jazz/lounge/ offer music from a range of jazz styles.

2. Share the book as a read-aloud. Pause at each setting—barbershop, diner, jazz lounge, and sidewalk—to add details using visualization. Ask questions such as "What colors are around you? What else do you see? What do you hear? Who is talking? What do they say?" to imagine the setting and the characters.

3. After the story, read the "Author's Note" and share Kane's photograph of the 57 musicians. The photograph is also available to view online at www.art kane.com. The site has an interactive feature to identify each musician in the picture. List the artists included in the photograph.

PROMOTING CONCEPTS

1. The Harlem Renaissance is celebrated as the most significant and influential artistic movement of the African American community in literature, art,

and music. Although it ended in the 1930s, the cultural impact of the era's musicians (such as those in Art Kane's photograph) on future musicians is quite evident.

2. Images of Harlem can be found online at sites such as the following:

    - http://nfo.net/usa/CottonClub-1936.jpg
    - www.pbs.org/wnet/americannovel/timeline/images/harlemrenaissance.jpg
    - www.phila.k12.pa.us/schools/harding/Images/harlem3.jpg
    - http://imagecache2.allposters.com/images/pic/KNO/7100P~The-Harlem-Renaissance-Posters.jpg

3. Look at the images and discuss their mood and tone. What was happening in Harlem during this era?

4. Use the timeline of the Harlem Renaissance from www.si.umich.edu/CHICO/Harlem/timex/timeline.html to identify significant events of the era from 1900 to 1940. Some of the notable events include the founding of the Frogs, the first African American theatrical group, in 1908; the Silent Protest Parade in 1917; the establishment of the Black Swan Phonograph Corporation in 1921; and the opening of Langston Hughes's "Mulatto" on Broadway in 1935.

5. Have students use timelines of the history of the United States to contextualize the significant events of the Harlem Renaissance. What else was happening in the country? (*end of World War I, the Roaring Twenties, migration of blacks to northern cities*) When did the era end? Coinciding with what events in the country's history? (*the Great Depression and start of World War II*)

6. Have students complete an inquiry on a notable figure of the Harlem Renaissance from a range of areas using the online resource from ArtsEdge: www.artsedge.kennedycenter.org/content/2248. Examples of inquiry subjects include writers such as Langston Hughes and Zora Neal Hurston; actors such as Charles Gilpin; musicians such as Louis Armstrong and Duke Ellington; and businesses such as Black Swan Records, Cotton Club, and Apollo Theater. Who or what is the subject? What are the notable works by the subject? What is the significance of the work? How is the subject related to other notable figures of the Harlem Renaissance? How did these notable figures collectively create an era of such artistic creativity and cultural influence?

7. Record findings in the Inquiry Chart (Appendix A.14).

8. Let's consider a mathematical notation for a jazz rhythm. One beat can be notated in four simple ways: a quarter note, two eighth notes, four sixteenth notes, or a dotted-eighth sixteenth. Label four note cards with the four different notations for a beat A (quarter note), B (two eighth notes), C (four sixteenth notes), and D (a dotted-eighth sixteenth).

9. Have the students, working in pairs, rearrange the note cards to create as many different combinations (permutations) of groups of two. (*For example: AB, AC, BD, CD, AD, BD, etc.*) Encourage the students to make as many combinations as possible. Then record all the combinations (permutations). Ask if they have exhausted all the possibilities.

10. In jazz, there are essentially two beats, and one can choose between four different notations for each beat. What is the number of different combinations (permutations) that can be created to represent one beat? (*16*) Can you express that in an equation? (*4 x 4 = 16 or 4^2*)

11. Have students improvise a rhythm by clapping, tapping, snapping, humming, and so forth.

12. Extension: Given a certain number of ways to represent one beat, how many different ways can we represent one measure? (www.pbs.org/jazz/)

Assessment

1. *Performance:* Students will complete the Inquiry Chart (Appendix A.14).

2. *Performance:* Students will complete the timeline.

3. *Performance:* Students will share a pattern using snap or clap with the class.

Making Connections

OTHER CONCEPTS

History of jazz, NAACP, Civil Rights Movement, musical notes and rests in notations, fraction notation, musical notation, permutation, rhythm, patterns, tempo, march rhythms.

OTHER BOOKS

Bippity Bop Barbershop, Natasha Anastasia Tarpley (2002)

Ellington Was Not a Street, Ntozake Shange (2004)

Harlem: A Poem, Walter Dean Myers (1997)

Harlem Renaissance: Art of Black America, Charles Miers (1994)

Harlem Stomp: A Cultural History of the Harlem Renaissance, Laban Carrick Hill (2004)

Jazz Man, Mary Hays Weik (2006)

Jazzy Miz Mozetta, Brenda C. Roberts (2004)

Lookin' for Bird in the City, Robert Burleigh (2001)

Me and Uncle Romie: A Story Inspired by the Life and Art of Romare Bearden, Claire Hartfield (2002)

Uptown, Bryan Collier (2004)

Visiting Langston, Willie Perdomo (2005)

WEBSITES

http://42explore.com/jazz.htm

http://teacher.scholastic.com/activities/bhistory/history_of_jazz.htm

www.artsedge.kennedy-center.org/content/2248

www.artsedge.kennedy-center.org/content/2258/

www.artsedge.kennedy-center.org/content/2459/

www.harlem.org/

www.pbs.org/jazz/

www.pbs.org/jazz/classroom/

www.readwritethink.org/lesson_images/lesson252/websites.html

www.si.umich.edu/CHICO/Harlem/timex/timeline.html

9.14

LESSON

Weslandia

Paul Fleischman • **Kevin Hawkes, Illus.**

Wesley is "an outcast from the civilization around him." Living in an ordinary neigh-borhood with ordinary children with ordinary likes and dislikes, Wesley has plenty of tormentors, not friends. With the knowledge that "each civilization has its staple crop," Wesley decides to grow his own and create his very own civilization as a summer pro-ject. Using the unidentifiable crop that mysteriously plants itself in his backyard, Wesley begins to form his civilization, Weslandia, which includes its unique written language (based on an 80-letter alphabet), counting system (based on the number 8), complex games, and more. By the time Wesley returns to school, the tormentors trans-form into friends as they accept the ways of being in Weslandia.

GRADE LEVELS: **6–8**

MATHEMATICS STANDARDS ADDRESSED: numbers and operations; data analysis; problem solving

SOCIAL STUDIES STANDARDS ADDRESSED: people, places, and environments; production, distribution, and consumption

LANGUAGE ARTS EXPERIENCES: vocabulary, research, compare and contrast, writing, learning log

OBJECTIVES: to identify staple food crops around the world; to calculate daily calorie requirements; to analyze data on nutrition labels

KEY CONCEPTS: staple food crops, nutrition, production vs. consumption

MATERIALS: world map or globe, scale, calculator, Grains Exploration (Appendix A.44), Nutrition Evaluation Exploration (Appendix A.45), learning logs

Procedure

SHARING THE BOOK

1. As the story is read aloud, generate examples of how Wesley's staple crop, "swist," is used to support his civilization (*food, fiber, garments, oil for suntan lotion and mosquito repellent, sundial, instrument, ink, etc.*) Can you think of other uses for swist?

2. Ask students if they can predict what will happen to Wesley. What will hap-pen to Weslandia?

PROMOTING CONCEPTS

1. Staple crops are defined as those most commonly used in people's diets, such as rice, wheat, and corn. Much of the world's land is dedicated to grow-ing these crops.

2. According to the Food and Agricultural Organization of the United Nations, 12 plant species provide three-quarters of the world's food. More than half of the world's food comes from three "mega-crops"—rice, wheat, and maize (corn). In small groups, have students research staple crops around the world. Groups can form based on the three mega-crops. What are the nutritional benefits

of the crops? Where are the crops most often found? Mark the regions of production on the world map or globe. What accounts for the match between a particular staple crop and a particular region? (*climate, land formation, average precipitation, etc.*) Websites such as www.biologyreference.com/Fo-Gr/Grain.html and www.idrc.ca/en/ev-31631-201-1-DO_TOPIC.html provide many of the answers to these questions.

3. An easy way to estimate one's daily calorie requirements is to use this formula (Lahmayer, 1991):

   For sedentary people: Weight x 14 = estimated calories/day

   For moderately active people: Weight x 17 = estimated calories/day

   For active people: Weight x 20 = estimated calories/day

   Note: "Moderately active" is defined as 3–4 aerobic exercise sessions per week. "Active" is defined as 5–7 aerobic sessions per week.

   Have students calculate their estimated calories required per day based on their weight and general activity level. Using the calories in one cup of white long-grain rice (205 calories); corn flour masa (416 calories); and whole-grain wheat (407 calories), calculate the number of cups of each food item they will need each day. See Exhibit 9.9 and Appendix A.44a.

4. Using the calculations from item #3, have students calculate the number of cups of one of the grains needed per day to supply everyone in their city. (The U.S. Census Bureau, at www.census.gov/, has a "Population Finder" feature.) In their state? In the United States? In another country, such as China? In the world? In their city per week? Per month? Per year? In the world per year? See Exhibit 9.10 and Appendix A.44b. How much land do you think we need in order to grow rice/wheat/corn to feed the world's population for a year? How can you find out?

5. Using www.caloriecount.com, locate "Nutrition Facts" labels for Rice Krispies, Shredded Wheat, and Corn Flakes. Using the Nutrition Evaluation Exploration sheet in Appendix A.45, compare and contrast the nutritional value of the three cereal brands. Which should you have for breakfast? Why? Would that choice be same for everyone? Why or why not?

E X H I B I T 9.9 Daily caloric requirement.

Daily Calorie Requirement Based on Weight and Activity Levels	Calories/Day 120 x 17 = 2040	
CALORIES PER CUP	**APPROXIMATE NUMBER OF CUPS NEEDED PER DAY**	
1 cup of white rice = 205 calories	10	Cups
1 cup of corn flour masa = 416 calories	5	Cups
1 cup of whole-grain wheat = 407 calories	5	Cups

EXHIBIT **9.10** Chart for rice.

LOCATION	POPULATION	# CUPS/DAY	# CUPS/WEEK	# CUPS/MONTH	# CUPS/YEAR
Allentown, PA	107,294	1,072,940	7,510,580	32,188,200	391,623,100
Pennsylvania	12,432,792				
United States	304,684,931				
Costa Rica	4,195,914				
World	6,712,198,038				

6. International agricultural researchers report that consumption of staple crops such as rice is outpacing production. What will be the impact of this occurrence based on what you know about staple food crops? (*Many, especially in poor countries, will experience food shortage.*) What are some possible reasons for consumption outpacing production? (*overpopulation, agricultural practices, demand for biofuels due to high oil prices, etc.*) What threatens an adequate supply of a staple food crop?

Assessment

1. *Writing*: Students should respond to the following questions in their learning logs: What is a staple food crop? What is its significance in the lives of people around the world?

Making Connections

OTHER CONCEPTS

Identity development, agricultural practices around the world, ecosystems, biofuels.

OTHER BOOKS

Animal, Vegetable, Miracle: A Year of Food Life, Barbara Kingsolver (2007)

Life on a Crop Farm, Judy Wolfman (2001)

WEBSITES

www.biologyreference.com/Fo=Gr/Grain.html

www.caloriecount.com

www.census.gov/

www.echotech.org

www.fao.org/docrep/u8480e/u8480e07.htm

www.idrc.ca/en/ev-31631-201-1-DO_TOPIC.html

www.nytimes.com/learning/teachers/lessons/20030611 wednesday.html

9.15

LESSON

Flotsam

David Wiesner

An old-fashioned Melville underwater camera washes up ashore and is found by an inquisitive boy on a beach. When its film is developed, the pictures reveal the fantastical and astonishing world under the sea: a wind-up fish among a school of fish, a family of octopi lounging in their living room, tiny aliens encountering sea horses, and more. The most curious picture of all is of a girl holding a picture of a boy holding a picture of a boy holding a picture, and so on. Using his magnifying glass, the boy sees that the original photo shows a turn-of-the-century boy waving on a beach. Realizing the significance of the chain, the boy takes a picture of himself holding the photo before returning the camera to the sea. After going through another adventure under the sea, the camera is washed ashore and is found by a girl.

GRADE LEVELS: 6–8

MATHEMATICS STANDARD ADDRESSED: representation

SCIENCE STANDARD ADDRESSED: life science—organisms and environments

SOCIAL STUDIES STANDARDS ADDRESSED: people, place, and environments

LANGUAGE ARTS EXPERIENCES: vocabulary, retelling, making inferences, listening comprehension, research, writing

KEY CONCEPTS: iteration, flotsam and jetsam, ocean motion, biodegradable and nonbiodegradable materials, recycling, conservation

MATERIALS: Internet, mirror, rulers, compass

Procedure SHARING THE BOOK

1. Present this wordless picture book story in large or small groups using "picture walk" and retelling. Ask students:
   a. What is happening in the story?
   b. What inferences can you make about the camera? The boy? Other children in the photograph?
   c. What parts of the story are fantastical in nature? Have you ever found anything on the beach?

2. Hold a mirror in front of a larger mirror. Ask students:
   a. What do you see?
   b. Can you imagine the "picture within a picture"?
   c. Do you see the repetition in the image you see in the mirror? (*You end up with "mirror within a mirror."*)
   d. What are the similarities? This pattern in mathematics is referred to as *iteration*. Iteration is a repeating pattern.

3. Have the students construct their own "Triangles within a Triangle" Puzzle, as shown in Exhibit 9.11, and count all of the triangles. To complete the puzzle, use a ruler and a compass to draw an equilateral triangle that measures 6

EXHIBIT | 9.11 | Triangle within a triangle.

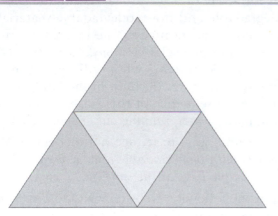

inches on each side. Find the midpoint of each side of the triangle. Draw line segments to connect the midpoints to create an inscribed equilateral triangle that measures 3 inches on each side. Next, find the midpoint of each side of the inscribed triangle. Draw line segments to connect the midpoints to create another inscribed equilateral triangle that measures 1½ inches on each side. Repeat these steps three more times for each of the equilateral triangles measuring 3 inches on each side. Then count the number of different triangles and the total number of triangles in the triangle puzzle. What is the total number of triangles? Have you counted all of the triangles? How many different sized triangles do you have? (*Hint: Trace a triangle of each different size and move these smaller triangles around the puzzle.*) What if we continued the pattern? Describe what would happen.

PROMOTING CONCEPTS

1. *Flotsam* refers to items floating or washed up ashore "as a consequence of the action of the sea," such as a ship wreck. *Jetsam* refers to items cast into the ocean by the crew of a ship. Ask the students if the camera is an example of flotsam or jetsam. Why do they think so?

2. *Tracking Trash: Flotsam, Jetsam, and the Science of Ocean Motion* by Loree Griffin Burns (2007) present objects in the ocean from accidental spills such as sneakers, rubber ducks, and bottles. The website http://beachcombersalert.org/index.html presents similar lists. How do these items end up in the ocean? (*Containers fall from cargo ships; scientists throw things in the ocean to track*) Are these examples of flotsam or jetsam? What do scientist who track these items learn? (*They learn about ocean motion that change with time.*)

3. Play for students "Team Hunts Deadly 'Ghost Nets' in the Pacific," a news clip from NPR's All Things Considered; it can be found online at www.npr.org/templates/story/story.php?storyId=4673939. Similar information is found at www.highseasghost.net of the High Seas GhostNet Project. What is a "ghost net"? (*Lost or abandoned nets that stretch for miles in the ocean and are becoming gigantic traps for trash and living things in the ocean*) Why is this a fairly new environmental problem? (*Materials used for fishing nets are no longer biodegradable.*) How are the ghost nets located? (*Computer models can predict where the ghost nets may be by using the motions in the ocean.*) What are the solutions to the ghost net problem? (*Clean-up projects when ghost nets are located, use biodegradable materials for fishing nets, take action by writing government representatives for tougher regulations, etc.*)

4. Biodegradable materials decompose naturally using agents such as bacteria, fungi, or other living organisms. Examples of other biodegradable materials include paper, wood, and leather. Nonbiodegradable materials such as glass, plastic, and metal may take a very long time to decompose or never decompose at all. An apple core will decompose in two months. Compare that to time it takes for a tin can (100 years), soda can (500 years), milk jugs (500 years), and glass (a million years) to break down.

5. Generate a list of trash we produce in our homes. Students may generate an inventory of trash in their homes for a day or a week. Have students sort their lists of trash items into biodegradable and nonbiodegradable materials; then sort the lists of trash into recyclable and nonrecyclable items. Of nonbiodegradable materials, which ones are nonrecyclable? (*vinyl; toys; Styrofoam; light bulbs; type 3, 5, and 7 plastic, etc.*) Ask students what will happen to these nonbiodegradable and nonrecyclable trash. (*Remain in the landfill or ocean for a very long time.*) What is the consequence of this trash in the environment? (*Harm living things; contaminate water; running out of space, etc.*)

6. Ask students to think about some possible ways to reduce nonbiodegradable, nonrecyclable trash. (*Purchase products with biodegradable and/or recyclable packaging; ask for paper bags or use reusable bags at the store; reuse, etc.*)

7. Share interesting recycling facts from the following website: www.dosomething .org/tipsandtools/11-facts-about-recycling; for example, "Americans use 2.5 million plastic bottles every hour," or "Recycling one aluminum can saves enough energy to run a TV for three hours."

8. Visit official websites for the local community and learn how to dispose and recycle properly. The resource www.ourearth.org/recycling/directory.aspx is good for locating disposal and recycling programs in communities around the United States. Have students generate a list of facts that may help their families improve their disposal or recycling practices. For example, items not included in curbside collection can be brought to drop-off centers, or cell phones should be disposed in designated drop-off centers for wireless products.

Assessment

1. *Writing:* Students should use the online resources from the lesson to create a brochure about recycling in their local community. Include recycling facts, local recycling policies, and other useful information for other people in the community.

Making Connections

OTHER CONCEPTS

Convergence zone, ocean currents, drift experiments, water and air pollution, fractals, magnification.

OTHER BOOKS

50 Simple Things Kids Can Do to Save the Earth, The Earth-Works Group (1990)

Garbage and Recycling (Young Discoverers: Environmental Facts and Experiments), Rosie Harlow and Sally Morgan (2002)

Washed Up: The Curious Journeys of Flotsam and Jetsam, Skye Moody (2006)

WEBSITES

http://beachcombersalert.org/index.html

http://web.stclair.k12.il.us/splashd/biodexp.htm

www.dosomething.org/tipsandtools/11-facts-about-recycling

www.earthcarecanada.com/EarthCare_Program/Lessons/ 5_trash_attack.pdf

www.ehow.com/how_9160_recycle-plastic.html

www.highseaghost.net

www.keepbanderabeautiful.org

www.microbeworld.org/resources/experiment/experiment_ now_you_see_it.aspx

www.npr.org/templates/story/story.php?storyid=4673939

www.ourearth.org/recycling/directory.aspx

www.sciencenetlinks.com/sci_update.cfm?DocID=19

REFERENCES

Burns, L. G. (2007). *Tracking trash: Flotsam, jetsam, and the science of ocean motion.* Boston: Houghton Mifflin.

Harste, J. C., Short, K. G., & Burke, C. (1996). *Creating classrooms for authors and inquirers* (2nd ed.). Portsmouth, NH: Heinemann.

Lahmayer, R. (1991). *American council on exercise, personal trainer manual: The resource for fitness instructors.* Boston, MA: Reebok University Press.

McGinley, W. J., & Denner, P. R. (1987). Story impressions: A pre-reading/writing activity. *Journal of Reading, 31,* 248–253.

National Council of Teachers of Mathematics. (2000). *Principles and standards for school mathematics.* Reston, VA: Author.

National Research Council. (1996). *National science education standards.* Washington, DC: National Academy Press.

CHILDREN'S LITERATURE

Anno, M., & Anno, M. (1983). *Anno's mysterious multiplying jar.* New York: Putnam.

Base, G. (1996). *The eleventh hour: A curious mystery.* New York: Puffin.

Demi. (1997). *One grain of rice: A mathematical folktale.* New York: Scholastic.

Fleischman, P. (1999). *Weslandia* (K. Hawkes, Illus.). Cambridge, MA: Candlewick Press.

Jenkins, S. (1999). *The top of the world: Climbing Mount Everest.* Boston: Houghton Mifflin.

Miller, D. S. (2002). *The great serum race: Blazing the Iditarod trail* (J. V. Zyle, Illus.). New York: Walker.

Nagda, A. W., & Bickel, C. (2000). *Tiger math: Learning to graph from a baby tiger.* New York: Holt.

Neuschwander, C. (1999). *Sir Cumference and the dragon of Pi: A math adventure* (W. Geehan, Illus.). Watertown, MA: Charlesbridge.

Neuschwander, C. (2001). *Sir Cumference and the great knight of Angleland: A math adventure* (W. Geehan, Illus.). Watertown, MA: Charlesbridge.

Scieszka, J. (1995). *Math curse* (L. Smith, Illus.). New York: Viking.

Spier, P. (1980). *People.* New York: Doubleday.

St. George, J. (2002). *So you want to be an inventor?* (D. Small, Illus.). New York: Philomel Books.

Taylor, D. A. (2004). *Sweet music in Harlem* (F. Morrison, Illus.). New York: Lee & Low.

Wiesner, D. (2006). *Flotsam.* New York: Clarion Books.

Wick, W. (1997). *A drop of water: A book of science and wonder.* New York: Scholastic.

Appendix

Principles of child development and learning

1. Domains of children's development—physical, social, emotional, and cognitive—are closely related. Development in one domain influences and is influenced by development in other domains.

2. Development occurs in a relatively orderly sequence, with later abilities, skills, and knowledge building on those already acquired.

3. Development proceeds at varying rates from child to child as well as unevenly within different areas of each child's functioning.

4. Early experiences have both cumulative and delayed effects on individual children's development; optimal periods exist for certain types of development and learning.

5. Development proceeds in predictable directions toward greater complexity, organization, and internalization.

6. Development and learning occur in and are influenced by multiple social and cultural contexts.

7. Children are active learners, drawing on direct physical and social experiences as well as culturally transmitted knowledge to construct their own understandings of the world around them.

8. Development and learning result from interaction of biological maturation and the environment, which includes both the physical and social worlds that children live in.

9. Play is an important vehicle for children's social, emotional, and cognitive development as well as a reflection of their development.

10. Development advances when children have opportunities to practice newly acquired skills as well as when they experience a challenge just beyond the level of their present mastery.

11. Children demonstrate different modes of knowing and learning and different ways of representing what they know.

12. Children develop and learn best in the context of a community where they are safe and valued, their physical needs are met, and they feel psychologically secure.

From S. Bredekamp and Copple (Eds.). (2009).

Name: _____   Date: _____

_____ plus

me

makes _____

A.3 *Number cards 1–12*

Lesson 6.1

3	6	9	12
2	5	8	11
1	4	7	10

1	6
2	7
3	8
4	9
5	10

Name: _____   Date: _____

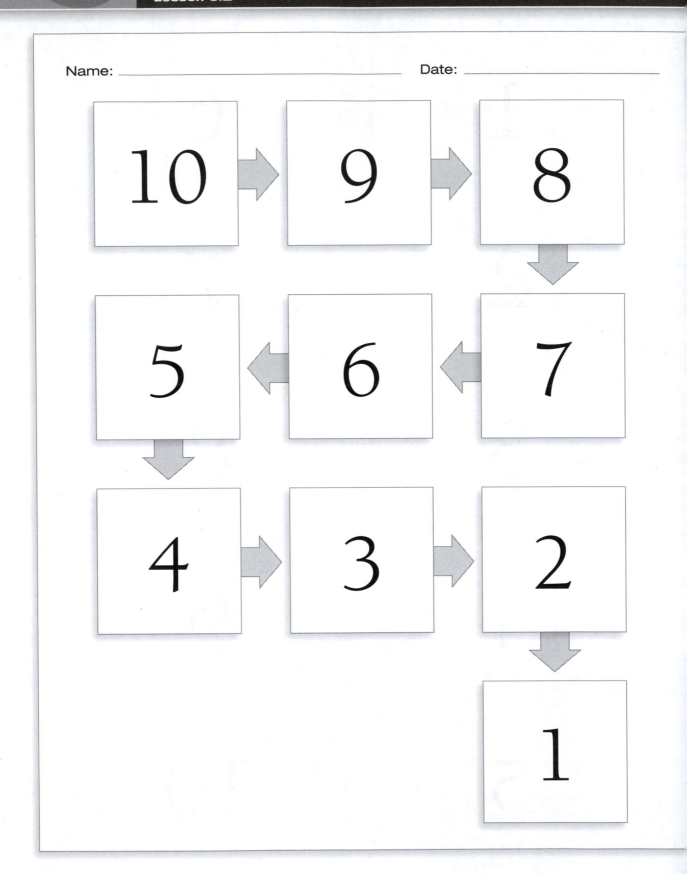

Hundreds chart

Name: _____ Date: _____

1	2	3	4	5	6	7	8	9	10
11	12	13	14	15	16	17	18	19	20
21	22	23	24	25	26	27	28	29	30
31	32	33	34	35	36	37	38	39	40
41	42	43	44	45	46	47	48	49	50
51	52	53	54	55	56	57	58	59	60
61	62	63	64	65	66	67	68	69	70
71	72	73	74	75	76	77	78	79	80
81	82	83	84	85	86	87	88	89	90
91	92	93	94	95	96	97	98	99	100

Name: _____ Date: _____

Title of Graph: _____

										10
										9
										8
										7
										6
										5
										4
										3
										2
										1

A.8

Questions for a dinner party

I would like to ask _____ (character's name) these questions.

1. _____
   _____

2. _____
   _____

3. _____
   _____

I would like to ask _____ (character's name) these questions.

1. _____
   _____

2. _____
   _____

3. _____
   _____

I would like to ask _____ (character's name) these questions.

1. _____
   _____

2. _____
   _____

3. _____
   _____

I would like to ask _____ (character's name) these questions.

1. _____
   _____

2. _____
   _____

3. _____
   _____

From Oczkus (2004).

Name: _____ Date: _____

Name: _____

Title: _____

Date: _____

Text-to-Self	Text-to-Text	Text-to-World

From Keene and Zimmermann (1997).

Prediction chart

Lesson 6.13

Name: _____

Title: _____

Date: _____

I think the story will be about . . . .

The story really was about . . . .

Exploration: Calendar for the Month

Make a calendar for this month. Write the month and the dates.

SUNDAY	MONDAY	TUESDAY	WEDNESDAY	THURSDAY	FRIDAY	SATURDAY

Exploration: Clocks vs. calendars

Lesson 6.14

Name: _____   Date: _____

Write or draw your answers to the following questions.

How are a clock and a calendar alike?	How are a clock and a calendar different?	Can you think of anything else that measures time?

GUIDING QUESTIONS

TOPIC	1.	2.	3.	4.	INTERESTING FACTS AND FIGURES	NEW QUESTIONS
WHAT WE KNOW						
1.						
2.						
3.						
4.						
SUMMARY						

SOURCES

From Hoffman (1992).

A.15

Estimation recording sheet I

Name: _____   Date: _____

STATION	ESTIMATION	ACTUAL

Name: _____   Date: _____

Name: _____ Date: _____

A.18

Observation log

Lesson 7.7

Name: _____

Date: _____

TIME	OBSERVATION NOTES

Date: _____

Name: _____

K-W-L chart

Name: _____

Date: _____

what we know	what we want to know	what we have learned
K	W	L

K-W-H-L-H chart

K what is known	
W what we want to know	
H how we think we can find out	
L what we learned	
H how we learned about it	

From Soderman, Gregory, and O'Neill (2004).

Name: _____   Date: _____

What do you think will happen?	Draw what you observe	Describe what you observe

Name: _____ Date: _____

STATION	ESTIMATION	ACTUAL	DESCRIBE STRATEGY

Name: _____ Date: _____

Write as much as you can about the topic.

What do you know about it?   How do you know about it?

Pass this on to a friend.

Respond to the writing above.

Pass this on to a friend.

(Teacher: Allow enough spaces for the number of responses you wish to get.)

Name: _____   Date: _____

Frog leaps	Rank from shortest to longest

Subtract the shortest frog leap from the longest frog leap. This is the *range* of your data set. _____

What distance appears most frequently? This is your *mode.* _____

What is the middle frog leap in your data set? This is your *median.* _____

Looking at the 15 frog leaps, what is an estimate of the average leap of your frog? _____

What is the average or *mean* of your data set? Add up all 15 leaps and divide by 15 to determine the mean. _____

A.26

Static electricity observation chart

Lesson 8.5

Name: _____ Date: _____

1. After rubbing a balloon on the carpet and then holding it next to your hair, what happened?

   _____

   _____

2. Did the same balloon stick to the wall? Why do you think this happened?

   _____

   _____

3. Record observations:

Balloon rubbed with wool cloth	Balloon rubbed with plastic wrap	Comb rubbed with wool cloth	Comb rubbed with plastic wrap

4. Describe what happens when you rub a comb with a wool cloth or a piece of plastic wrap.

   _____

   _____

Name: _____   Date: _____

How close was your prediction of distances to the actual scale model?

_____

_____

What did you learn about the solar system by completing the scale model?

_____

_____

What are some problems that may result from the vast distances between the planets in the solar system?

_____

_____

What new questions do you have about the solar system?

_____

_____

How could you find out the answers to these new questions?

_____

_____

Return to the story *Starry Messenger*. What additional challenges do you think Galileo faced as he studied the stars in the 1600s?

_____

_____

_____

_____

Why do you think Galileo is considered a genius of his time and the father of modern astronomy?

_____

_____

Name: _____ Date: _____

Event	Draw your predictions	Why do you think so?	Draw your conclusions
Winter Solstice			
Vernal Equinox			
Summer Solstice			
Autumnal Equinox			

A.29

Talking drawings

Name: _____   Date: _____

Talking Drawings—Before

Talking Drawings—After

From McConnell (1992/1993).

Estimating the measurement of boxes exploration

Name: _____   Date: _____

Benchmarks (Explain your reference point or mental picture that you use when you estimate):

BOX NUMBER 1	ESTIMATE	ACTUAL
Length		
Width		
Height		
Weight		

BOX NUMBER 2	ESTIMATE	ACTUAL
Length		
Width		
Height		
Weight		

BOX NUMBER 3	ESTIMATE	ACTUAL
Length		
Width		
Height		
Weight		

BOX NUMBER 4	ESTIMATE	ACTUAL
Length		
Width		
Height		
Weight		

BOX NUMBER 5	ESTIMATE	ACTUAL
Length		
Width		
Height		
Weight		

BOX NUMBER 6	ESTIMATE	ACTUAL
Length		
Width		
Height		
Weight		

A.31 Exploration: Longest rivers in the world

Lesson 8.15

Name: _____   Date: _____

LONGEST RIVERS IN THE WORLD

Continents/Countries	First (in miles)	Second (in miles)
Asia		
North America		
South America		
Europe		
Antarctica		
Australia		
Africa		
India		
China		

Name: _____ Date: _____

1. Rank the ten longest rivers in the world from longest to shortest (in descending order). Include their length in miles. (*Hint:* Use the data collected from the Longest Rivers in the World Exploration.)

RIVERS	Length (in miles)
1.	
2.	
3.	
4.	
5.	
6.	
7.	
8.	
9.	
10.	

2. If you added the length of the Mississippi River and the Missouri River together, would they make the longest river in the world? Where would it rank? Explain.

_____

_____

_____

Determine if the length of the following rivers are *greater than*, *less than*, or *about the same*. Record the data used to determine your answer.

3. The Amazon River is _____ the Mississippi River.

4. The Mississippi River is _____ the Yangtze River.

5. The Congo River is _____ the Mississippi River.

6. The Mississippi River is _____ the Niger River.

7. The Mississippi River and the Missouri River are _____ the Nile River.

A.33 *Metric scavenger hunt*

Name: _____   Date: _____

(*a.*) *Directions:* In your classroom, find each object on the list. Estimate the length in centimeters. After you have estimated the lengths of all the objects, measure the objects with a centimeter ruler and record the actual measurement.

Object Length	Estimated Measurement	Actual Measurement
1. your pencil		
2. marker		
3. magnet		
4. pencil box		
5. math book		
6. your shoe		
7. stapler		
8. tape dispenser		
9. quarter		

Describe the benchmark that you are using when you make your estimation.

(*b.*) *Directions:* Using a centimeter ruler, find objects in the classroom that have these lengths (or as close as possible).

Find objects in the classroom that have these lengths	Name of Object	Actual Measurement
1. 1 meter		
2. 65 centimeters		
3. 3 decimeters		
4. 38 millimeters		
5. 93 centimeters		
6. 1 decimeter		
7. 2 meters		
8. 1 centimeter		
9. 10 millimeters		

Describe the benchmark that you are using to help you find your object in the classroom.

Name: _____   Date: _____

METRIC RIDDLES

Directions: Replace the standard measurements, below, with metric vocabulary: mm, cm, dm, m, or km to make a funny riddle. Remember to have fun, and the metric term does not have to have an exact numerical equivalent. We are not converting between systems, just using metric vocabulary. *Hint:* Use your benchmark or visual estimation to determine the metric unit; for example, the width of your pinky is about one centimeter.

1. Mom asked us to wipe our (**feet**) ____*decimeters*____ before we come into the house.

2. I saw an (**inch**) _____ worm on the leaf in the green bush.

3. My brother ran a 50 (**yard**) _____ dash in the race yesterday.

4. There is a huge one-eyed monster at 20,000 (**leagues**) _____ under the sea.

5. Let's play baseball in my (**yard**) _____ today.

6. A diamond is only one-eighth of an (**inch**) _____ long.

7. It is 75 (**miles**) _____ by train between Lewiston and Grangeville.

8. My nails grow one-sixteenth of an (**inch**) _____ per week.

YOUR OWN RIDDLE

Directions: Write a riddle using inches, feet, yards, or miles and then replace with metric vocabulary—millimeters, centimeters, decimeters, meters, or kilometers.

MORE METRIC VOCABULARY:

Directions: Complete each statement with mm, cm, dm, m, or km.

1. A walking trail is 1 _____ long.

2. A button is 4 _____ thick.

3. The flagpole is 5 _____ long.

4. The notebook is 3 _____ long.

5. A paperclip is 4 _____ long.

6. A piece of toast is 1 _____ wide.

7. My house is 6 _____ from school.

8. My hand span is 1 _____ long.

9. My pencil box is 1 _____ wide.

Name: _____

Date: _____

Directions: Complete the following table. Start the exploration with the suggestions recorded.

NUMBER OF 1/2 TWISTS	CUT POSITION	NUMBER OF SIDES	PREDICTION	RESULTS			
				LENGTH BEFORE CUTTING	LENGTH AFTER CUTTING	NUMBER OF LOOPS	PATTERNS/OTHER OBSERVATIONS
0	No cuts	2					
1	1/2	1					
1	1/3	1					

Explain any patterns you observe.

In a small group, write a report about what happened during your exploration and your observations and results.

Exploration: Permutations

Lesson 9.1

Name: _____   Date: _____

Anno's Mysterious Multiplying Jar
Masaichiro and Mitsumasa Anno

Calculate the number of permutations for the following experiments. Use the factorial notation.

1. Different types of ice cream cones with six scoops (all different flavors).

2. Number of ways seven runners can be arranged at the starting line.

3. Number of ways eight children can be lined up in the classroom.

4. Number of ways nine passengers can be arranged on an airplane, each in a different row.

5. Number of ways 10 houses can be arranged on a block.

6. How many ways can the letters in MATH be arranged?

7. Find the value of the following: 5!   7!   (3!)(2!)

Name: _____   Date: _____

Clues	My Prediction
raja ↓ rice ↓ famine ↓ feast ↓ plan ↓ wish ↓ double	

Name: _____ Date: _____

Record the number of grains of rice.

Day 1	Day 2	Day 3	Day 4	Day 5
_____ grain of rice	_____ grains of rice	_____ grains of rice	_____ grains of rice	_____ grains of rice

Day 6	Day 7	Day 8	Day 9	Day 10
_____ grains of rice	_____ grains of rice	_____ grains of rice	_____ grains of rice	_____ grains of rice

Day 11	Day 12	Day 13	Day 14	Day 15
_____ grains of rice	_____ grains of rice	_____ grains of rice	_____ grains of rice	_____ grains of rice

Day 16	Day 17	Day 18	Day 19	Day 20
_____ grains of rice	_____ grains of rice	_____ grains of rice	_____ grains of rice	_____ grains of rice

Day 21	Day 22	Day 23	Day 24	Day 25
_____ grains of rice	_____ grains of rice	_____ grains of rice	_____ grains of rice	_____ grains of rice

Day 26	Day 27	Day 28	Day 29	Day 30
_____ grains of rice	_____ grains of rice	_____ grains of rice	_____ grains of rice	_____ grains of rice

How many grains of rice did Rani receive in all? _____

Name: _____ Date: _____

Gina ($12.45 per hour)		
Monday	Tuesday	Wednesday
6:30–12:30	7:00–4:00	5:00–9:00
Total Amount Paid		

Keith ($8.35 per hour)		
Thursday	Friday	Saturday
9:00–5:00	1:00–6:00	9:00–3:30
Total Amount Paid		

Name ($0.00 per hour)		
Day	Day	Day
Time	Time	Time
Total Amount Paid		

A.40 Exploration: Standard/scientific notation

Lesson 9.5

Name: _____

Date: _____

CONTINENTS/ COUNTRIES	POPULATION IN STANDARD NOTATION										POPULATION IN SCIENTIFIC NOTATION
	BILLIONS			MILLIONS			THOUSANDS			ONES	
	10^{11}	10^{10}	10^9	10^8	10^7	10^6	10^5	10^4	10^3	10^2	10^1	10^0	Powers of 10
Asia			3	6	7	4	0	0	0	0	0	0	3.674×10^9
North America													
South America													
Europe													
Antarctica													
Australia													
China			1	2	3	7	0	0	0	0	0	0	1.237×10^9
India													
Indonesia													
United States													
World													

Name: _____   Date: _____

See how many different angles you can find. Estimate the measure of each angle. Then, measure to check your estimate. Is the angle *right*, *acute*, *obtuse*, or *straight*?

1.

No. of Angles	Est. Measure	Actual Measure	Type
1.			
2.			
3.			
4.			
5.			
6.			
7.			

2.

No. of Angles	Est. Measure	Actual Measure	Type
1.			
2.			
3.			
4.			
5.			
6.			
7.			

3.

No. of Angles	Est. Measure	Actual Measure	Type
1.			
2.			
3.			
4.			
5.			
6.			
7.			

4.

No. of Angles	Est. Measure	Actual Measure	Type
1.			
2.			
3.			
4.			
5.			
6.			
7.			

5.

No. of Angles	Est. Measure	Actual Measure	Type
1.			
2.			
3.			
4.			
5.			
6.			
7.			

Exploration: Pi

Lesson 9.8

Name: _____   Date: _____

Work in pairs to complete this activity.

- At each center, record the name of the item being measured, such as a plastic lid or a soda can.
- Measure the diameter of each item.
- Record your measurement.
- Measure the circumference of each item.
- Record your measurement.
- Then, using a calculator, divide the circumference by the diameter for each item and record your approximation of pi.

Circle	Diameter Measurement	Circumference Measurement	Circumference Divided by Diameter
Plastic Lid			
Soda Can			
Coffee Can			
Soup Can			
Oatmeal Container			

Using your observations, measurements, and calculations, write a definition of pi.

_____

_____

_____

_____

_____

Name: _____ Date: _____

		HOT WATER	COLD WATER
1.	Temperature		
2.	What do you think will happen? Which jar will turn into colored water faster?		
3.	Why do you think so? How do you know?		
4.	Other responses you liked.		
5.	How long did it take for the entire jar to turn into colored water? (Measure until one of the jars has completely turned into colored water.)	Seconds	Seconds
6.	How did the colored water drop travel throughout the jar? Describe.		

(continued)

Continued.

		HOT WATER	COLD WATER
7.	Draw what you saw.		
8.	Why do you think one jar turned into colored water faster?		
9.	How do you know?		
10.	Summarize. What do you know now about water molecules?		
11.	How else could you illustrate this? Can you think of another experiment?		

Name: _____   Date: _____

(a)

Daily Calorie Requirement Based on Weight and Activity Levels	Calories / Day _____ × _____ = _____
CALORIES PER CUP	**APPROXIMATE NUMBER OF CUPS NEEDED PER DAY**
1 cup of white rice = 205 calories	Cups
1 cup of corn flour masa = 416 calories	Cups
1 cup of whole-grain wheat = 407 calories	Cups

(b)   Grain: _____

LOCATION	POPULATION	# CUPS/DAY	# CUPS/WEEK	# CUPS/MONTH	# CUPS/YEAR
City					
State					
United States					
Other Country					
World					

Name: _____   Date: _____

% DAILY VALUE/1 CUP	RICE KRISPIES	SHREDDED WHEAT	CORN FLAKES
Calories			
Total Fat			
Cholesterol			
Sodium			
Total Carbohydrates			
Dietary Fiber			
Sugars			

Bredekamp, S., & Copple, C. (Eds.). (2009). *Developmentally appropriate practice in early childhood programs serving children from birth through age 8* (3rd ed.). Washington, DC: National Association of the Education of Young Children.

Hoffman, J. V. (1992). Critical reading/thinking across the curriculum: Using I-Charts to support learning. *Language Arts, 69,* 121–127.

Keene, E. O., & Zimmermann, S. (1997). *Mosaic of thought: Teaching comprehension in a reader's workshop.* Portsmouth, NH: Heinemann.

McConnell, S. (1992/1993). Talking drawings: A strategy for assisting learners. *Journal of Reading, 36,* 260–269.

Oczkus, L. (2004). *Super 6 comprehension strategies: 35 lessons and more for reading success.* Norwood, MA: Christopher-Gordon.

Ogle, D. (1986). K-W-L: A teaching model that develops active reading of expository text. *The Reading Teacher, 39,* 564–570.

Soderman, A. K., Gregory, K. M., & O'Neill, L. T. (2004). *Scaffolding emergent literacy: A child-centered approach for preschool through grade 5* (2nd ed.). Boston: Pearson.

Index